25 CONCEPTS IN MODERN ARCHITECTURE

25 CONCEPTS IN MODERN ARCHITECTURE
A GUIDE FOR VISUAL THINKERS

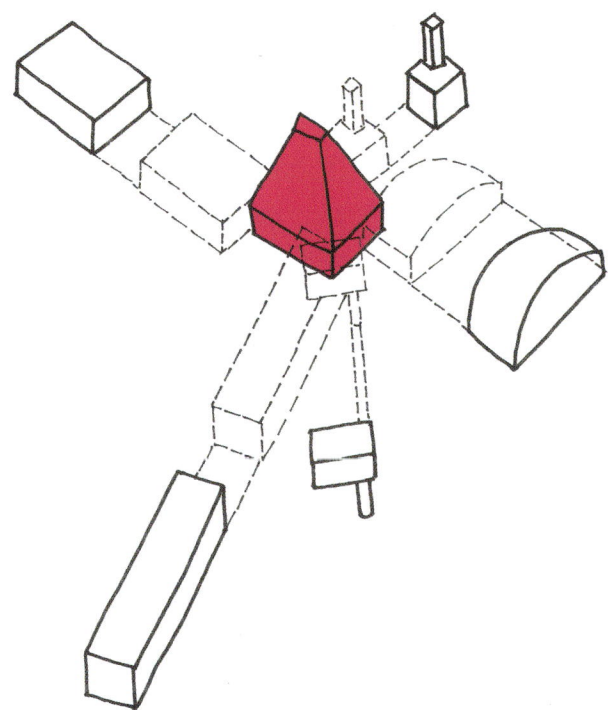

Stephanie Travis + Catherine Anderson

BLOOMSBURY VISUAL ARTS
NEW YORK • LONDON • OXFORD • NEW DELHI • SYDNEY

BLOOMSBURY VISUAL ARTS
Bloomsbury Publishing Plc
50 Bedford Square, London, WC1B 3DP, UK
1385 Broadway, New York, NY 10018, USA
29 Earlsfort Terrace, Dublin 2, Ireland

BLOOMSBURY, BLOOMSBURY VISUAL ARTS and the Diana logo are trademarks of
Bloomsbury Publishing Plc

First published in Great Britain 2021

Copyright © Stephanie Travis and Catherine Anderson, 2021

Stephanie Travis and Catherine Anderson have asserted their right under the
Copyright, Designs and Patents Act, 1988, to be identified as Authors of this work.

For legal purposes the Acknowledgments on p. 8 constitute an extension of this
copyright page.

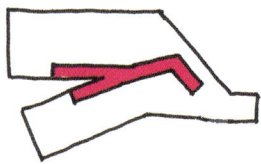

Cover design: Stephanie Travis and Catherine Anderson
Cover image: Kaufmann House

All rights reserved. No part of this publication may be reproduced or transmitted
in any form or by any means, electronic or mechanical, including photocopying,
recording, or any information storage or retrieval system, without prior permission
in writing from the publishers.

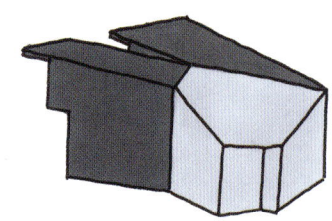

Bloomsbury Publishing Plc does not have any control over, or responsibility for, any
third-party websites referred to or in this book. All internet addresses given in this
book were correct at the time of going to press. The author and publisher regret
any inconvenience caused if addresses have changed or sites have ceased to exist,
but can accept no responsibility for any such changes.

A catalogue record for this book is available from the British Library.

Library of Congress Cataloging-in-Publication Data
Names: Travis, Stephanie, author. | Anderson, Catherine (Catherine K.), author.
Title: 25 concepts in modern architecture : a guide for visual thinkers /
    Stephanie Travis + Catherine Anderson.
Other titles: Twenty five concepts in modern architecture : a guide for visual thinkers
Identifiers: LCCN 2019049167 | ISBN 9781350055605 (paperback) | ISBN
    9781350055575 (pdf) | ISBN 9781350055582 (epub) | ISBN 9781350055599
Subjects: LCSH: Architecture, Modern--Philosophy. | Architecture, Modern—
    Pictorial works.
Classification: LCC NA500 .T73 2021 | DDC 720.1—dc23
LC record available at https://lccn.loc.gov/2019049167

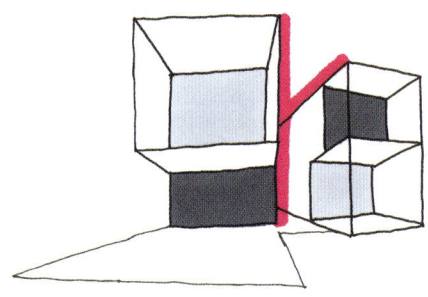

ISBN: PB: 978-1-3500-5560-5
           ePDF: 978-1-3500-5557-5
           eBook: 978-1-3500-5558-2

Typeset by Lachina Creative, Inc.
Printed and bound in India

To find out more about our authors and books visit www.bloomsbury.com
and sign up for our newsletters.

DEDICATIONS

stephanie travis
to mark, samantha + matthew

catherine anderson
to scott + caroline

CONTENTS

Acknowledgments		8
About the authors		9
Introduction		11

1	**Rotating L-Shapes** Schindler Chace House, Rudolph Schindler 1922		12
2	**Manipulating Volumes** Masters' Houses, Walter Gropius 1926		18
3	**Shifting Space** Lovell Beach House, Rudolph Schindler 1926		24
4	**Sliding Planes** Barcelona Pavilion, Ludwig Mies van der Rohe 1929		30
5	**Moving Perspectives** Villa Savoye, Le Corbusier 1931		36
6	**Compressing Horizontals** Jacobs House, Frank Lloyd Wright 1937		46
7	**Expanding Volumes** Fallingwater, Frank Lloyd Wright 1937		54
8	**Extending Rectangles** Kaufmann House, Richard Neutra 1947		64
9	**Splitting Zones** Eames House, Charles and Ray Eames 1949		72
10	**Offsetting Interior/Exterior** Glass House, Philip Johnson 1949		80
11	**Layering Planes** Farnsworth House, Ludwig Mies van der Rohe 1951		88
12	**Undulating Forms** Casa das Canoas, Oscar Niemeyer 1953		96
13	**Manipulating Light** Chapel of Notre-Dame du Haut at Ronchamp, Le Corbusier 1955		106
14	**Interlocking Cubes** Trenton Bath House, Louis Kahn 1955		114
15	**Connecting Forms** Miller House, Eero Saarinen 1957		122
16	**Lengthening Views** Stahl House, Pierre Koenig 1960		130
17	**Overlapping Circles** Pre-Columbian Gallery, Philip Johnson 1963		136
18	**Rotating Blocks** Fisher House, Louis Kahn 1967		144
19	**Embedding Components** Koshino House, Tadao Ando 1984		152
20	**Clustering Objects** Winton Guest House, Frank Gehry 1987		160
21	**Engaging Procession** Church on the Water, Tadao Ando 1988		168
22	**Lifting Elements** Maison à Bordeaux, Rem Koolhaas 1998		174
23	**Branching Masses** Y House, Steven Holl 1999		182
24	**Nesting Rectangles** House N, Sou Fujimoto 2008		188
25	**Stacking Shapes** Tokyo Apartment, Sou Fujimoto 2010		194

Notes	202
Bibliography	207
Index	213

ACKNOWLEDGMENTS

Our deep gratitude goes to James Thompson, Alexander Highfield, and the entire team at Bloomsbury Publishing for their guidance and unwavering support throughout the process. A special thanks goes to Abigail Zola, Rebecca Landwehr, Caitlin MacGregor, Shannon Turner, and Grace Poillucci—each of you moved the multiple iterations of the book ever forward. Lastly, we want to acknowledge the GW Interior Architecture faculty, staff, and, most importantly, the myriad students we have had the privilege of teaching.

All illustrations are copyright the authors, except:

Schindler Chace House (p. 12). Photo: Joshua White/JWPictures.com

Masters' Houses (p. 18). Photo by Fishman/ullstein bild via Getty Images

Lovell Beach House (p. 24). Nick Bonetti)/Eye Ubiquitous/Alamy Stock Photo

Barcelona Pavilion (p. 30). Photo by Quim Llenas/Cover/Getty Images

Villa Savoye (p. 36). © ADAGP, Paris and DACS, London/© FLC/ADAGP, Paris and DACS, London 2020. Photo by Thierry PERRIN/HOA-QUI/Gamma-Rapho via Getty Images

Jacobs House (p. 46). Photo by James Steakley via Wikimedia Commons.CC BY-SA 4.0. https://commons.wikimedia.org/wiki/File:Jacobs_First_House_-_back_02.jpg, accessed 09/09/2020

Fallingwater (p. 54). Photo © Richard A. Cooke/CORBIS via Getty Images

Kaufmann House (p. 64). © J. Paul Getty Trust. Getty Research Institute, Los Angeles (2004.R.10)

Eames House (p. 72). © J. Paul Getty Trust. Getty Research Institute, Los Angeles (2004.R.10)

Glass House (p. 80). Photo by Ramin Talaie/Corbis via Getty Images

Farnsworth House (p. 88). Photo by Carol M. Highsmith/Buyenlarge/Getty Images

Casa das Canoas (p. 96). © leonardo finotti

Chapel of Notre-Dame du Haut at Ronchamp (p. 106). © FLC/ADAGP, Paris and DACS, London 2020. Photo by Jose-Fuste RAGA/Gamma-Rapho via Getty Images

Trenton Bath House (p. 114). Photo by Smallbones via Wikimedia Commons.CC0 1.0. https://commons.wikimedia.org/wiki/File:T_bath_house_3.jpg, accessed 09/09/2020

Miller House (p. 122). Photo by Nyttend via Wikimedia Commons. https://commons.wikimedia.org/wiki/File:Miller_House_in_Columbus.jpg, accessed 09/09/2020

Stahl House (p. 130). © J. Paul Getty Trust. Getty Research Institute, Los Angeles (2004.R.10)

Pre-Columbian Gallery (p. 136). © Dumbarton Oaks, Archives, Washington, DC

Fisher House (p. 144). National Trust/Tom Crane, Photographer

Koshino House (p. 152). From Tadao Ando/Koshino House. A Rax Rinnekangas Film © Oy Bad Taste Ltd

Winton Guest House (p. 160). Morgan Sheff Photography

Church on the Water (p. 168). Kaedeenari/Alamy Stock Photo

Maison à Bordeaux (p. 174). Photo by Hans Werlemann, courtesy Office for Metropolitan Architecture (OMA), Weena-Zuid 158, 3012 NC Rotterdam, The Netherlands. www.oma.com

Y House (p. 182). Alon Koppel Photography

House N (p. 188). Photo by View Pictures/Universal Images Group via Getty Images

Tokyo Apartment (p. 194). Photo by Forgemind ArchiMedia via Flickr. CC BY 2.0. https://bit.ly/3m6fkdC, accessed 09/09/2020

ABOUT THE AUTHORS

Stephanie Travis received her Master of Architecture with distinction and Bachelor of Science in Architecture from the University of Michigan, Ann Arbor. Since 2009, she has been an associate professor and program head of interior architecture at The George Washington University (GW) in Washington, DC. Prior to GW, Stephanie worked in New York City for Gensler and Vicente Wolf Associates; she is also a LEED Accredited Professional. She brings her passion for modern architecture and design to her courses and research; her love of drawing led to her best-selling book, *Sketching for Architecture + Design* (Laurence King Publishing, 2015), which has been published in seven languages and is sold in museums around the world. She has brought students abroad to study modern and contemporary architecture in cities such as Paris, London, Copenhagen, Berlin, and Milan. Stephanie has also published and presented many peer-reviewed articles on the topics of design pedagogy and modern architecture, and was the 2018 recipient of the Design Principles and Practices International Award for Excellence for her article *Pure Form: The Interior of the Hirshhorn Museum in Washington, DC.*

Prior to her position as an assistant professor at the George Washington University Interior Architecture Program in Washington, DC, **Catherine Anderson** worked in a variety of architecture and interior design firms for over twelve years. Her primary practice experience was focused on commercial projects for a wide range of clients such as law firms, nonprofits, associations, and embassies. She earned a Bachelor of Science in Architecture and a Master of Architecture from The Catholic University of America's School of Architecture + Planning that included a summer semester abroad in Rome and Slovenia. She was awarded the American Institute of Architects' (AIA) Henry Adams Medal, the highest honor for a graduating student in an accredited architecture program. A LEED Accredited Professional, her teaching focus is on sustainability as well as the design process and design thinking. Her work includes participation in the US Department of Energy's 2013 Solar Decathlon with Team Capitol DC's submission, *Harvest Home*, which won a 2014 AIA DC Design Award.

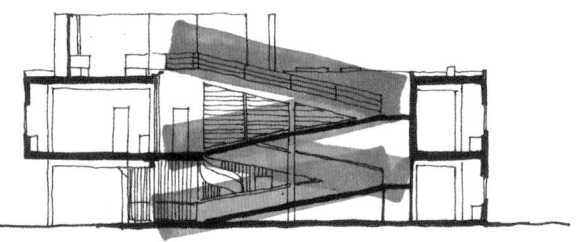

INTRODUCTION

When an educator inquires about the concept as the impetus for work, the beginning design student is often perplexed. After all, what exactly *is* a concept (or *parti*, the word often used in architecture school)? How does one derive a "correct" concept? Why is it even necessary? This initial step in the design process is met with frustration and angst for many—yet without it, one cannot truly begin to design. It would be akin to writing an essay without knowing the paper's topic. The architect Steven Holl rigorously adheres to an overarching idea, stating that he is "almost obsessive about following the concept" as it "drives the design, it guides the design."[1]

There are many different ways of generating a concept; as with design, a prescriptive or correct way to proceed does not exist. Inspiration and observation often go hand in hand when thinking divergently during the initial phase of design. However, going too far afield can lead to "wandering" as more words enter the ever-crowded space of possible contenders to be *the* concept. Indecision (or "analysis paralysis") sometimes becomes the default position when students face too many ideas. To avoid being stymied at this early stage, many students half-heartedly select a word or phrase, hoping that their selection is a best guess or assuring themselves that they can abandon their concept if (when) another idea seems more appropriate.

This book offers offers one approach to demystify this seemingly elusive process: select a verb and a noun that come together to create a concept. We believe that this method highlights or elucidates an action (verb) that is *visible* in the forms (nouns) that shape the architecture. It is important to note that not all verbs are appropriate to use. Suggesting that the creative process can be harnessed into an equation is not our intention; however, beginning design students can benefit from using this framework for concept development.

As educators, we underscore that the concept must be seen or evidenced when asking students to describe and defend their work. To this end, we have curated words that describe the process of *doing* (such as *sliding*) demonstrated in existing works; this is not unlike the *Verblist* that the artist and sculptor Richard Serra developed in 1967.

This is not to suggest that the concepts identified in this book are the definitive ideas that were intended when these seminal works of architecture were created. At times, our words and the architects' characterization of the structures do align; for others, we have distilled the predominate contours of the buildings and interpreted them in our own way. We also acknowledge that by parsing these great works of architecture into two words, it may appear that we intend to oversimplify the multiple layers of meaning that historians, theorists, and architects have carefully observed. Instead, our objective is to be straightforward by using less jargon that has to be unpacked and providing more diagrams when explaining the design strategies of architecture.

We gave ample consideration to the book's title, understanding that the featured buildings are classified as either modern *or* contemporary. The former word refers to a time period in history that roughly spans early to late twentieth century, while the latter calls to mind any work that is of the present era; what is *contemporary* continually progresses and is redefined. While the majority of the structures we selected fall under the designation of *modern*, our intention is not to use the word in the historical sense but, rather, to describe something as novel and engaging or to express a sensibility that abandons traditional norms.

Our hand-drawn diagrams serve a purpose: during the formative and initial process of concept formation, the connection between the hand, eyes, and brain creates a feedback loop. Steven Holl states: "I believe in the analogue as the beginning of architecture . . . The very first thought, the meaningful first diagram, the 'concept' for the building, is a combination of eye and mind and hand, and, one hopes, the spirit. I always begin with these little five by seven drawings in my watercolor notebooks."[2]

The precise lines of a computer-generated drawing can appear sterile, final, and complete; at times, they nearly eliminate room for process and exploration. The initial stages of the design process—iterative, messy, and unpredictable—only benefit from a forgiving and intuitive method that permits imprecise lines and the looseness afforded by hand drawings.

Our diagrams are an abstraction, another way of communicating ideas through representation. They are not intended to be precise documentation of a building; rather, each drawing in this book is meant to convey a supporting idea. Together, they provide a broader understanding of the architecture in each chapter, in addition to the main concept. We hope this book inspires many—from the beginning design student to the architecture enthusiast—to see the myriad ways an idea can be articulated in form, drawings, and words.

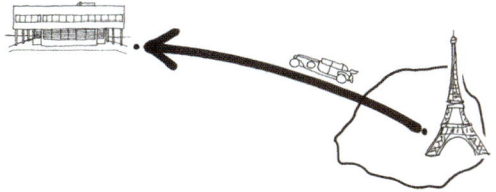

1 ROTATING L-SHAPES
Schindler Chace House

When configured in a pinwheel arrangement, multiple L-shapes create a dynamic form, providing a visual and physical expanse between inside and outside.

Schindler Chace House

A Viennese by birth, Rudolph M. Schindler traveled to the United States in 1914 and found employment in Chicago as a young architect. However, grander ambitions were in his sights as he wrote to Frank Lloyd Wright, only eight months after his arrival from Austria, in the hopes of securing a position at his firm. Schindler deeply admired the American architect's work, as noted in his own words about Wright: "his art is spatial art in the true sense of the word . . . The room is not a box—the walls have disappeared and free nature flows through his houses as in a forest."[1]

His aspiration was realized as he initially worked in Wright's home and studio, Taliesin, in Wisconsin. When the firm received the commission of the Hollyhock House for Aline Barnsdall, he was sent to Los Angeles to oversee its construction. Schindler consummately embraced life in California and stayed, deeply moved by the natural beauty of the environment while creating architecture that responded to the mild, temperate climate.

Stepped back from the edge of Kings Road in West Hollywood and integrated with the landscape stands a modest house of wood and concrete that Schindler designed in 1922 for his wife, Pauline, and another couple, Clyde and Marian Chace. The architect would describe the home as a "cooperative dwelling for two young couples." Writing to his in-laws, the Giblings, he notes that "the utility room therefore must be in the center of the structure" in order for all the inhabitants to access the kitchen, storage, and laundry facilities—a communal and democratic use of space. The floor plan is completely unorthodox; gone are the confined, dimly lit rooms that would have been prevalent in its time. Typical rooms—such as a dining room or living room—were dispensed; instead, each person had an ample-sized studio with direct access to an expansive, outdoor space and a fireplace. The studios afford ultimate flexibility, with the furniture arranged to suit the occupant's hourly or daily needs. Rather than allotting bedrooms, the roof provides space for "sleeping baskets" or frames of wood, supporting a platform for a bed. In his correspondence to the Giblings and in a brief written description of the house for a publication, Schindler refers to the experience of this dwelling as "a social 'campfire' affair" while fulfilling the "basic requirements for a camper's shelter." The catalyst for this romantic view of rustic domestication likely comes from a camping trip to Yosemite; he made a deep, emotional connection to the place as he wrote about it was "one of the most marvelous places in America." Pauline would observe, in later years, that her husband's residences "are intimately related to the earth. Meant for a life which flows naturally from the house out of doors but which at the same time maintains an intense privacy."[2]

Diagram 1. This view, looking east, shows the guest bedroom and garage on the left; to the right, the studios belonging to Pauline and Rudolph Schindler surround an outdoor courtyard, seen as an extension of their rooms.

Rotating L-Shapes

The **rotating, L-shaped** arrangement suits three purposes. First, the entrances into each couple's suite as well as a shared bathroom are located where the two arms meet. This supports the notion that the couples are together but separate—a radical departure from the way households were perceived at the time. Secondly, few doors separate the studios; the 90-degree placement of them provides adequate privacy. Lastly, the two studios embrace an ample exterior garden space that serves to spatially extend each room. Moveable screens and glass create ambiguity between inside and outside, allowing the inhabitants to fully soak in the mild California weather as a natural part of daily living. Conceiving the landscape as an extension of the architecture—while seemingly obvious—was not a common approach. Schindler took great pains to design the site with the same rigor and attention to detail as the house; he writes, "The shape of the rooms, their relation to the patios and the alternating roof levels, create an entirely new spatial interlocking between the interior and the garden."[3]

In his words, Schindler firmly believed that an architect "needs a unit dimension which is large enough to give his building scale, rhythm and cohesion." The preoccupation with this unit, integral to a proportional system, based on "a simple relation to human stature" had to be flexible and "small enough to fill all needs for detail sizes by sub-dividing into simple fractions . . . 1/2, 1/3, 1/4 at the most." Pragmatically, the length of the unit had to align with industry-established standards for dimensioned construction elements, such as "lumber lengths, door and ceiling heights." He confidently states that "the four-foot unit will satisfactorily fulfill all specifications"; consistently, throughout Schindler's architecture, the employment of this unit is evident, and the house at King's Road is no exception. He adheres to this "four-foot unit," establishing an underlying order with rigor: the concrete panels that were poured in place and tilted up are four feet wide; the wooden vertical members as well as the roof joists are spaced every two feet; the lattice-like articulation of windows is further reduced with vertical strips of wood, placed every twelve inches. Yet, visually and spatially, there is a great deal of variety, which speaks to Schindler's adroitness and confidence as an architect who believes, as he wrote, that "proportion is an alive and expressive tool in the hands of the modern architect who uses its variations freely to give each building its own individual feeling."[4]

Diagram 2. Schindler positioned the structure to take advantage of the outdoor areas directly to the east and west of the house, as also shown in Diagram 3.

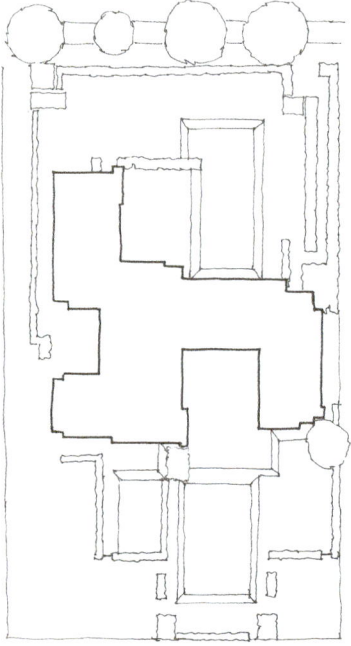

Diagram 3. It is common today to incorporate the landscape with the architecture; however, when Schindler designed his home, this comprehensive approach was unconventional. As seen in this diagram, the linear hedges and rectangular areas of lawn provide privacy while extending the vocabulary and proportions of the house, establishing connections with the outdoor spaces and the interiors.

Schindler Chace House

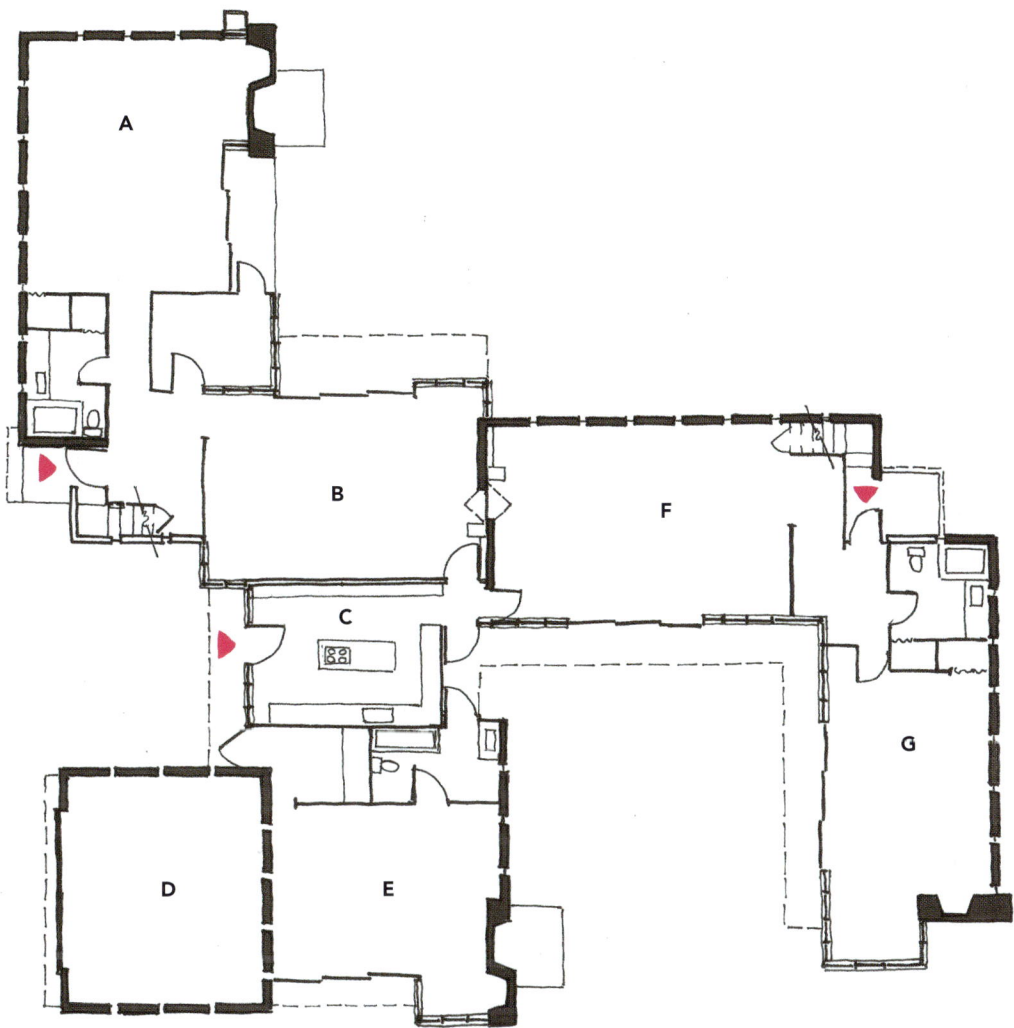

Diagram 4. With so much variety of spaces and the interplay of concrete and wood-framed walls, the complexity of the floor plan corresponds to the experiential diversity of the spaces. Schindler shunned the accepted use of nomenclature as he identified the largest spaces as studios rather than bedrooms; they were ample enough to support many activities.

A. Clyde Chace Studio
B. Marian Chace Studio
C. Utility / Kitchen
D. Garage
E. Guest Bedroom
F. Pauline Schindler Studio
G. Rudolph Schindler Studio

Rotating L-Shapes

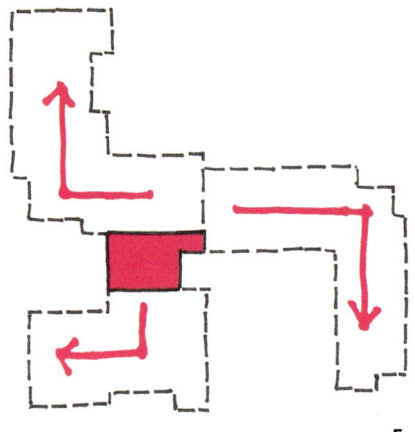

5

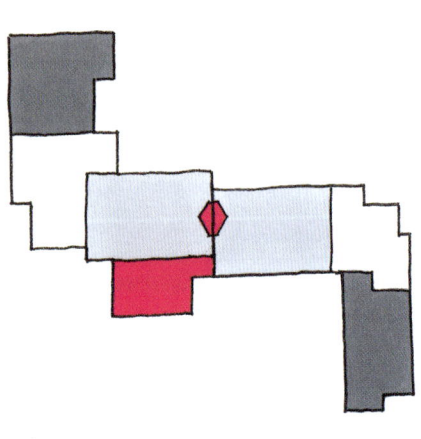

7

Diagram 5. The arms of house—shaped as "L"s—appear to rotate out from the center or core (the utility room), in pink.

Diagram 6. The line designates where the house "split" between the Chaces and the Schindlers. Although the utility room (in pink) was on the Chaces' side, Schindler's intention was for all residents to use it.

Diagram 7. Shown in pink, the utility area and fireplaces in Pauline and Marion's studios (light gray) were used for meal preparations. Schindler centrally located the utility area as a democratic gesture, allowing everyone to access this space. White represents zones each couple shared, and the dark gray boxes are the studios of Clyde and Rudolph.

Diagram 8. Each person had their own studio, shown in gray: Clyde (upper left), Marion (middle left), Pauline (middle, right), and Rudolph (lower right). The areas in white are areas that were shared and not designated for a specific individual.

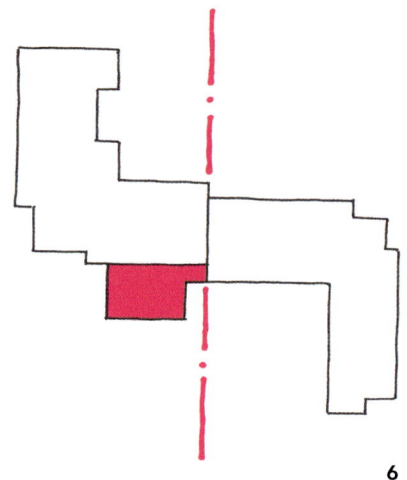

6

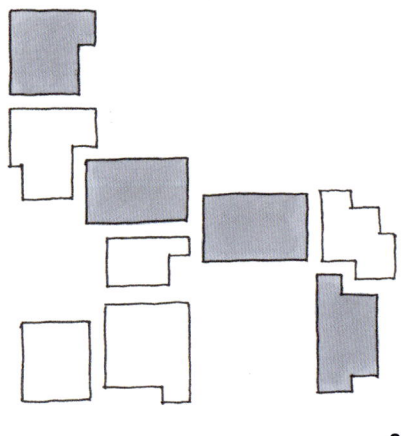

8

Schindler Chace House

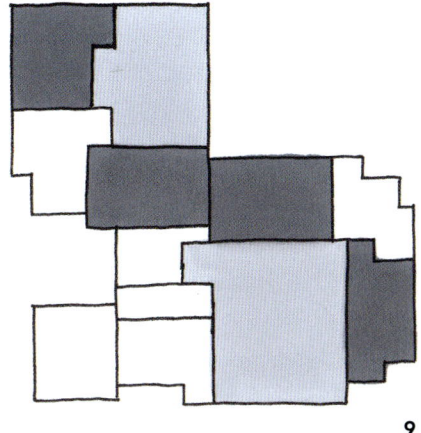

Diagram 9. In this diagram, the dark gray areas represent the studios with the medium gray spaces showing the generous outdoor spaces each couple shared. Communal or non-designated spaces are in white.

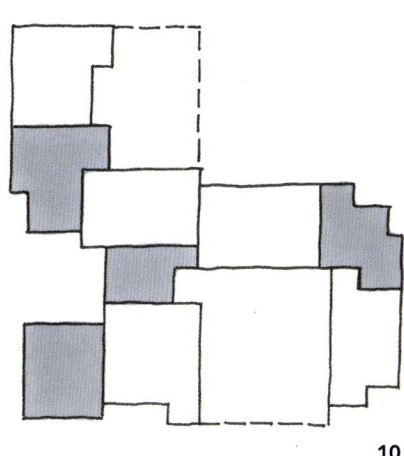

Diagram 10. Each couple shared two spaces: an entry (that included a bathroom), shown in gray, and outdoor space (bordered by the studios and dashed lines). A garage (lower left) and the kitchen/utility room were also used by all members of the household.

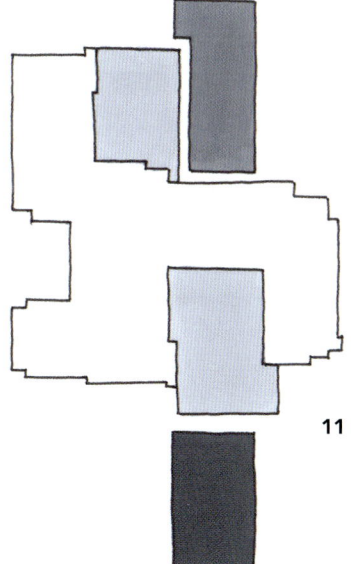

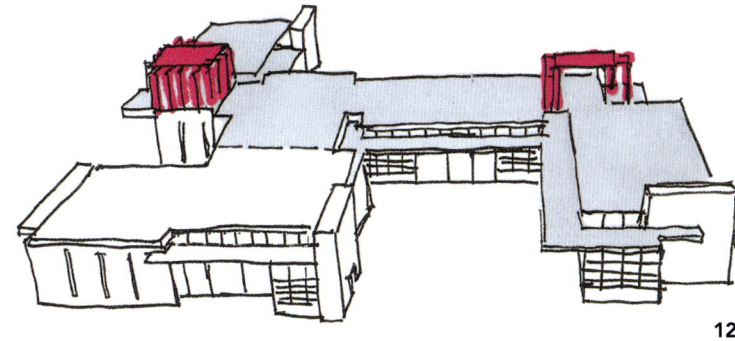

Diagram 11. The outdoor spaces were differentiated by Schindler as "patio" (shown in light gray), "garden" (in medium gray) and "sunken" (shaded the darkest gray).

Diagram 12. Schindler designated roof-top spaces (in pink) for sleeping during the warmest nights for each couple. Studios and shared spaces are shown in medium gray.

2 MANIPULATING VOLUMES
Masters' Houses

Playfulness and manipulation of volumes provide expressions of novelty by using forms that are modular and mass produced.

Masters' Houses

Due to political forces that were unsympathetic to the ethos and philosophy of the school in the city of Weimar, Germany, the Bauhaus shut its doors there in 1925. The search for a new location ended when the progressive mayor of Dessau, Fritz Hesse, welcomed the institution with a generous agreement to fund the construction of a large building for classes and housing for faculty. It was a serendipitous turn of events for Walter Gropius, the founder and director of the Bauhaus. At its previous location, housing for students and faculty did not exist; this *tabula rasa* enabled the architect to promulgate the doctrines and spirit of the Bauhaus in the *Meisterhauser*, or the Masters' Houses, which were completed in July of 1926.

In total, Gropius designed four houses for seven faculty members on a quiet, residential street, located conveniently within a very short walking distance from the main campus of studios, workshops, and students' dorms. The house that he shared with his wife, Ise, was the only detached residence; the other three structures were semi-detached, each housing two instructors and their families: Laszlo Moholy-Nagy and Lyonel Feininger, Georg Muche and Oskar Schlemmer, and Wassily Kandinsky and Paul Klee.

The philosophy of the Bauhaus and the severe housing shortage in Germany after World War I were the actuators for Gropius' approach to the design of the residences. He envisions a utopian way of life, writing: "The overarching principle of the Bauhaus is the bringing together of many arts to form a new unity . . . that . . . requires life itself to attain purpose and meaning." Acutely aware of the dire need for housing, he addresses this concern by penning the essay, "How Do We Build Decent, Beautiful, and Inexpensive Housing?" In it, he defines the paramount role of the architect as the visionary, the one who literally gives form to his query, "How do we want to live?" This new, modern way of life would be hygienic, efficient, and facilitated by machines to ease the burdens of mundane tasks.[1]

Diagram 1. Asymmetric and box-like volumes of the Masters' Houses, as viewed looking southeast, defied the conventional ideals of a typical dwelling when they were built in 1926. Even today, their appearance sharply contrasts with the traditional houses on the quiet, tree-lined residential street of Ebertallee.

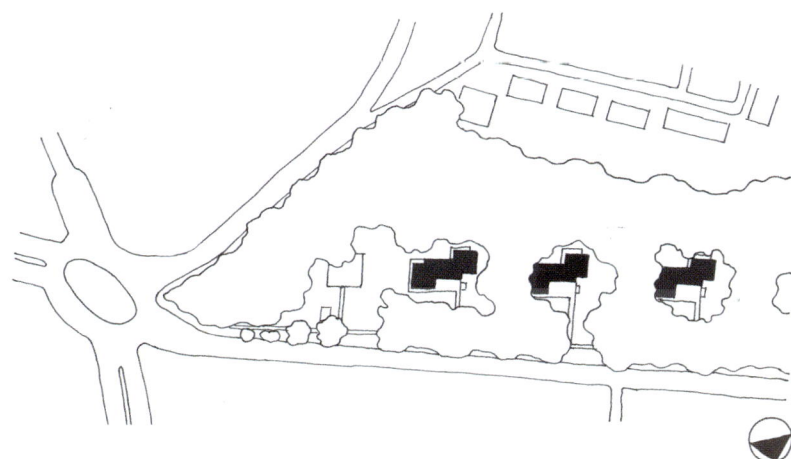

Diagram 2. Only a short walk to the Bauhaus, the homes were conveniently located for the instructors and their families. Each structure accommodated two instructors and their families (shown in black); Gropius designed a fully detached house for himself and his wife, located on the left.

Manipulating Volumes

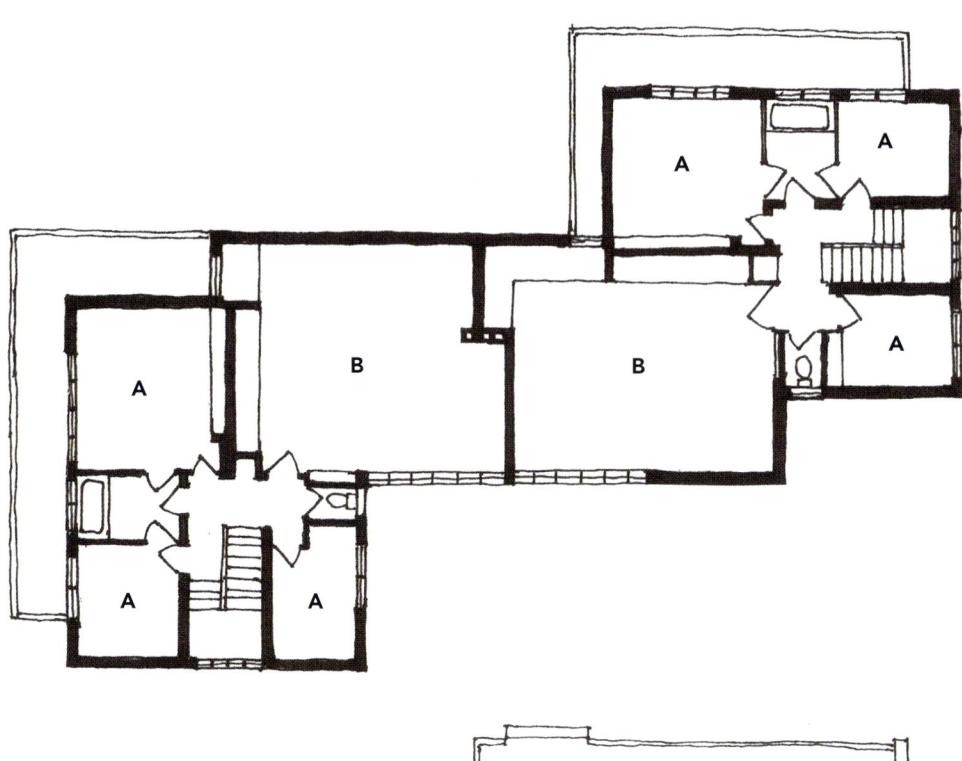

Diagram 3. On the second floor plan, the ample studio space demonstrates the importance of pursuing artistic and design endeavors on a daily basis for the inhabitants.

A. Bedroom
B. Studio

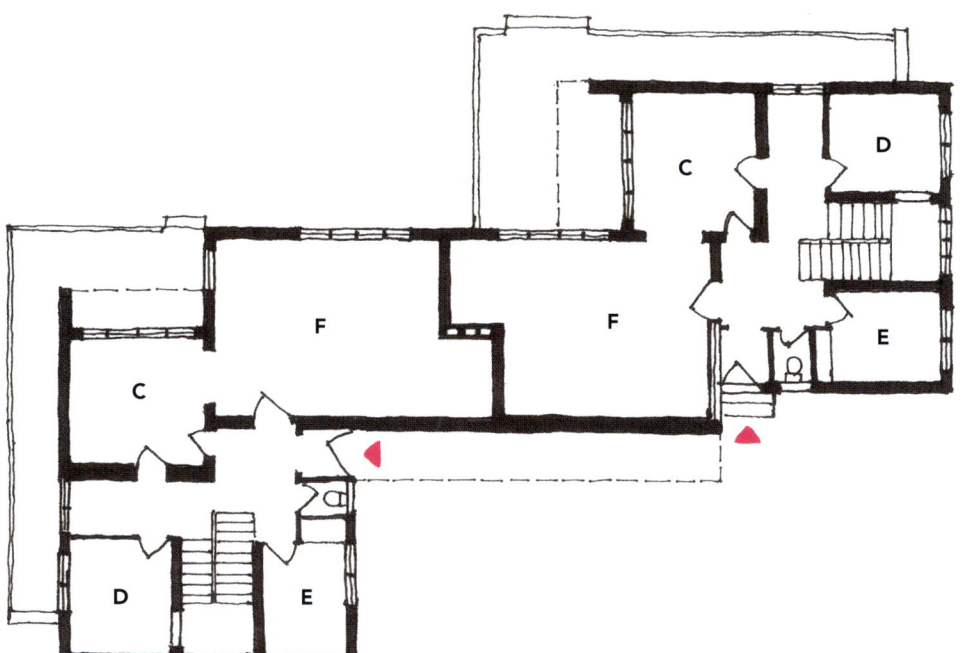

Diagram 4. The ground floor plan depicts a semi-detached house that was adjoined at the living room.

C. Dining
D. Kitchen
E. Storage
F. Living

Assembly of mass-produced "large-scale modular building blocks," as Gropius describes them, where each box accommodates a particular function—such as bathing—gives shape to the structure or, in his words, "give[s] the whole design of the house its form." Rather than perceiving the homogeneity of machine-made goods pejoratively, the architect believes there is inherent worth in these products. He writes: "The particular nature of the machine is such that it develops its own novel 'authenticity' and 'beauty.'" Gropius rationalizes that modularity and uniformity can be embraced, noting, "One need not fear that such standardization will violate the individual" as this approach "provides a sense of order and calm." From this perspective, the Masters' Houses follow the logic of this additive architecture of "building blocks" or orthogonal rooms that cluster together near the hierarchical spaces of the large living rooms and the lofty studios.[2]

Despite his enthusiasm for simple, machine-made building components, Gropius recognizes the potential for architecture, devoid of novelty, to produce soulless and monotonous structures. In the architect's capable hands, thoughtful composition of the parts or **manipulation** of the **volumes** allows for self-expression. He argues, "Complete standardization . . . is not to be recommended, since the violation of all individuality is always shortsighted and wrong."[3]

Variation is achieved in several ways with the Masters' Houses. First, Gropius mirrors the plan twice, along its x and y axes, creating two areas that are then matched and pushed together like puzzle pieces. Then, he volumetrically emphasizes specific rooms—the living area and studio—and differentiates the heights of the flat roofs, so that from the exterior, the semi-detached house is an artful collection of proportionally composed cubes. There is no semblance of modularity or symmetry. Lastly, balconies and projections further reduce the monolithic cubes and provide additional articulation of the house, affording a surprising degree of visual complexity while reducing glare.

Color, used sparingly on the exterior, is applied more liberally inside, depending on the resident. In varying degrees, each master experimented with color for the interior walls. Some, such as Feininger, took great care and delight with the palette he selected; he wrote that "[t]he stairwell is my pride and joy, so cheerful with red banisters." Restoration of the Klee-Kandinsky House during 2017 to 2018 would reveal extensive experimentation with color. More than 170 different shades and hues were discovered, underscoring Gropius' beliefs when he wrote: "Despite the standardized homogeneity of the parts, the individual still has ample room for personal variation."[4]

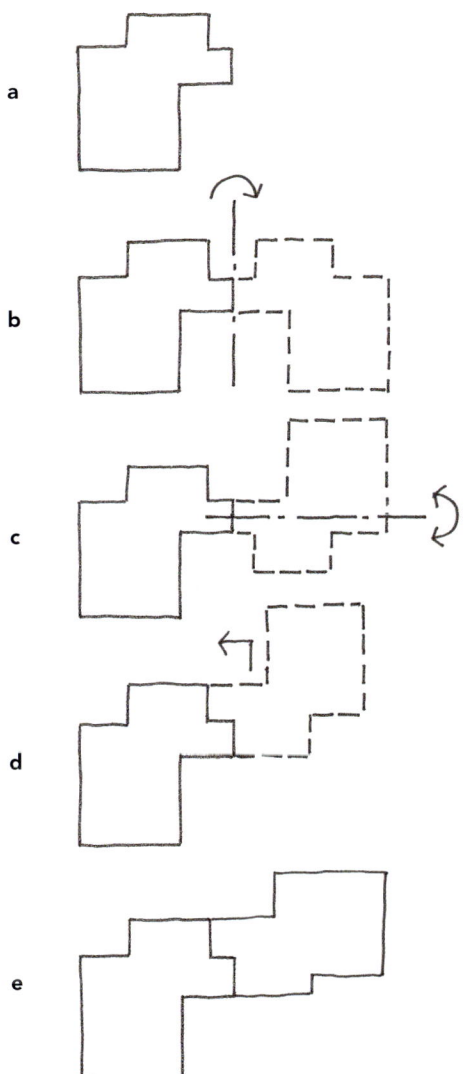

Diagram 5. Gropius' scheme was to take a simple module (a) and mirror it (b). To avoid symmetry, the mirrored portion was flipped along the axis as shown (c) and moved (d), fitting together in a similar way to a double-rabbet wood joint. Lastly, minor modifications were made, elongating the form horizontally (e).

Manipulating Volumes

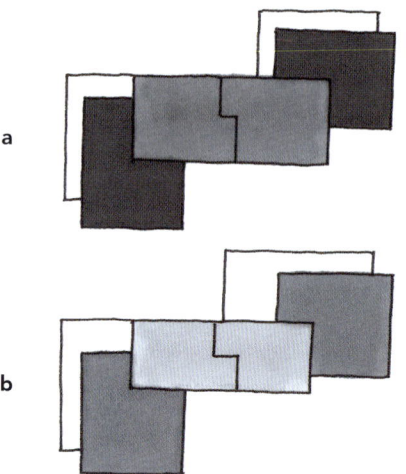

Diagram 6. The light gray shading in 6b represents the most public areas (living rooms) and the darker areas are more private on the ground level. 6a is the second floor where studio spaces are shown in medium gray while the bedrooms, the most private, are colored dark gray. In both diagrams, the white spaces are either patios or balconies.

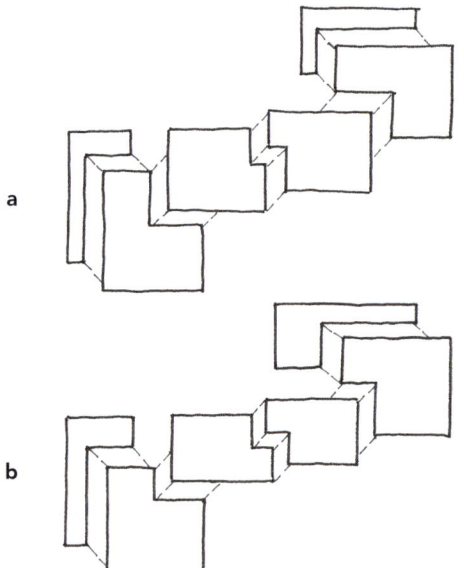

Diagram 7. All the components of both floor plans fit together like a puzzle. In this diagram, they have been drawn as separate pieces so that it is easier to see them as a series of "L" shaped spaces.

Masters' Houses

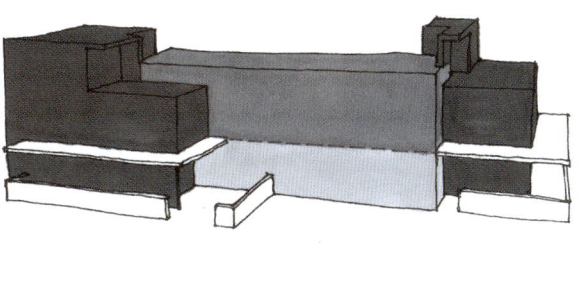

8

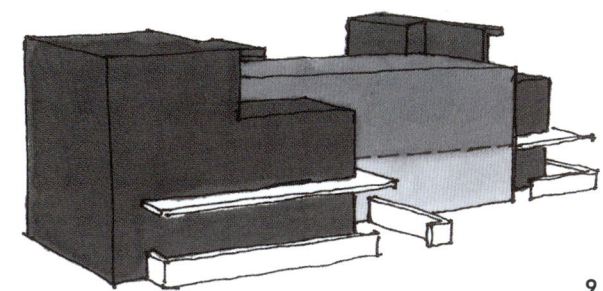

9

Diagrams 8, 9, 10, 11. Studying the architecture in three dimensions from various views emphasizes its complexity. In all four diagrams, the darkest gray represents the most private spaces while the lightest is the most public. Medium gray is semi-public or semi-private. Diagrams 8 and 9 are views looking predominately south or towards the front of the house. Articulation of the forms continue at the back, as seen in Diagrams 10 and 11, looking north.

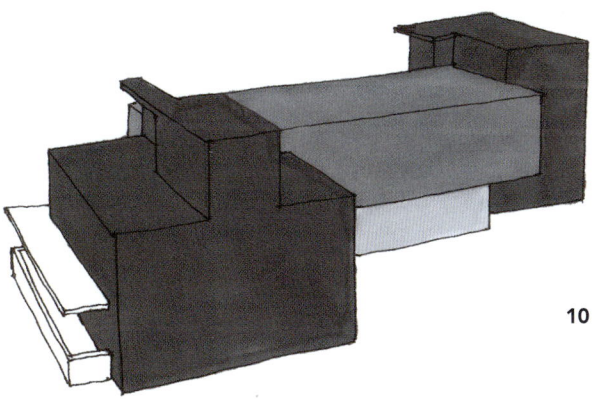

10

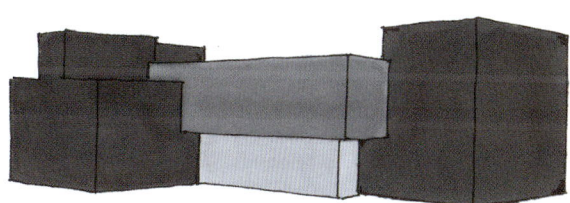

11

3 SHIFTING SPACE
Lovell Beach House

Shifting spaces create a complex form, with voids and overhangs, as well as a certain unpredictability that is absent with neatly stacked shapes.

Lovell Beach House

When Dr. Phillip Lovell first encountered the young Rudolph Schindler, he most likely thought he had met a kindred spirit. The unconventional physician shunned the use of drugs and instead relied on natural approaches to healing through organic remedies, such as living in spaces filled with sunshine and fresh air. Schindler, believing that the benefits of living a natural life and a healthy environment fully complimented one another, wrote six essays for Dr. Lovell's "Care of the Body," a column in the *Los Angeles Times*. In one of the articles, entitled "Shelter or Playground," it is evident that Schindler's opinions align with those of the physician: "It is not enough appreciated how directly and clearly our attitude toward life is expressed through our houses."[1] As the architect, his responsibility would be to "try to divine the possible development of his client, and . . . design a building which may grow with him. The house will be a form . . . And life will regain its fluidity."[2] So resolutely did Dr. Lovell believe in Schindler's architectural sensibilities that he hired the architect to design three residences for him in various locations in southern California. Schindler started work on the house at Newport Beach, south of Los Angeles, in 1922 and completed in 1926.

The structure today does not appear so anomalous; years later, Dr. Lovell would comment that his vacation home was known as "the upside down house." Viewing the west elevation, the cantilever gives the appearance of **shifting space** or a top-heavy upper level moving forward as the lower levels begin to show the framing or "legs" of the structure. Rather than stacking the floors in a conventional manner, the offset of the top floor provides spatial complexities unseen in other contemporaneous dwellings of the 1920s. While still a student studying architecture at Vienna's Academy of Fine Arts, Schindler penned, "Modern man . . . sees the freedom of the cantilever, the openness of the span, the space-forming surfaces of the large partition walls."[3] The cantilever of the second floor provides a porte cochere at the entrance while also allowing an unencumbered, voluminous two-story space for the living room. With its views to the ocean and natural light streaming in from three sides, this space exemplifies the ideals of healthy living, where, as Schindler writes, "Nature becomes a friend" to man in the hostile environment in which "high mechanical development" impedes this vital and rejuvenating connection.[4]

Diagram 1. A view of the house looking northeast. The balcony at the left, with small, rectangular cut-outs, depicts the beach house before Dr. Lovell requested this area to be closed in with glass.

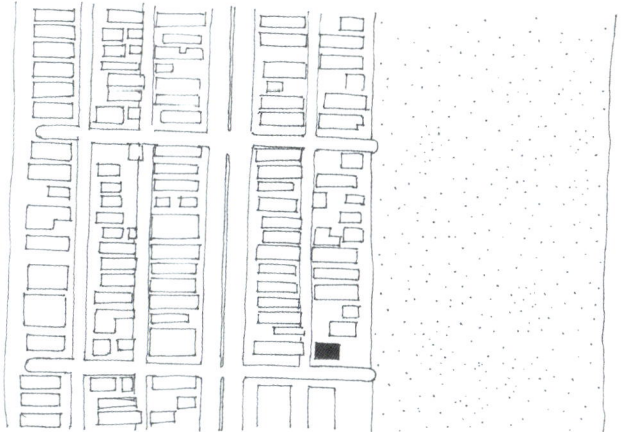

Diagram 2. The house, situated on a corner lot, is very close to the beach, as shown in the site plan. Dr. Lovell believed that the proximity to the ocean and sunbathing were energizing aspects of healthy living.

Shifting Space

Diagram 3. The third floor accommodates four bedrooms; Schindler's original intent was to have the sleeping porches open to the elements. Even for the nature-loving Dr. Lovell, they exposed the family to an excessive amount of sand and wind. Shortly after the family moved in, he requested the architect to close the porches with glass.

A. Bedroom
B. Sleeping Porch
C. Interior Balcony

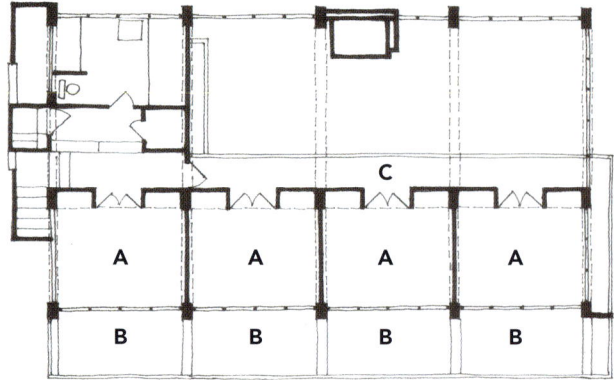

Diagram 4. This second floor shows the house with the stairs at the northeast corner of the house, leading to the maid's room and kitchen. It was removed in 1961 when the Lovells sold the adjacent lot, southeast of the house.

D. Maid's Bedroom
E. Kitchen
F. Dining
G. Fireplace
H. Living
I. Balcony

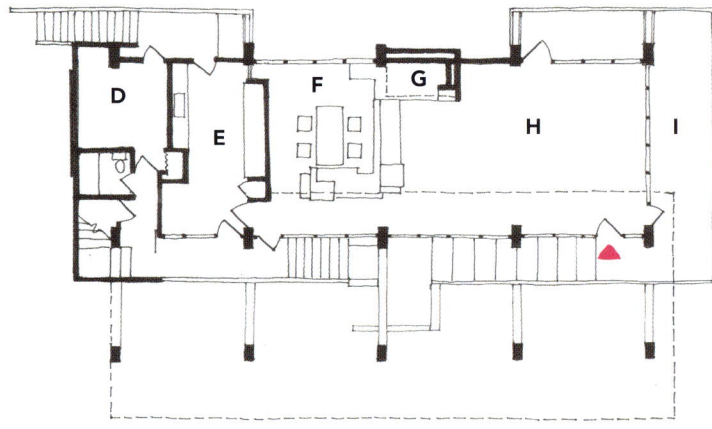

Diagram 5. The ground floor of the house, complete with a garage, shower, fireplace, and playground for the Lovell children.

J. Garage
K. Shower
L. Fireplace
M. Playground

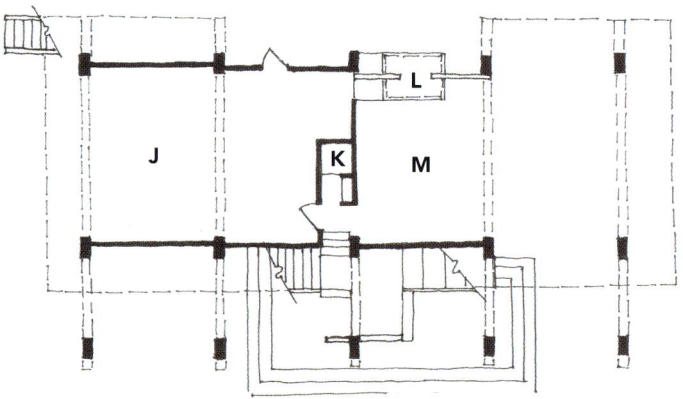

Lovell Beach House

Diagrams 6, 7. When drawn without the context of the building, the slabs appear as if they have moved from their starting point, the dashed line. None of the floors align, projecting the illusion that the structure is shifting.

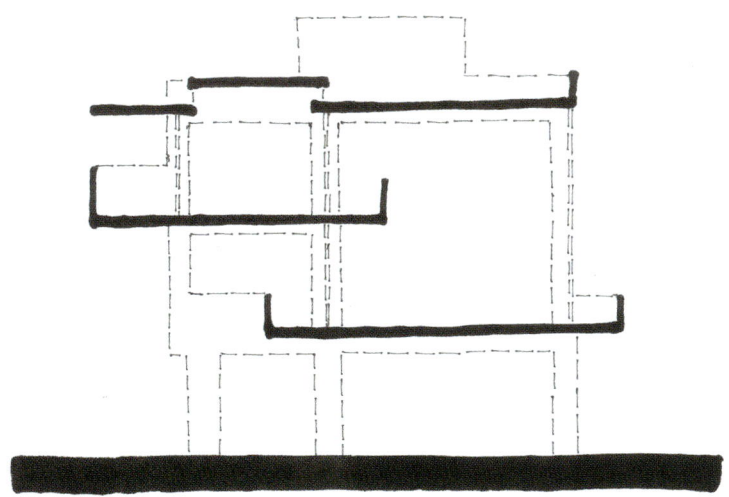

Diagram 8. Although the slabs are not stacked directly above each other, they are well supported and are centered within vertical concrete frames.

Shifting Space

Schindler, always keenly responding to the attributes of the site, observed that, "The motif used in elevating the house was suggested by the pile structure, indigenous to all beaches."[5] Additionally, raising the house above the ground level ensures privacy and better views of the Pacific Ocean. At the ground level, the continuation of the beach becomes a playground for the Lovell children; a fireplace, a small shower, and a garage is also located here. Two staircases at the west elevation travel in opposite directions, highlighting the programmatic and spatial differences between the extreme ends of the house. Towards the south, the stair treads are noticeably deeper, bringing the visitor up the second level with a slower cadence, to the light-filled and airy living room and balcony facing the ocean. The stairs leading north have much steeper treads, as they bring the housekeeper to a utilitarian suite, complete with an enclosed kitchen, maid's room, and small bathroom. Additional stairs nearby provide access to the third level bedrooms—each with a sleeping porch—and a large bathroom. In plan and section, it is straightforward: Schindler uses three of the four bays for communal spaces while the remaining bay is stacked with two levels of utilitarian spaces. The volume of this latter portion is emphasized on the roof above, where walls form an enclosure around a private outdoor deck for nude sunbathing, one of the programmatic requirements as specified by Dr. Lovell, as he felt that this activity was essential to healthy living.

At the heart of Schindler's work, a four-foot module exists in order to maintain proportion and harmony of the whole structure. Aside from five vertical concrete frames that are set twelve feet apart, the rhythm of this unit is not readily apparent. However, within the bays, elements such as the mullions on the windows as well as the built-in furniture he designed are comprised of dimensions derived from this module. Its versatility was noted when he listed how "the four-foot unit" was compatible with:

> Human height = 1½ units = 6'0"
>
> Standard door height = 1⅔ units = 6'8"
>
> Standard room height = 2 units = 8'0"[6]

Believing that a harmonic relationship between man and his built environment can facilitate his fullest level of self-maturation was the inspiration for the Lovell Beach House. More broadly, architecture, in Schindler's view, serves a higher purpose than mere shelter. It is "a cultural agent—stimulating and fulfilling the urge for growth and extension of our own selves."[7]

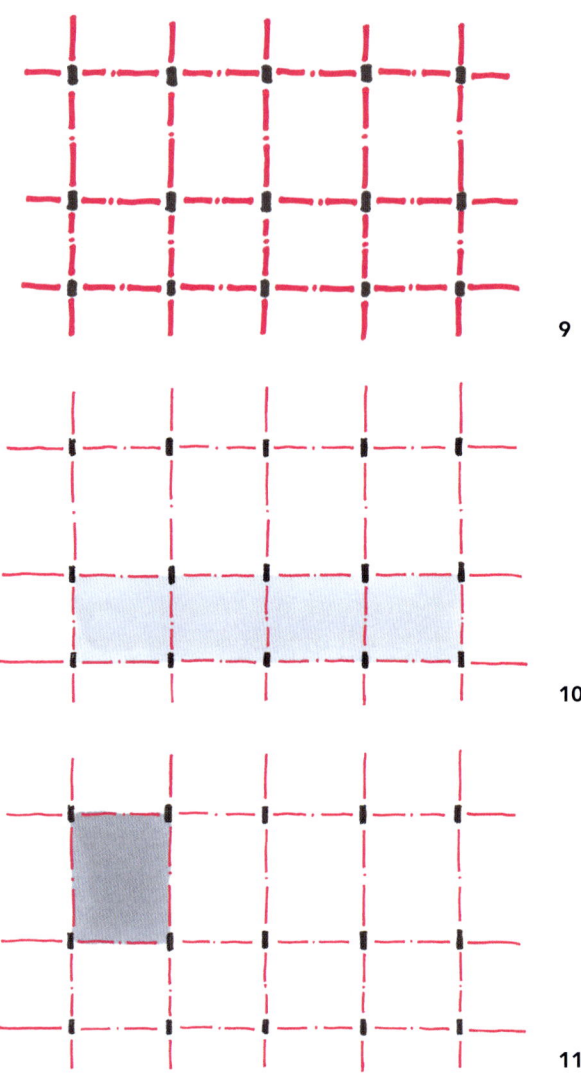

Diagrams 9, 10, 11. Seeing the basic structural rhythm of the house in Diagram 9 provides a basic understanding of the layout and sizes of spaces. In Diagram 10, the gray spaces are the bedrooms on the second floor (the living and dining spaces are in white). The dark gray area in Diagram 11 is the utility space on all three levels.

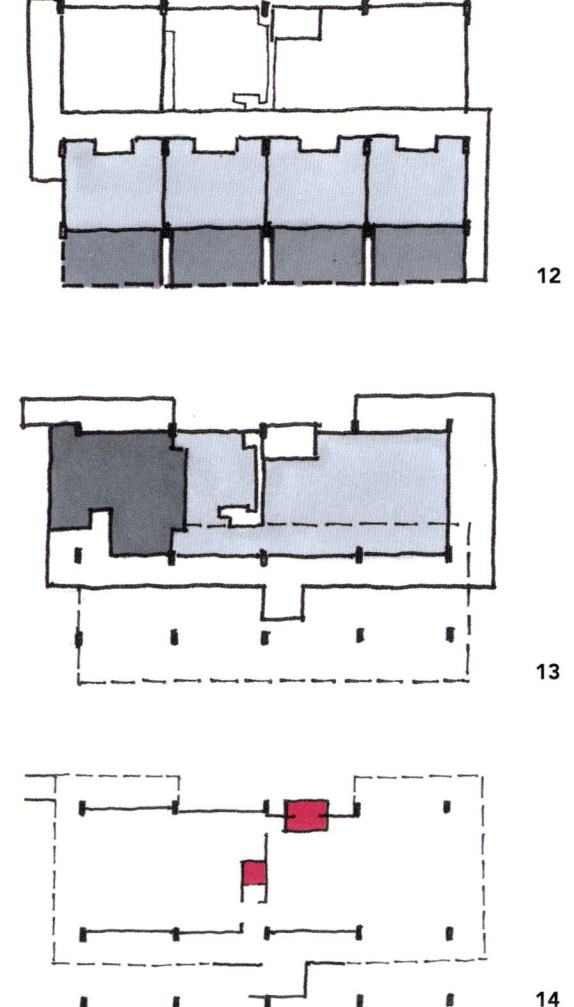

Diagram 12. On the 3rd floor, the dark gray areas are the sleeping porches that are immediately adjacent to the bedrooms, in light gray. All four are adjoined by a hallway and overlook the living room.

Diagram 13. On the second floor, the public, main living area is shown in light gray while the private spaces (kitchen and maid's room) are shown in dark gray.

Diagram 14. Outdoor living was integral to Dr. Lovell's philosophy of good health, and Schindler also subscribed to this point of view. A shower was necessary after swimming in the ocean (shown as the small pink box) and the fireplace (larger pink box) would be ideal to ward off the cool evening air as the family enjoyed their time outside. The ground level was seen as an extension of the beach.

4 SLIDING PLANES
Barcelona Pavilion

By utilizing a minimal number of vertical planes, configured to appear to slide past each other, a remarkable variety of spaces are created in the simplest manner.

Barcelona Pavilion

The structure that Ludwig Mies van der Rohe designed to represent Germany for the 1929 Barcelona International Exposition was described by the German High Commissioner Georg von Schnitzler (who selected the architect) as a building that would be the "voice to the spirit of a new era."[1] Even the most ardent supporter—including the architect himself—could not have envisioned how the German National Pavilion (now simply known as the Barcelona Pavilion) would become an architectural icon and one of most celebrated designs by Mies. It was never meant to be a permanent building; a pavilion, by its very nature, is a temporal, ethereal structure (the etymology of the word pavilion is *papillon*, or butterfly, in French), and so, after six months, the entire building was disassembled.

Although physically absent, its presence endured through photographs and critical acclaim. Its efficacy as a structure to represent the new German spirit was wholly realized; it has been identified as "the most beautiful modern building to have been constructed anywhere." Fervor for its reconstruction gave way to Mies granting permission to commence the project in the late 1950s. While the architect never saw its completion in 1986, his crystalline vision of the Barcelona Pavilion was "no less than a reinvention of architectural space."[2]

Without a specific need to satisfy or a list of required spaces to accommodate, the structure has generated speculation regarding its function, ranging from a place of repose for visitors of the International Exposition to "a modern country house ennobled and abstracted into a monument."[3] Others have noted it as an opportunity for Mies to develop his penchant for "flowing" spaces and study this as an exercise in spatial compositions and choreography of movement.[4]

A cursory inspection of the floor plan hardly reveals virtuosity: asymmetrical layouts of various lengths of opaque and transparent walls dominate the area opposite of the large pool. Similar to parentheses, walls tightly bind both ends of the pavilion. The pool edges align with the conventional grid of travertine slabs, uniformly blanketing the ground plane. Highly reflective, chrome-plated columns that dot the plan appear uncoordinated and out of step with the position and measurement of the walls. The entire structure is on a plinth; stairs leading up to the top provide a sense of monumentality. However, this deceptively simple composition observes a syncopated rhythm that considers the spatial and dimensional relationships of every element in the pavilion.

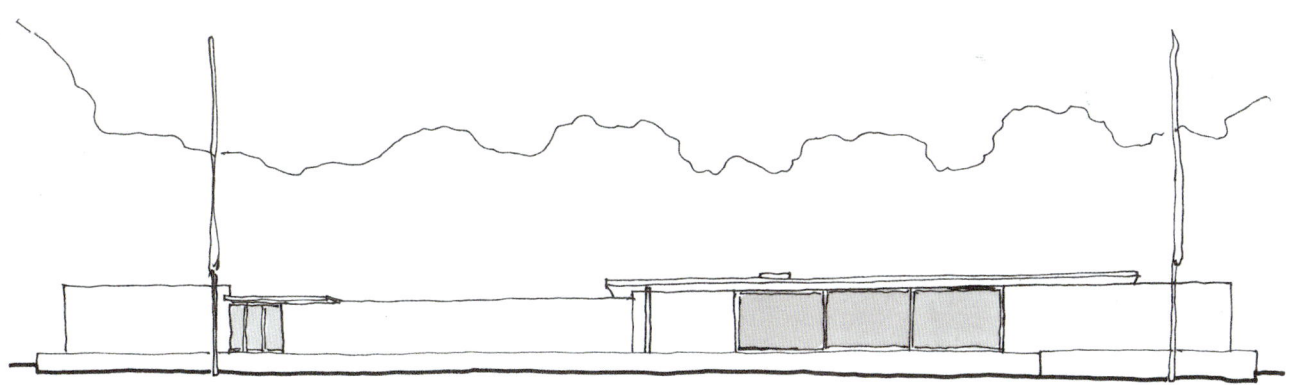

Diagram 1. A view of the pavilion, looking southwest.

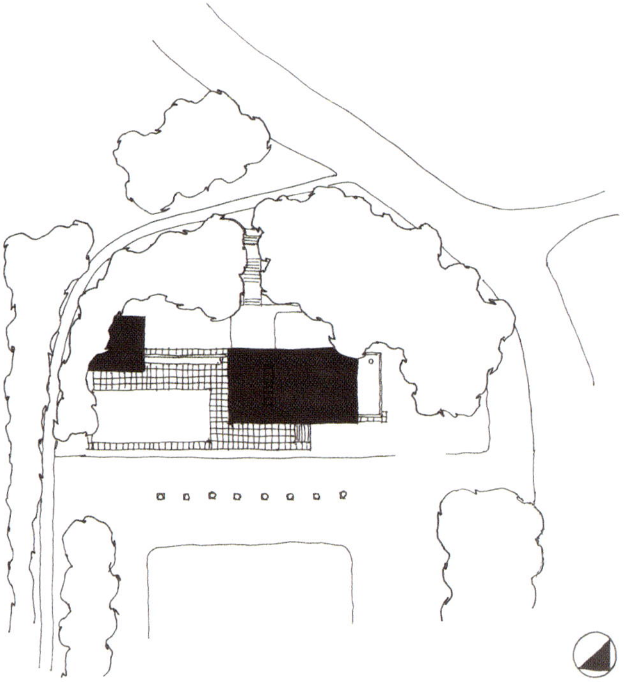

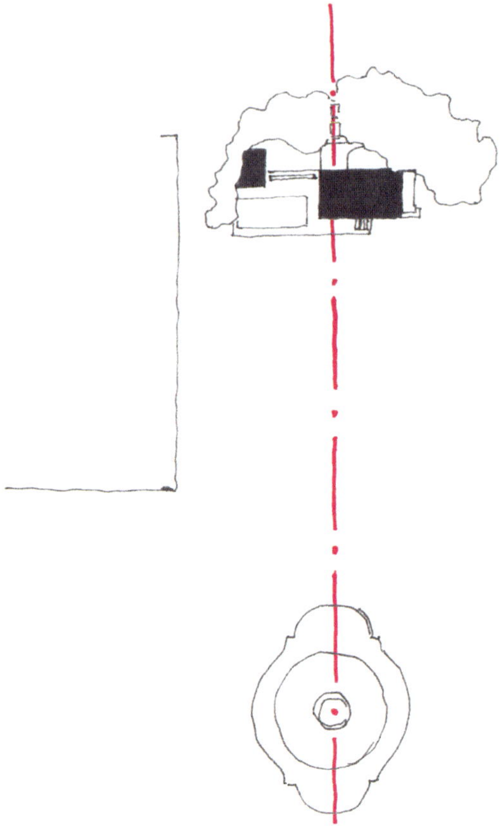

Sliding Planes

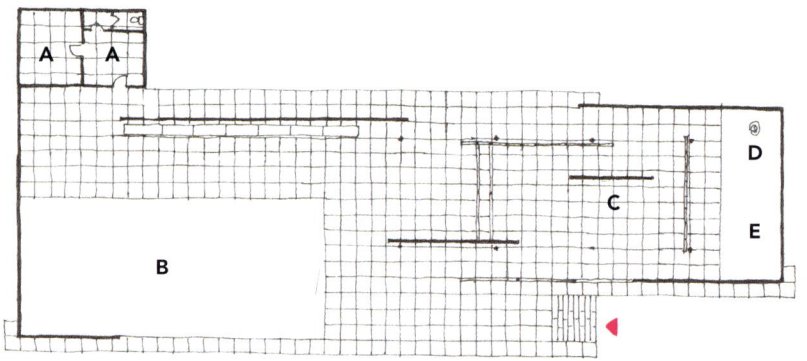

A. Office   **B.** Large Pool   **C.** Seating   **D.** Sculpture   **E.** Small Pool

Diagram 2 (above left). The site plan of the Barcelona Pavilion as constructed in 1929. When it was originally built, eight Ionic columns stood as a screen in front of the building. By the time it was reconstructed in 1986, the elegant vertical elements had been removed.

Diagram 3 (below left). The floor plan of the pavilion as it was in 1929; the current configuration includes doors.

Diagram 4 (above right). The pavilion was never intended to occupy its current site within the Gran Plaza de la Fuente Magica as shown; Mies requested this location. With this calculated move, a strong axial relationship between his building and the center of the plaza was realized.

Barcelona Pavilion

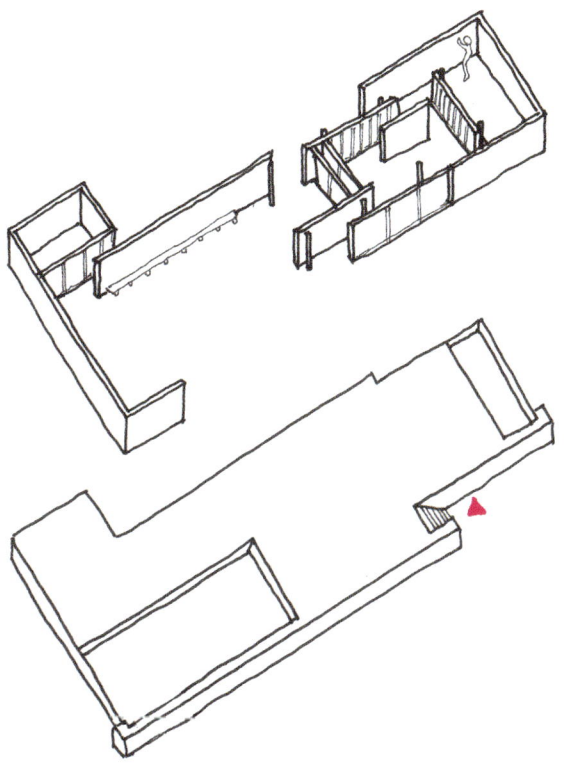

Diagram 5. In this drawing, the partitions have been drawn as a separate entity from the plinth to highlight the latter and its two pools. By elevating the structure on a travertine-covered base, it requires the visitor to make the procession up a flight of stairs before experiencing the space.

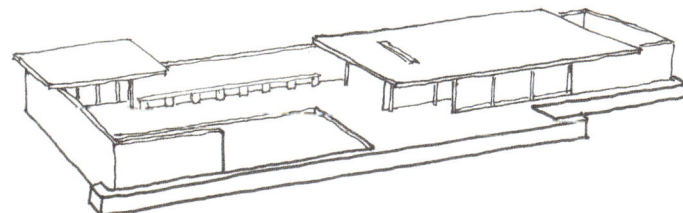

Diagram 6. Long, taut, horizontal lines dominate the elegant composition of the pavilion.

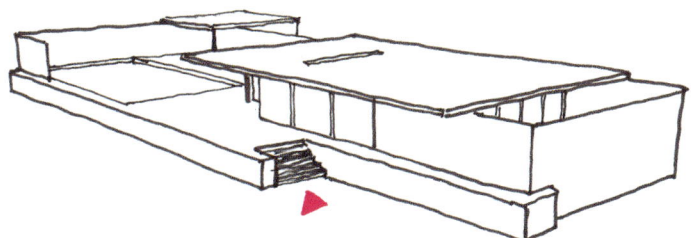

Diagram 7. Entrance stairs come into view when the visitor walks parallel to the building along its northeast side.

Sliding Planes

At 1.1 meters (3'7") square, the travertine floor maintains an overall sense of order and measure—literal and figurative—in plan and section. Each slab of the dark green marble surrounding the small pool and at the entrance, along with the travertine wall behind the large pool, is 1.1 meters high by 2.2 meters (7'2") wide. Lastly, the height of three slabs placed on top of each other establishes the overall height of 3.3 meters (10'10"). One wall, however, is the exception to this rule of thirds. While it is the same height as all the others, it is the only freestanding wall within the pavilion and its rare onyx cladding carries a horizontal seam exactly in the middle, accentuating the intense veining pattern that is characteristic of the stone.

All of the eight slender, cruciform-shaped columns follow the longitudinal seams of the travertine and are spaced apart evenly; only half of them intersect perfectly with the corresponding vertical seams. Nearly all the walls fail to terminate or initiate at a joint line. Seams of the travertine bench behind the large pool as well as its length and position ignore the 1.1- and 2.2-meter distances on the floor and wall. The spacing of mullions at every location observes its own rhythm. By the small pool, the overhead plane's edge aligns exactly with the pale travertine floor but correspondence with the dark green marble walls is nonexistent.

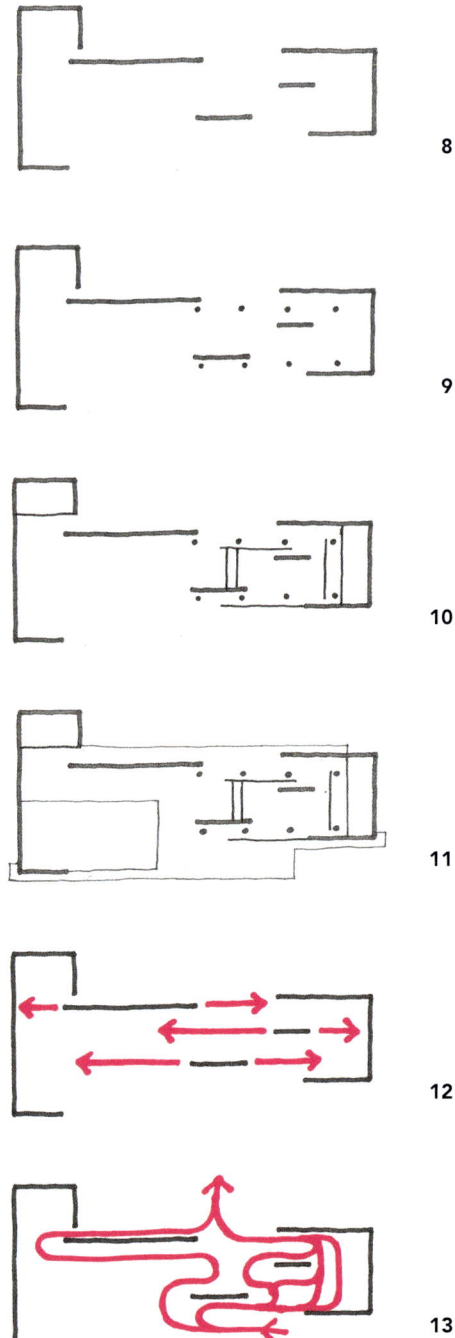

Diagrams 8, 9, 10, 11. Solid walls, made of travertine, marble, and onyx, define the perimeter as well as interior spaces in Diagram 8. Eight slender metal-clad columns, added in Diagram 9, provide more delineation of the pavilion. Diagram 10 includes glazing; the two pools have been added and the edges of the plinth are drawn in Diagram 11.

Diagram 12. The walls are perceived to be in motion, sliding in front of and past each other. It cannot be overstated that Mies devoted much of his attention to the space created by the relationship of these walls.

Diagram 13. Possible circulation routes that allow "people [to] explore its space like a labyrinth."[6] Carefully positioned elements negate a straight line in order to maximize one's experience throughout the pavilion.

Barcelona Pavilion

14

By no means could the Barcelona Pavilion be described as dissonant. The cumulative effect, visually and experientially, is strikingly modern, proportional, and beautiful. **Planes** of travertine, marble, and glass appear to be **sliding**, only stopping as Mies captures a snapshot of their movement. The elegant statue *Alba*, by Georg Kolbe, stretches her graceful form; the soft lines of her body are framed by the rigid and precisely cut stone that surrounds her. Due to the highly reflective surfaces of glass, chrome, water, and polished stone, a profusion of images accumulates, creating ambivalence and duplicity between what is perceived and what is real.

Ultimately, the visitor's movement within the space is fundamental to understanding the complexity of the pavilion; it is through the senses that the experience is magnified, and the beauty of space is brought to life. Accomplishing this intricacy with so little is the genius of the architect. Mies, in later years, would state: "The free plan asks for just as much discipline and understanding from the architect as a conventional plan."[5]

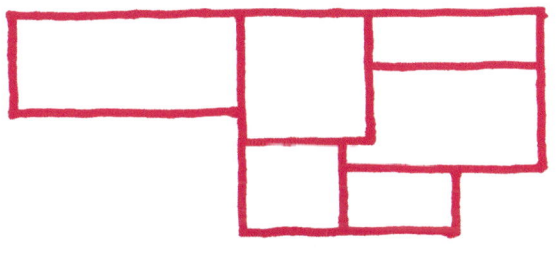

15

16

Diagrams 14, 15, 16. The pavilion can be interpreted as a series of rectangles configured in myriad ways. Historians have alluded to the similarities between the Barcelona Pavilion's composition and DeStijl paintings.

5 MOVING PERSPECTIVES
Villa Savoye

Experiencing architecture activates the participant's senses; shifting and moving perspectives unfold to visually and physically engage the viewer.

Villa Savoye

Nearly forty years old when he was commissioned by the wealthy Pierre Savoye to build a weekend retreat outside of Paris, Le Corbusier designed what was to become one of the most iconic houses of modern architecture. By then, the architect, who was also a painter and prolific writer, had penned a manifesto entitled *Vers Une Architecture* (*Towards a New Architecture*), which was a collection of essays. In addition to noting that "[A] house is a machine for living in,"[1] he posited a series of principles called "The Five Points of a New Architecture" that included: *pilotis*, or columns that supported a building rather than load-bearing walls; open plans that allowed freedom for placement of interior partitions; free *façades*, or walls that had no structural restraints; long ribbon or horizontal windows, providing ample light into even the deepest recesses of the interiors; and flat roofs for gardens.[2] These architectural strategies are visible in the Villa Savoye, which was completed in 1931, five years after he had written this modern thesis.

While Le Corbusier is a towering figure in the Modernist movement of the early twentieth century, his abiding respect for historical structures and the novel ways he sought to reinterpret the works of antiquity is evident. Although the villa appears to share no traits with a Greek temple, Le Corbusier was deeply impressed by the Parthenon and its site, the Acropolis. An appreciable amount of his book, *Towards a New Architecture*, is devoted to this site through observations and sketches. Some have observed that the villa's tripartite form—the pilotis on the ground, the second floor horizontal *piano noble* (the main living area above the ground level), and the roof garden—recalls the base, shaft, and capital of a column; others have compared it to the columns, entablature, and pediment of a classical building.

As a weekend home for the Savoye family to retreat from the hectic tempo of city life, the villa's location in Poissy, a two-hour drive from Paris, initiated the concept of movement. The turning radius of the automobile was the impetus for the semi-circular form at the ground level, which afforded glimpses of the interior through full-height vertical slats of glass at the southeast side of the house, where the entry was located. After the chauffeur brought the Savoyes to the door, a gentle and smooth turn to the left welcomed the vehicle into a large garage.

Diagram 1. The entry elevation is customarily the "face" or front of a structure. Le Corbusier chose to locate the doors into the villa at the back or southeast elevation as shown. Driving past the front and circling to the rear was the choreographed movement that was integral to the design and experience of the house.

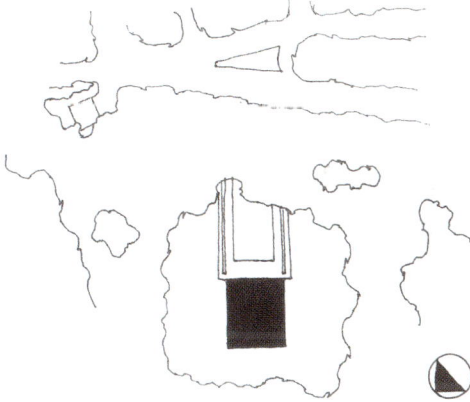

Diagram 2. Site plan; the entrance is located at the southeast. The clearing, carved out of the wooded landscape, was created to be the setting of this refined, white structure.

Moving Perspectives

Once inside on the ground level, the visitor immediately encounters a ramp; its full width is axially aligned with the entry. A spiral staircase is in clear view to the left; its sculptural nature stands in slight tension with its proximity to the taut lines of the ramp. The eye is drawn upward to trace the elegant curve of the stairs as it twists up to reach the first floor. Mainly used by the servants of the house, this spiral staircase acts to counter the overwhelming sense of horizontality. At the roof garden, a semi-circular wall follows the arc of these stairs, recalling the initial encounter at the entry *porte cochere*, with its half-circular glass and vertical mullion façade.

The idealized experience that Le Corbusier envisioned for individuals was through the ramp, the start of a choreographed architectural promenade. The spaces unfold; views and **perspectives move**, rotate, and vary as the occupant moves through the house. His sentiment on movement can be understood as he writes with admiration for North African architecture in his book, *Oeuvre Complete*: "Arab architecture has a precious lesson for us. You appreciate it on foot, walking. Only on foot, in movement, can you see the developing articulation of the architecture."[3] Situated at the center of the house in plan, the ramp is an organizing element, connecting the levels seamlessly while dividing inside and outside. It also made manifest his belief that "one rises imperceptibly by means of a ramp, which is a completely different sensation from going up a flight of stairs. A staircase separates one floor from another; a ramp connects."[4]

On the second floor, the seemingly endless horizontal windows provide a view that is an integral component of the interiors, inviting its inhabitants to visually access nature at all times. In the living room, this thin opening can be seen as it runs uninterrupted—like a ribbon—from one end of the room to the far end of the adjacent terrace. Floor to ceiling glass planes between the living room and outdoor terrace—with one of them on a track to slide away—only reinforces the ambiguity of separation between these spaces as circulation, the sun's path, and the elements are free to move seamlessly from interior to exterior.

The final portion of the promenade along the ramp concludes at the roof garden, a composition of curved, organic-shaped walls that provide a discrete, framed opening to view the bucolic landscape. These sculptural walls sit juxtaposed with the static, rigid lines and structured rhythm of the columns that are prevalent throughout the villa. In similar fashion, Le Corbusier sought to encourage the freedom of movement within, writing that experiences within the house are "constantly varied, unexpected and sometimes astonishing."[5]

Diagrams 3, 4, 5. Drawings of the ground floor plan (Diagram 3), second floor plan (Diagram 4), and the roof garden (Diagram 5).

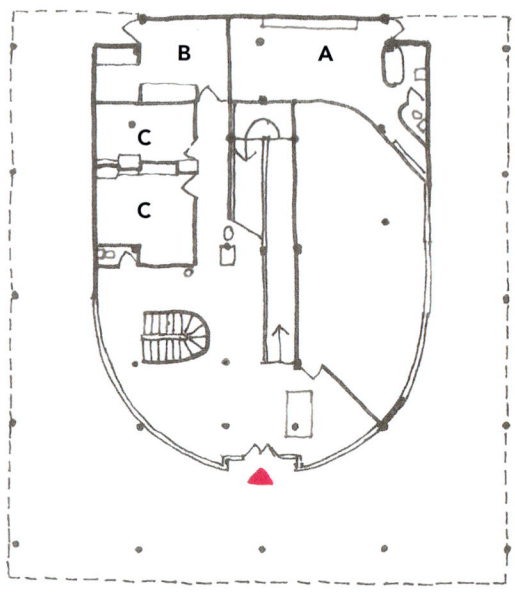

3

A. Chauffeur's Room
B. Laundry
C. Maid's Room

Villa Savoye

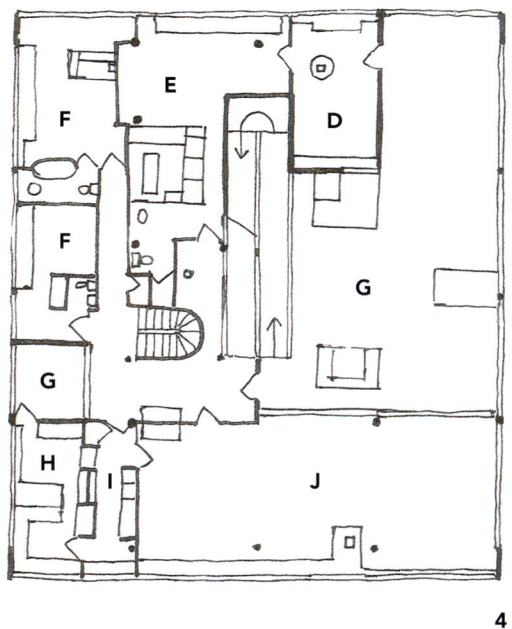

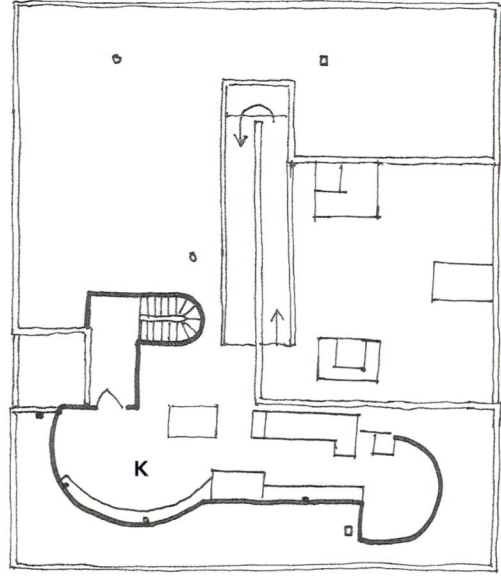

4

5

D. Boudoir
E. Master Bedroom
F. Bedroom
G. Terrace
H. Kitchen
I. Pantry
J. Living

K. Roof Garden

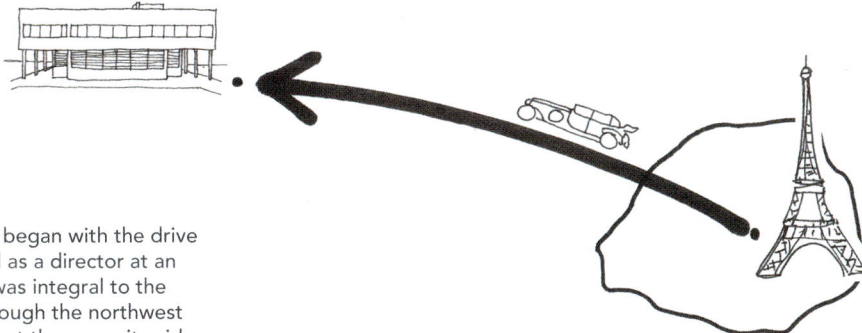

Diagram 6. The arrival to the villa in Poissy began with the drive from Paris, where Monsieur Savoye worked as a director at an insurance company. The vehicular journey was integral to the semi-circular form of the ground level. Although the northwest façade shown is the initial view, the entry is at the opposite side.

Moving Perspectives

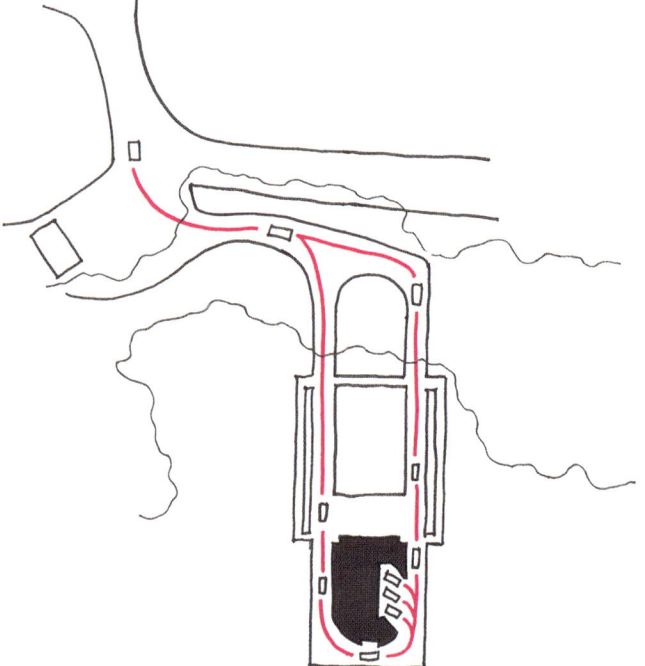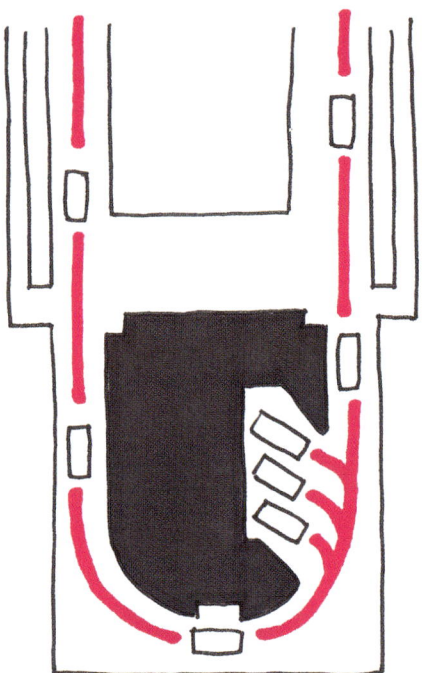

Diagrams 7, 8. Driving counterclockwise, the car went past the front and brought the visitor to the north side of the house. This facilitated the vehicle's entry into the garage as well as its exit.

Villa Savoye

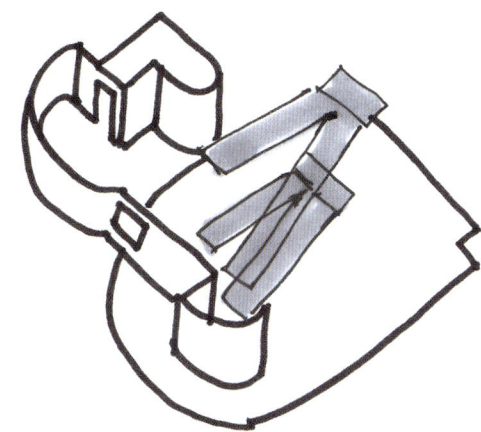

Diagram 9. Access to the floors was mainly via the ramp, rendered in gray. This movement, Le Corbusier wrote, was "a completely different sensation"[6] from that of stairs, and it mirrored the freedom of the forms that were on the roof garden.

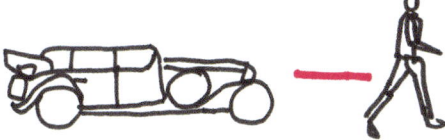

Diagram 10. After the visitor approached the house in the car, the architectural promenade was contingent upon the movement of the visitor.

 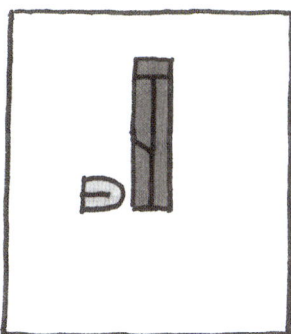 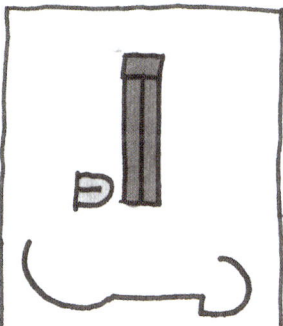

Diagram 11. Circulation between the levels depended mostly on the ramp (in dark gray) that bisected the floor plan and a circular stair (in light gray).

Moving Perspectives

Diagram 12. A study of interior and exterior areas underscores how intrinsic the outdoor spaces were to Le Corbusier's aspiration for this house. White denotes enclosed spaces; dark gray areas are exterior zones. On the far right, even though the entire roof garden is open and there are no complete enclosures, the area in white suggests an "outdoor room"[7] that is shaped by the screen of curved and straight partitions.

Diagram 13. Le Corbusier imagined how "[t]he human eye, in its investigations, is always on the move and the beholder himself is always turning right and left, and shifting about."[8] While he was not specifically referring to Villa Savoye, the architect's agenda to create a meandering experience was realized in this house.

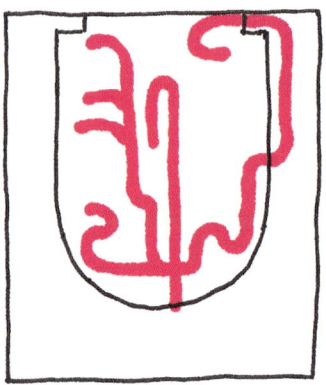 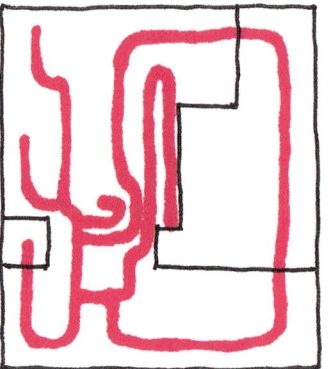 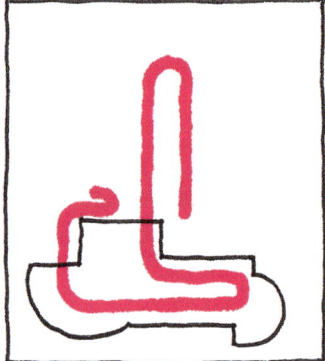

Villa Savoye

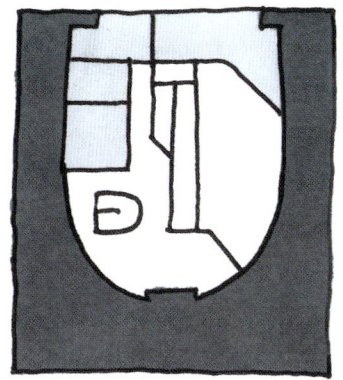 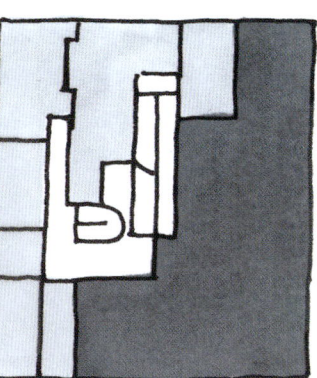 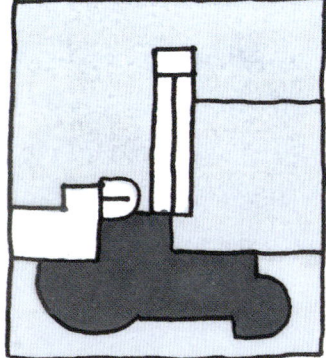

Diagram 14.
The white areas indicate circulation, the light gray represents private spaces, and the dark gray zones are exterior and public spaces.

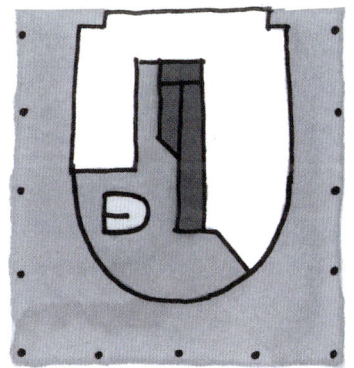 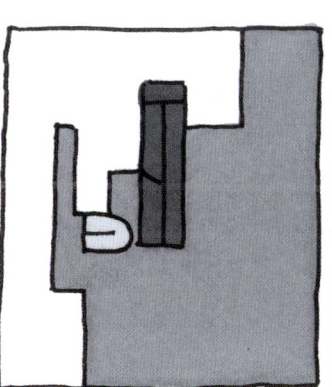 

Diagram 15.
Gray areas correspond to areas of circulation as well as public zones on each level.

Moving Perspectives

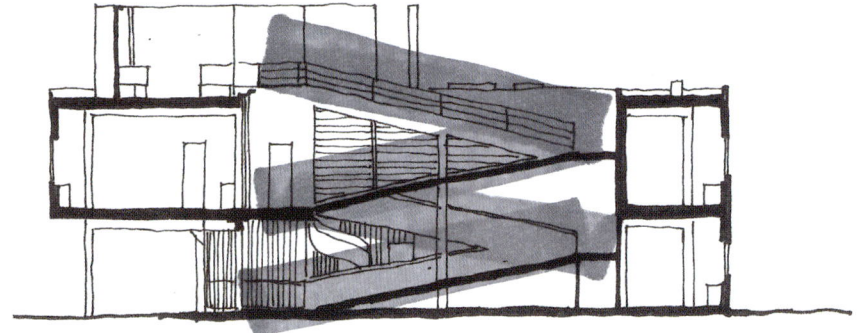

Diagram 16. Viewing the ramp and building in section illustrates the architectural promenade through the center of the house.

Villa Savoye

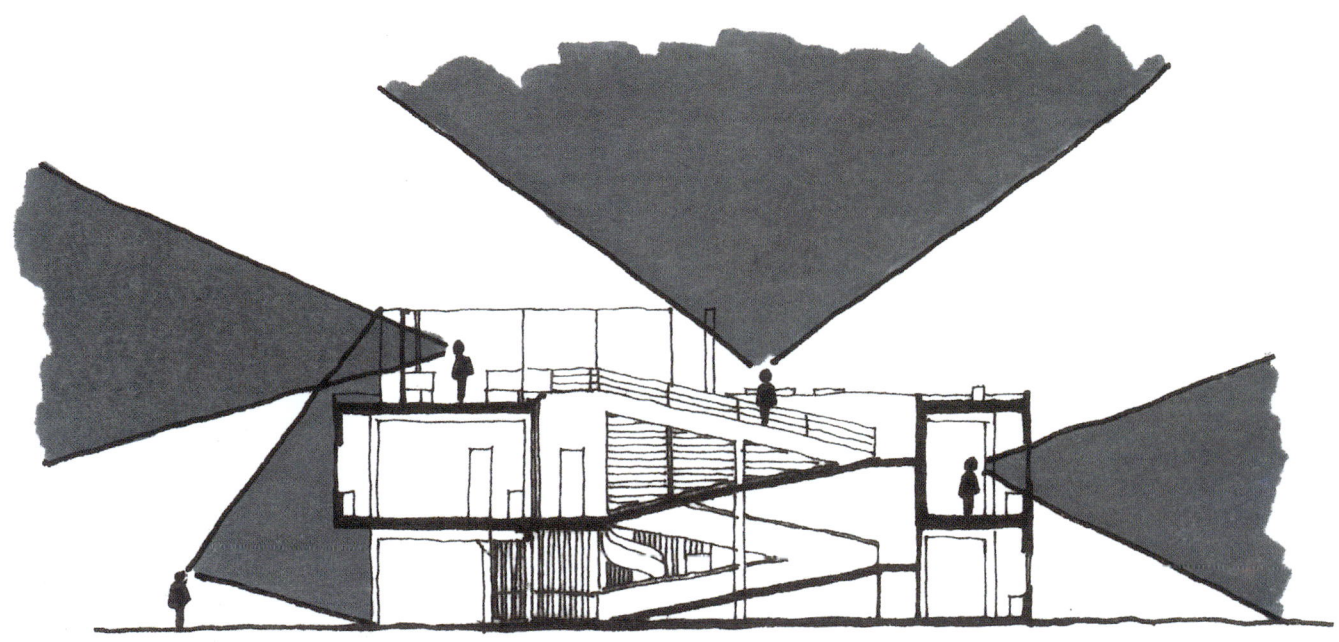

Diagram 17. Villa Savoye was to be viewed as a refine, pristine object within a clearing; the integral experience of the house involved the opportunities to look at the landscape and sky that enveloped the site.

6

COMPRESSING HORIZONTALS
Jacobs House

Compressing horizontals relate intimately with the ground plane, harmonizing with the line where sky and earth meet, identifying with the landscape.

Jacobs House

Little did Herbert and Katherine Jacobs realize that when they approached Frank Lloyd Wright in 1936 with a seemingly improbable proposal—to design and build their house for a total of $5,500, including his fee—their faith in the architect would yield a prototype for Usonian Houses, eventually leading to many variations to be built across the United States.

The etymology of Usonia is believed to be derived from the acronym for United States of North America. While other architects might have had qualms about undertaking the commission for such a paltry sum of money, Wright most likely reveled in the challenge of such a severe limitation. He understood that to be frugal, his years of experience and his innovative methods would be tested; he was also primed for the task. During this time, many Americans, still reeling from the financial devastation of the Great Depression, clamored for affordable housing. Although he had many affluent clients, he was aware that this issue, in his words, was "pressing, needy."[1]

Some strategies—such as the floor heating coils, embedded in sand and covered with a concrete mat—had never been installed before in a residence. Wright experienced this sensation of a heated floor for the first time when working in Japan and it deeply impressed him, as he wrote in his autobiography: "The indescribable comfort of being warmed from below was a discovery." Utilizing this novel approach, he noted that he could dispense with "ugly electrical heat fixtures" that he "always hated" and, at the same time, save the Jacobses money as this strategy would keep Wisconsin winters at bay.[2]

Other cost-saving strategies include: eliminating a full basement; designing a carport that provides sufficient overhead protection from the elements rather than a garage; and removing gutters and downspouts, superfluous because of the deep overhangs of the roof that divert the rainwater away from the structure. There is an honesty with the use of materials—the bricks and wood panels for interior and exterior are one and the same, identified as "thoroughbred" by Wright. This dispensed with the need for extra labor and materials to finish the interiors with lathing, plaster, and paint.[3]

Completed in 1937, the house is arranged in a simple "L" shape: one wing stretching east contains two bedrooms and a study; the other wing reaching south is dedicated to an ample living room and a small dining area. At the intersection of these two arms, constructed entirely from bricks, the bathroom, kitchen and hearth meet, centralizing the piping for water and sanitation for economy. This "L" configuration on the site provides privacy as the two arms facing Toepfer Avenue to the west and the neighbor to the north have very few openings. The space that the arms of the "L" embrace is a garden and lawn; the boundary between backyard and house is blurred, due to the abundance of glass doors at the east edge of the living room and the south side of the bedrooms. Although this strategy was an expense that strained the humble budget, Wright viewed it as a necessity rather than a luxury.

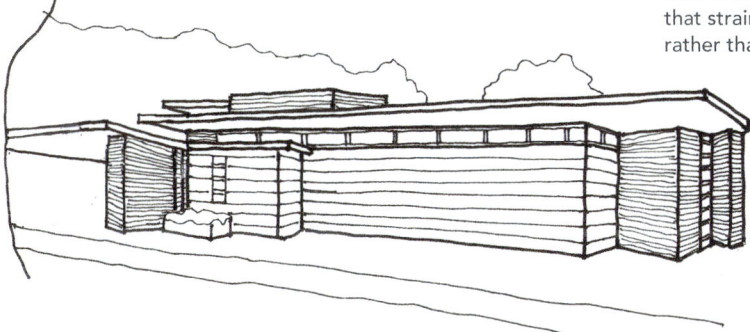

Diagram 1. The horizontality of the Jacobs House figures prominently in this front view, looking east.

Diagram 2 (right). Originally, the Jacobses selected a plot of land that was 60 feet wide by 120 feet deep. Wright designed the house to be exactly 60 feet wide; this was too large for this site, when factoring setback distances from the property lines. The young couple, draining nearly all of their savings, was forced to purchase the adjacent plot, creating enough space for the house, garden, and yard that Wright intended as a part of the design.

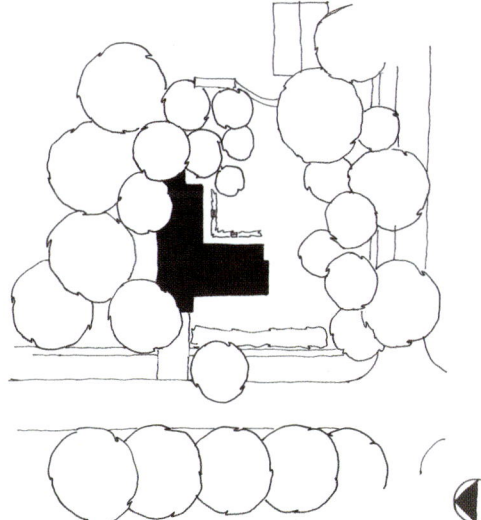

Compressing Horizontals

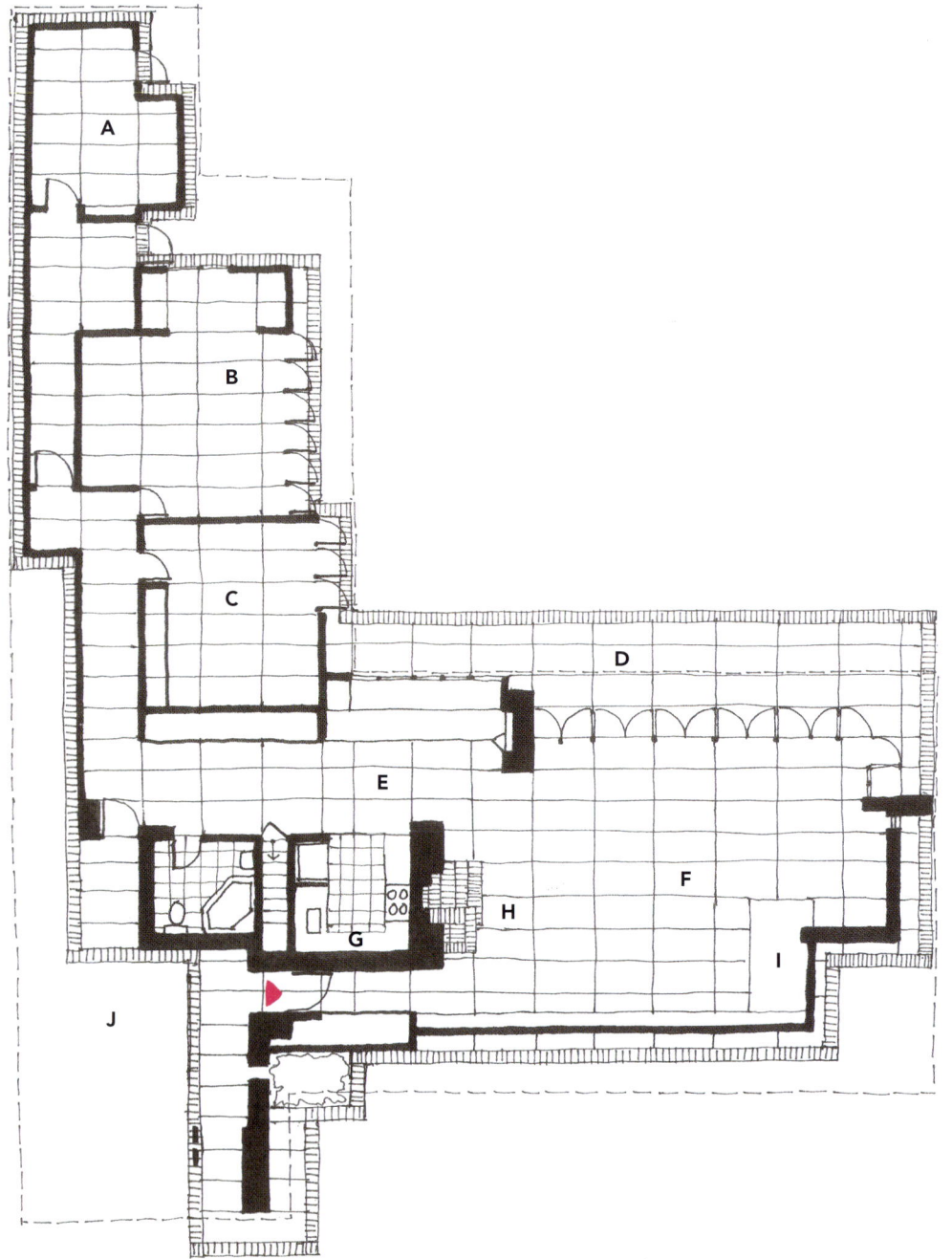

Diagram 3. The floor plan of Usonia Number 1, as Wright occasionally referred to it. He frequently used this "L" configuration for other Usonian houses.

A. Study
B. Master Bedroom
C. Bedroom
D. Patio
E. Dining
F. Living
G. Kitchen
H. Fireplace
I. Built-In Desk
J. Carport

Jacobs House

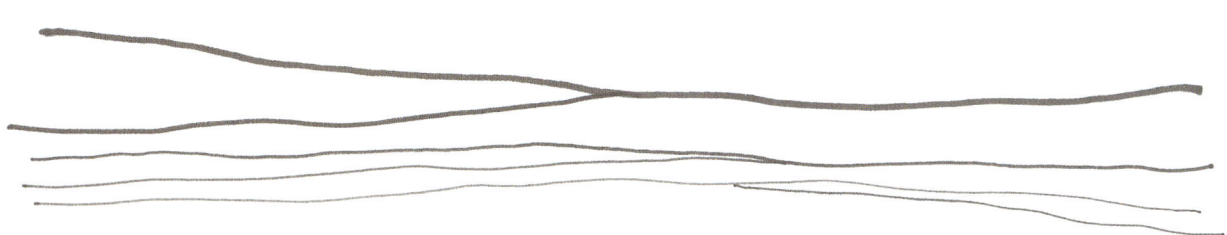

Diagram 4. The horizon in the landscape is a lasting reminder of how Wright integrated this endless line into his architecture and his deep affinity for it.

Diagram 5. The flat roofs, brickwork, and wood panels, expressed as neatly stacked horizontal lines of various thicknesses, appear to compress the house.

Compressing Horizontals

The architect's affinity for the horizontal line is well-known; in fact, he writes that, "this Usonian house . . . extends itself in the flat parallel to the ground."[4] Due to this strong emphasis, the dwelling appears to be a series of **compressed horizontals**; however, this impression is only apparent from the street. Inside, the house opens to the outdoors; Herbert Jacobs later wrote about this "abundance of light that flooded the whole interior through the glass doors of the living room and bedrooms."[5]

The concrete floors are marked off with a two-foot by four-foot grid, as Wright believed that this would greatly facilitate the construction process by delineating the placement of nearly every wall. Perhaps more importantly, it enabled the architecture to accomplish a sense of harmony and proportion. However rigid this grid might appear, he would occasionally deviate from this "unit system," as he referred to it, relying on his well-honed sensibilities when designing. To avoid static, rectangular spaces, the brick and wood paneled walls step back and forth, providing visual and spatial variety.

The Jacobses, fully admitting that owning "a fifty-five hundred dollar house" would preclude them from living a life of extravagance, were nonetheless delighted with their home. A dwelling of "beauty and convenience," as Herbert wrote, was their reward for placing their trust and unwavering belief in Wright. Katherine Jacobs said it best, when she summed it as "[a] simple, luxurious life in a simple luxurious house."[6]

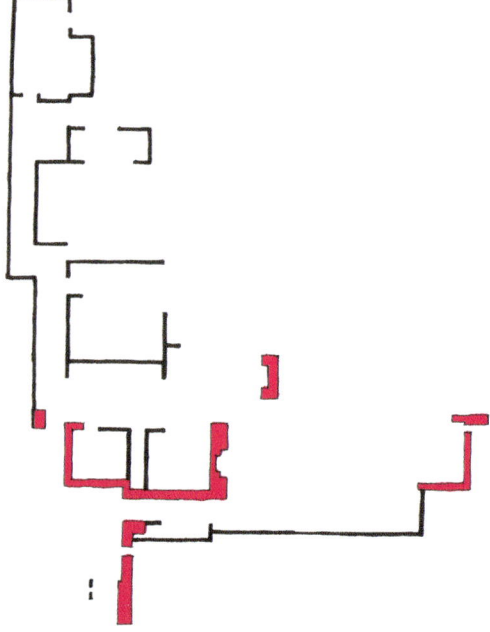

Diagram 6. The areas shaded in pink represent the brickwork that is concentrated mostly around the bathroom, kitchen, and hearth, and located where the arms of the "L" intersect. The thinner lines represent the wood walls, made to be suited for interior and exterior walls, as they were to be one and the same. Lastly, the absence of glass in this diagram underscores its abundant use throughout the house.

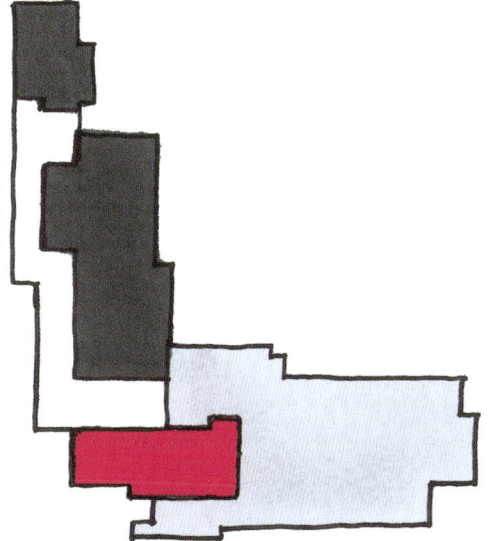
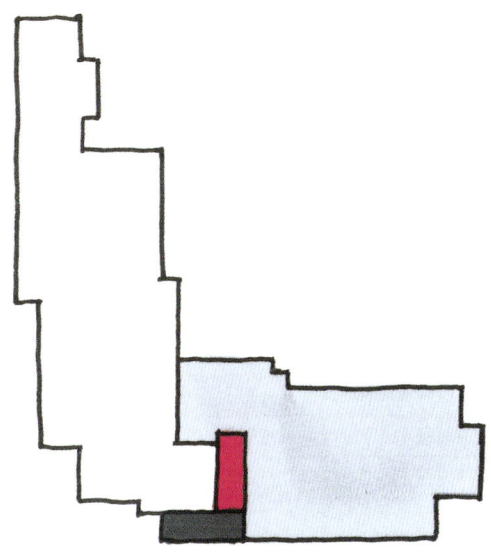

Diagram 7. The core and hearth are the areas shaded in pink. For Wright, the fireplace was the metaphorical heart of the home and it was always an integral part of the design. The dark gray represents private areas—the study and two bedrooms—and a hallway (in white) connects them and the wing to the living room, shown in the light gray. The living room is the most public of all the areas in this diagram.

Diagram 8. Wright frequently created a compact and tight entrance area, shown in dark gray, in order to enhance and contrast the large expanse of space that was the living area, represented in light gray. The fireplace is in pink.

Compressing Horizontals

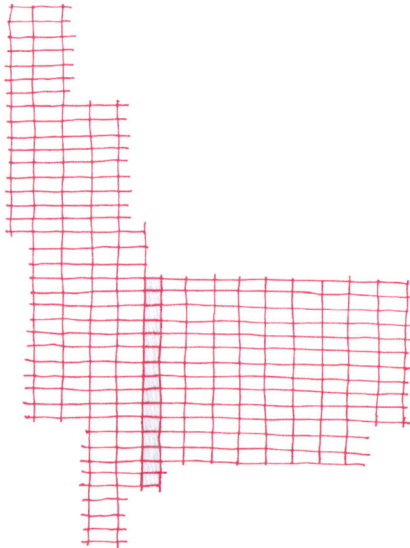

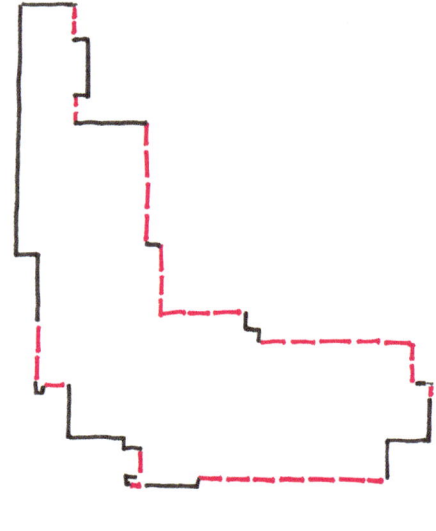

Diagram 9. Wright frequently used a "unit system," a grid that facilitates proportional cohesion of the architecture. This 2' × 4' grid is imprinted in the concrete floor of the Jacobs House; the gray zone shows a slight deviation from the 4' dimension. The two grids have joined along this seam, in a similar manner in which the programmatic differences are split along this line, separating the living area from the bedrooms, bath, and kitchen.

Diagram 10. Placed directly under the roof, clerestory windows provide the interior spaces with a "soft, even light," as described by Herbert Jacobs. He went on, noting that this contrasted with the "abundance of light that flooded the whole interior"[7] from the glass doors located along the bedroom and living areas. For a house of this size, there is a generous amount of glazing, as shown in dashed lines.

Jacobs House

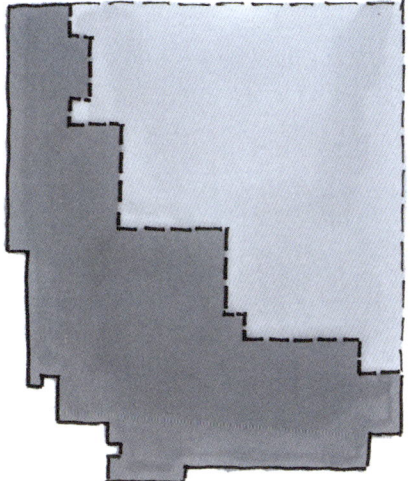

Diagram 11. Integral to the experience of dwelling in this house is the garden, shown in light gray. Wright conceived the two together, placing glass between them, to blur the edge where one ends and the other begins.

7 EXPANDING VOLUMES
Fallingwater

Expanding volumes push out in all directions, creating dynamic layers between cantilevers and overhangs that invite moments to engage with nature.

Fallingwater

Many architectural historians consider Fallingwater one of Frank Lloyd Wright's finest works. It could certainly be argued that it is one of the most famous residences in the United States, due in large part, to the publicity it received after it was completed in 1937. By then, Wright, who was in his early 60s, was enjoying a resurgence of his professional profile; he had been considered to be in the waning years of his illustrious career when he took the commission from Edgar J. Kaufmann, owner of the eponymous department store in Pittsburg, Pennsylvania. Fallingwater, in the January 1938 issue of *Time* magazine, noted that Wright's masterpiece was his "most beautiful."[1]

Arriving at the site in 1934, Wright must have felt a deep affinity for the pristine landscape; prior to this visit, he had observed: "The rock-ledges of a stone-quarry are a story and a longing to me. There is suggestion in the strata and character in the formations. I like to sit and feel it." A topographic map was requested and sent to Wright in early spring of 1935. Keen to review the initial designs and drawings of his house, Kaufmann stopped by Wright's studio, Taliesin, in September. An architectural apprentice, Bob Mosher, who would help oversee the construction of the house recalls: "In the studio, Mr. Wright explained the sketches to his client. Mr. Kaufmann, a very intelligent but practical gentleman, merely said, 'I thought you would place the house near the waterfall, not over it.' Mr. Wright said quietly, 'E.J., I want you to live with the waterfall, not just look at it, but for it to become an integral part of your lives.'" Wright would also later note in an interview that "the natural thing seemed to be to cantilever the house from that rock bank over the falling water . . . Then came Mr. Kaufmann's love for the beautiful site. He loved the site where the house was built and liked to listen to the waterfall. So that was a prime motive in the design."[2]

Diagram 1. This image is a perspective looking west, as one approaches the entry of the house from a walkway that bridges over the river, Bear Run.

Expanding Volumes

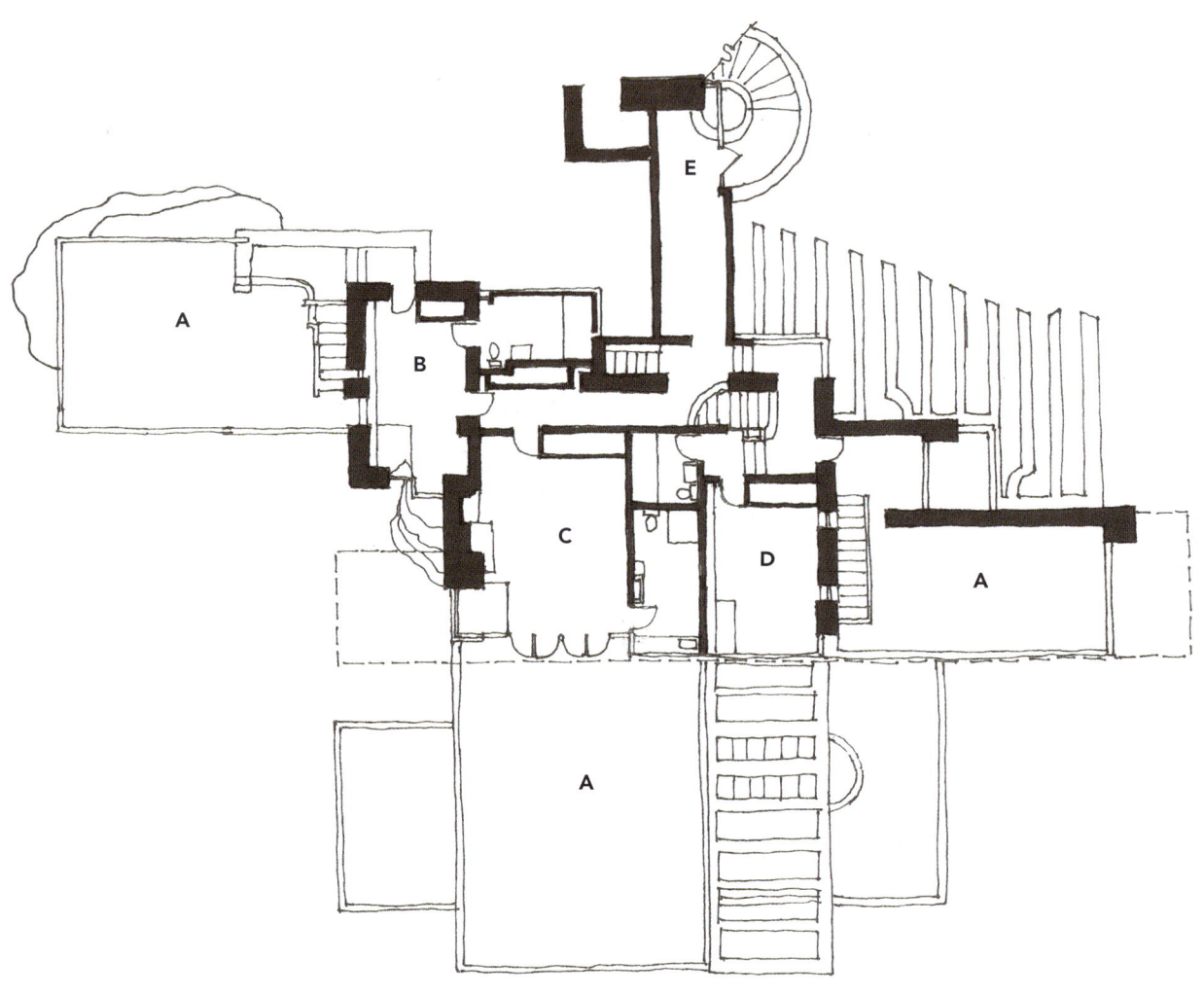

Diagram 4. The second floor is composed mainly of bedrooms and terraces. At the northwest end of the plan, a bridge leads to the separate guest house.

A. Terrace
B. Dressing Room
C. Master Bedroom
D. Guest Bedroom
E. Bridge

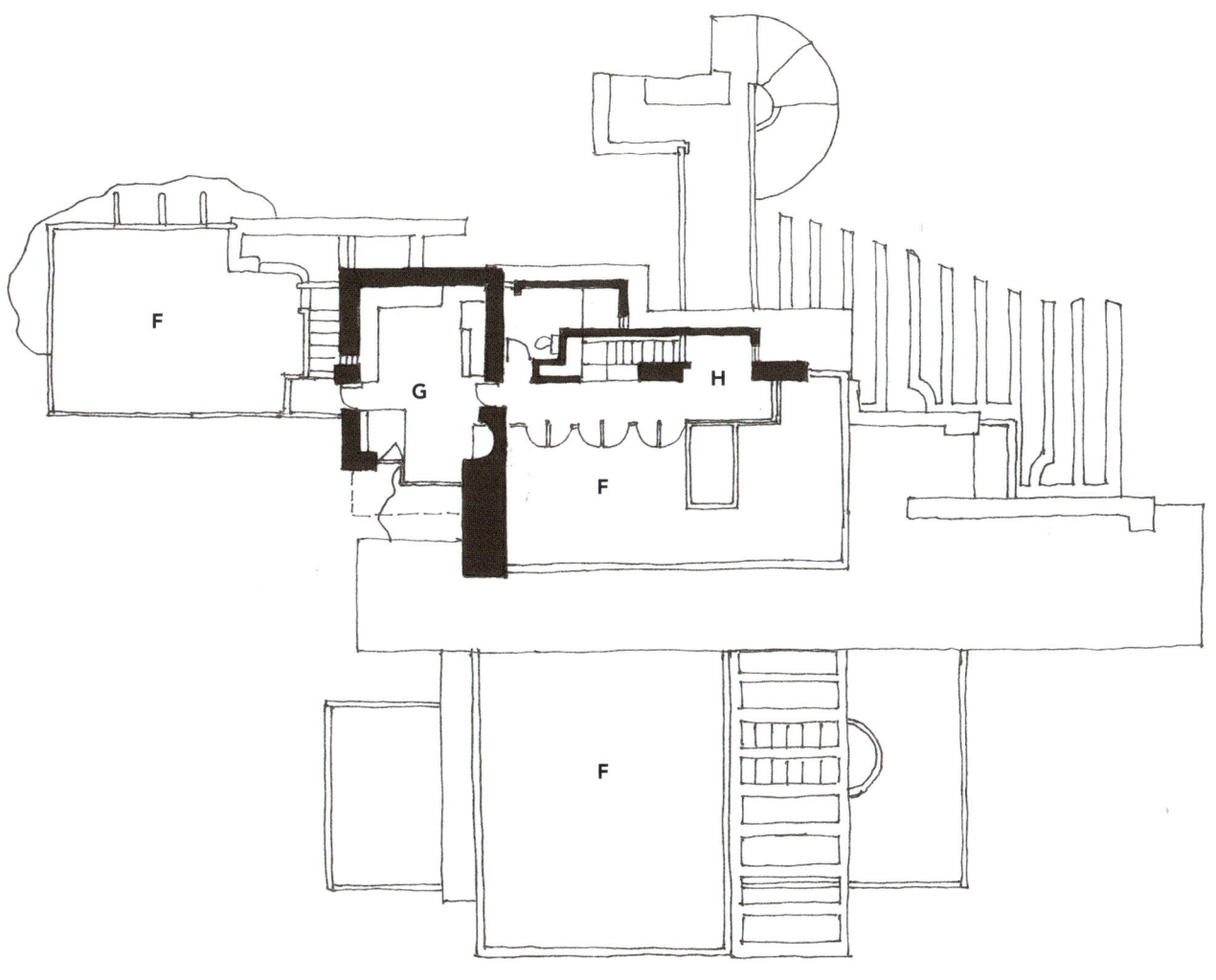

Diagram 5. Secluded and private, the entire third floor is dedicated to their son, Edgar Kaufmann, Jr., complete with a bedroom, study, and terraces.

F. Terrace
G. Study
H. Bedroom

Expanding Volumes

Visually, it is difficult to conceive of the structure as distinct floors; rather, it appears as various cascading levels that mediate between the surrounding forest, boulders, and the river below. The spatial complexity and visual variety of the house is immediately apparent; deep cantilevers, terraces bathed in light, glazing held in frames painted Cherokee red, dark recesses that suggest introverted, interior spaces—these elements hover above the waterfall. Tightly stacked, roughly hewn rocks, casting irregular lines of horizontal shadows, are used for walls that literally and visually ground the structure. Wright orchestrates an unforgettable entry sequence, providing a dynamic view of the house as the visitor crosses a bridge over the water. Surrounded by the beauty of nature and observing a structure that appears to be levitating over the falls, one is struck with the notion that this is no ordinary residence but a peerless work of architecture, or, as Mrs. Liliane Kaufmann wrote to Wright, "Living in a house built by you has been my one education."[3]

Although the house initially presents itself as a series of floating terraces, the barely detectable entrance at the north is hidden between the rock walls, making the entrance incongruous with the expansiveness. The sensation of *terra firma* is prominent as the driveway seems to cleave a path between the building and the boulders and the house seems to be a natural extension of the rocky hillside. Wright continues to "compress" the visitor through a small and confining entrance loggia; there is even a horizontal beam at the front door, seeming to limit the portal's height, but upon entering the living room, the **volume** immediately **expands** from all sides, unfolding towards the beautiful scenery of the surrounding trees. The room pushes beyond the confines of the glass; generous-sized terraces at the south and east invite the visitor to traverse the room and walk towards the light.

The waterfall is seen and heard from above—a staircase with a glass cover or hatch leads directly to the stream—while also providing cool air during hot summer days. Edgar Kaufmann, Jr., describes Wright's design as being able to "keep the main room in touch with the movement and energy of the run (the falls)."[4]

Directly above the staircase, a skylight pierces the roof, granting a simultaneous view of water, forest, sky—all at this location. This airy transparency is balanced by the massive stone hearth located near the dining table. Being inside the house allows an experience of the waterfall and nature in the way that Wright had intended—feeling the safety and enclosure of the rugged rock formations while providing the freedom of the expansion of space stretching into the horizon. His belief in the horizontal line was ever-present in his architecture: "I see this extended horizontal line as the true earth-line of human life, indicative of freedom. Always."[5]

Architecture never overpowers nature; Wright has a profound respect for the bond between his works and the environment. Perhaps Edgar Kaufmann, Jr., who spent many years at the house his parents commissioned, was most acutely aware of the architect's sensitivities as he wrote: "Wright's insights penetrated more deeply. He understood that people were creatures of nature, hence an architecture which conformed to nature would conform to what was basic in people."[6]

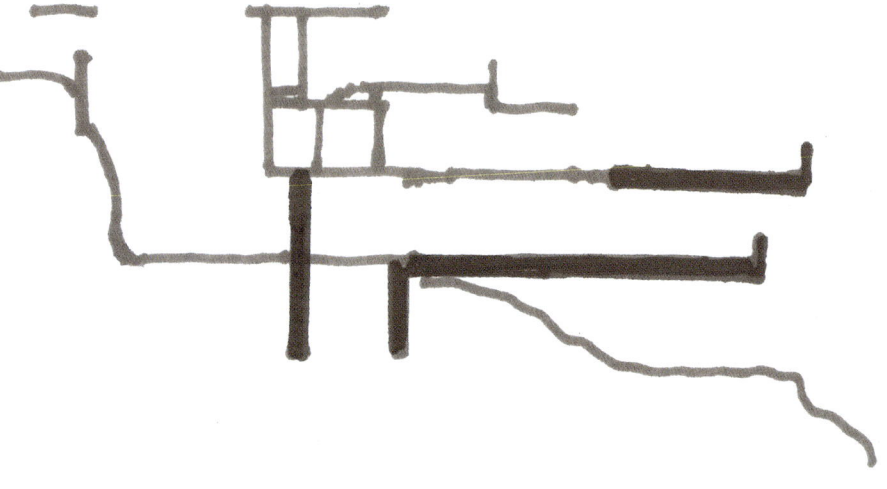

Diagram 6. Much of the house cantilevers over the falls of the river. Construction of the house would prove long, tedious, and difficult for many reasons, including contractors—as well as Mr. Kauffman—who would undermine the validity of the structural drawings that Wright provided.

Fallingwater

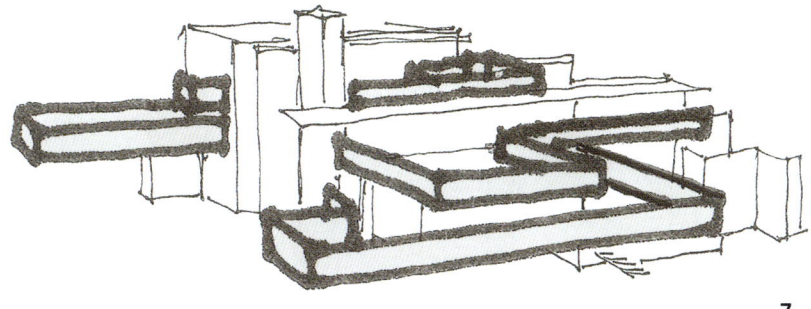

7

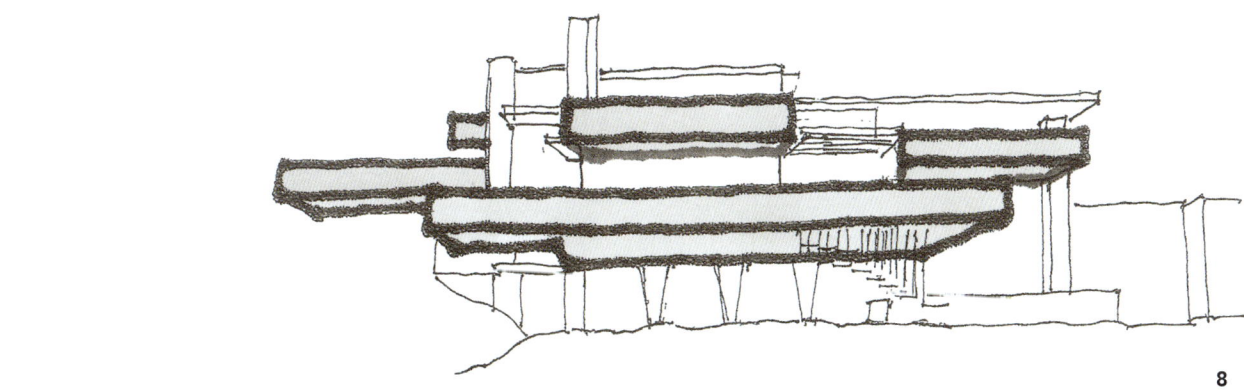

8

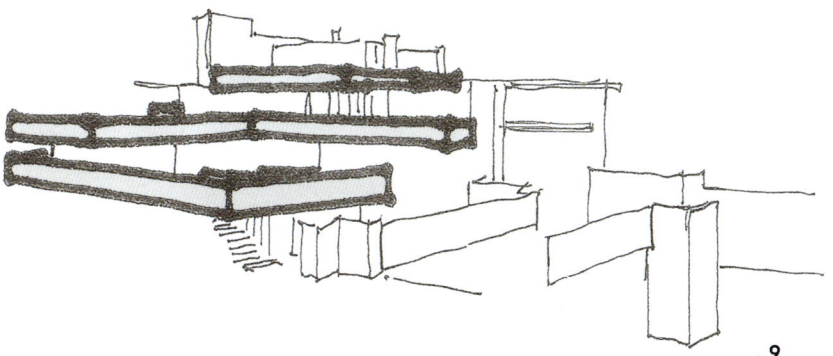

9

Diagrams 7, 8, 9. The many cantilevering terraces provide outstanding and ever-changing views of nature. These areas extend in nearly every direction into the landscape as "it is in the nature of any organic building to grow from its site, come out of the ground into the light,"[7] as noted by Wright. Diagram 7 is a view looking north; Diagram 8 is the view of the southeast elevation; Diagram 9 is the house seen from the east.

Expanding Volumes

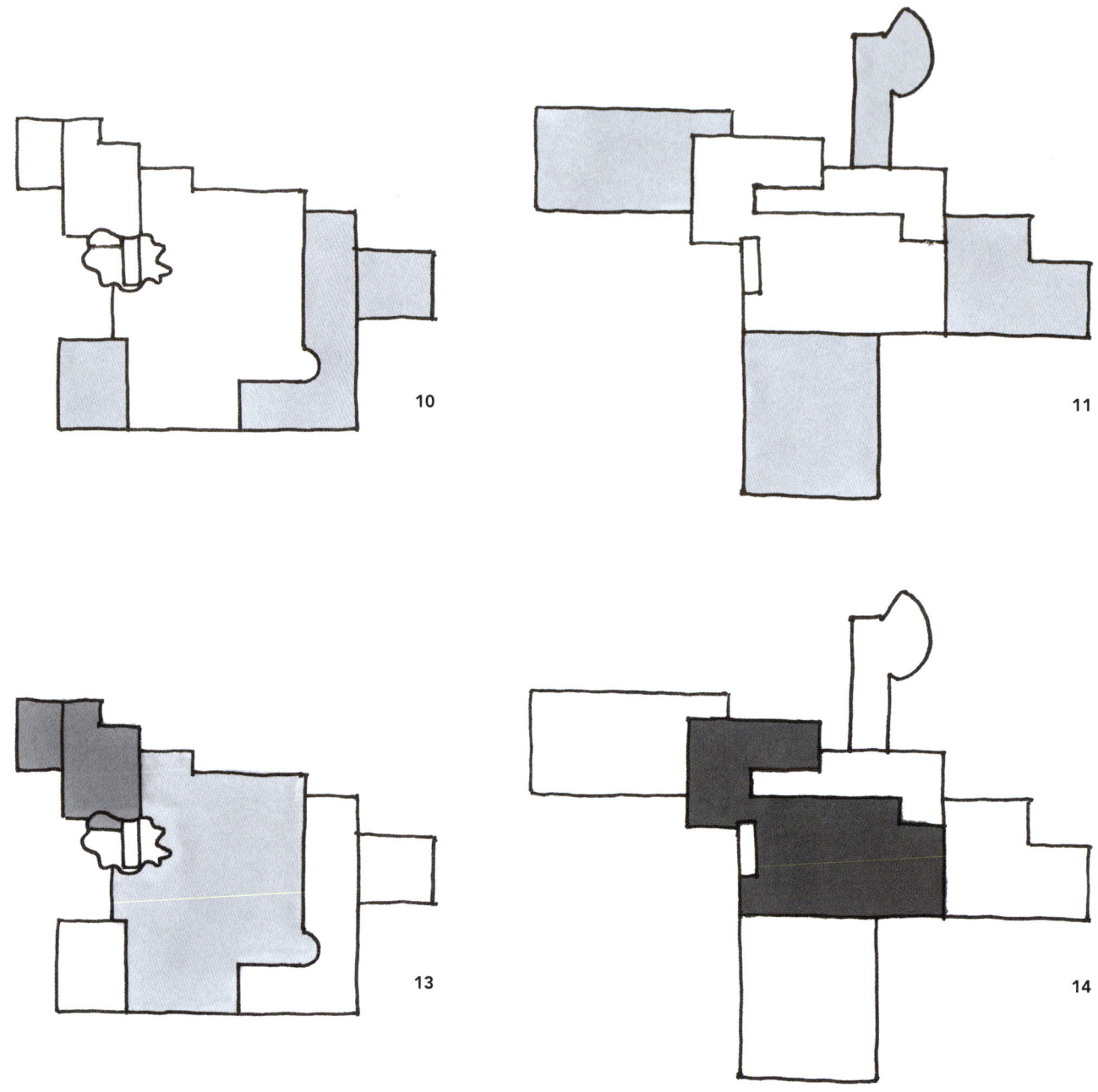

Fallingwater

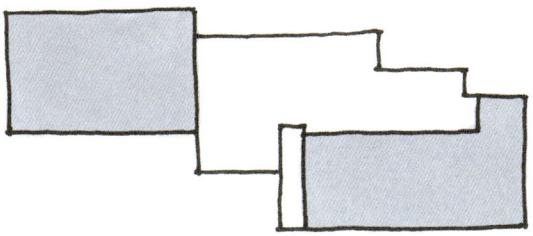

Diagrams 10, 11, 12. Due to the generous number of terraces (shown in light gray on each floor), the majority of the interior rooms have direct access to an outdoor space.

12

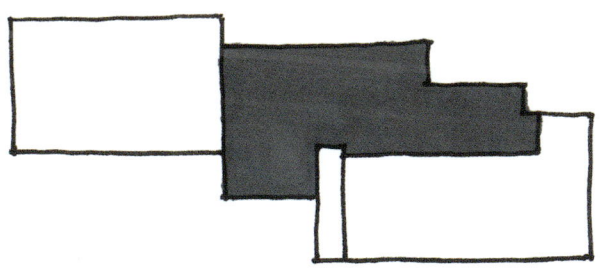

Diagrams 13, 14, 15. On the first floor (Diagram 13), the light gray represents the most public space while the medium gray identifies the semi-public spaces of the kitchen and sitting room. The second and third floors (Diagrams 14 and 15) are private spaces; the bedrooms are located there, rendered in dark gray.

15

8 EXTENDING RECTANGLES
Kaufmann House

Pristine, extending rectangles stretch across the expansive site, creating exterior zones that blur the boundary between interior spaces and the landscape.

Kaufmann House

In the town of Palm Springs, located in the Sonoran Desert of California, Edgar J. Kaufmann, built a house to escape the dreary winter months of the northeast. Over a decade earlier, his decision to hire Frank Lloyd Wright to build Fallingwater in Bear Run, Pennsylvania, had made headlines; the house graced the cover of *Time* magazine in 1938. He clearly favored an entirely different expression of architecture for this residence. Rather than commissioning Wright to design this winter home, Kaufmann sought another architect: the Viennese-born Richard Neutra. When describing the house, completed in 1947, Neutra unapologetically states that it "is frankly an artifact, a construction transported in many shop-fabricated parts over long distance. Its lawns and shrubs are imports, just as are its aluminum and plate glass." Rather than integrating the architecture as a form emerging from the land and appearing "organic," it is a refined object, with **extending rectangles** positioned within an oasis-like landscape. This stance should not be interpreted as his indifference to the context of the house nor seen as his diminished capability to be sensitive to the environment; in fact, Neutra writes passionately about connecting to the nuances of a place: "My experience, everything within me, is against an abstract approach to land and nature, and for the profound assets rooted in each site."[1]

The plan consists of two axes that align with the cardinal points; the majority of the house is positioned along the east-west direction. At the heart of the home, an open, generous living and dining space is partially separated by a fireplace. This space has the benefit of glazing on the north, south, and east; sunlight, views to the rugged mountains, and the pool are all accessible from this central location. The master bedroom and a pool stretch eastward from the living room and a wall extends beyond, defining a portion of the landscape that is strewn with rocks and native vegetation. Opposite this area to the west are two study rooms (formerly maids' rooms) and a kitchen. A carport at the south and a covered walkway leading from it terminates at a large entrance; continuing north, two guest bedrooms are separated from the main house by a large patio.

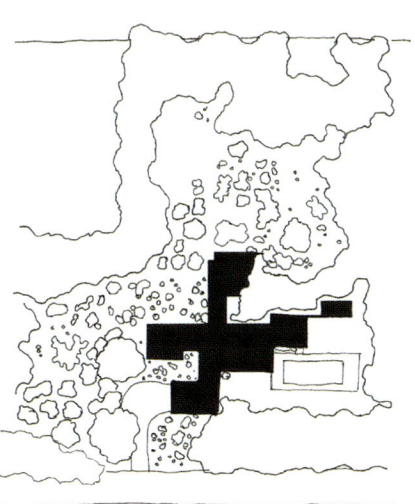

Diagram 1. The rugged, natural terrain is in sharp contrast to the rectilinear lines of the house, as seen from the southwest. Neutra never intended for the architecture to appear as an extension of the environment but, rather, to have "a design idea fitting sensitively into the landscape."[6]

Diagram 2 (right). The site plan shows the extensive use of rocks and native vegetation surrounding the house. Painstakingly restored, beginning in 1993, part of the renovation included the purchase of the adjacent plots of land, preserving the beautiful views of the desert terrain from the interiors that Neutra had once envisioned.

Extending Rectangles

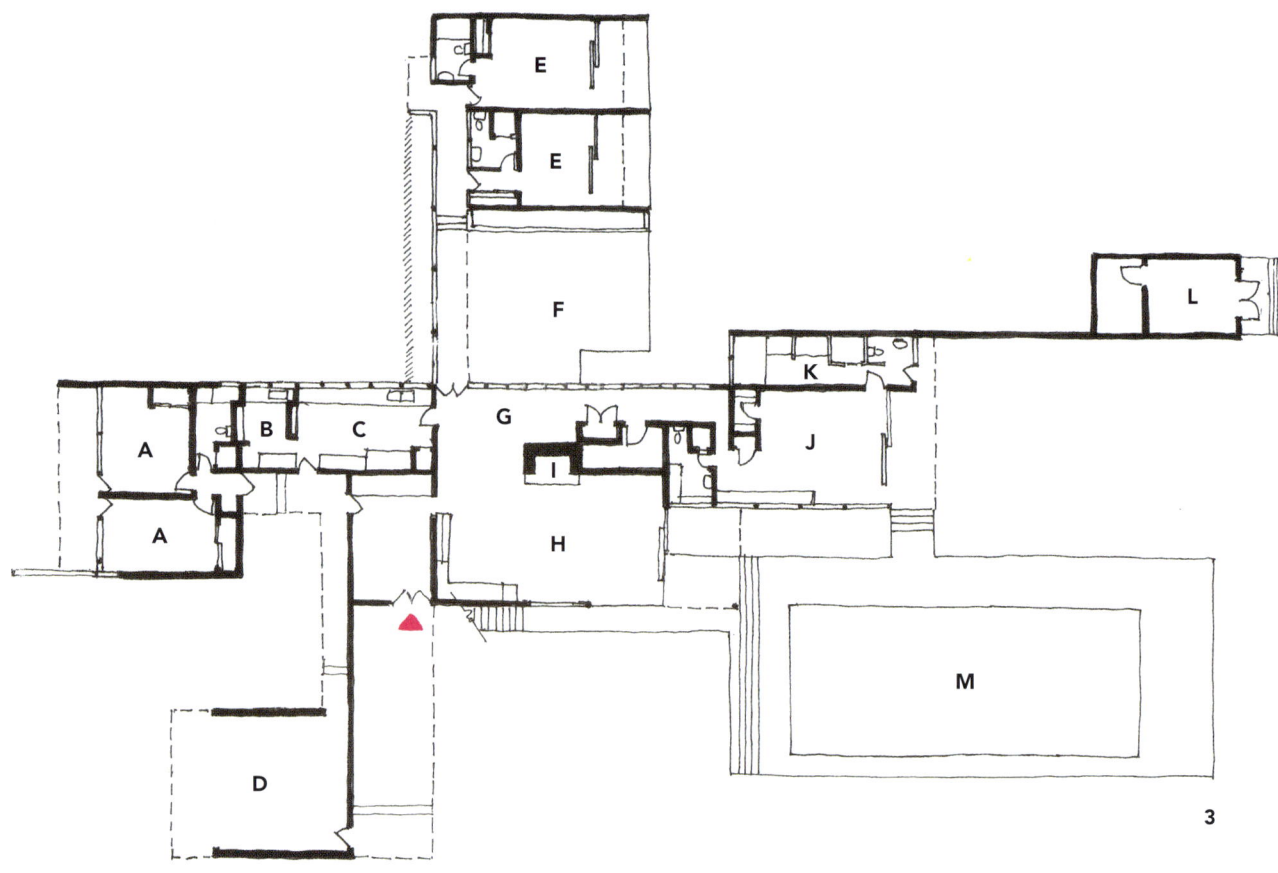

Diagrams 3, 4. Nearly the entire house is on the first floor as shown in Diagram 3. The plan reveals the long east-west axis configuration that intersects with the shorter north-south axis. The diminutive second level, or "gloriette," as identified by Neutra, in Diagram 4, is accessible via an exterior staircase, located south of the living room. This upper area facilitates a visual connection to the various mountain ranges and landscapes beyond the immediate site.

A. Maid's Room
B. Storage
C. Kitchen
D. Carport
E. Guest Room
F. Patio
G. Dining
H. Living
I. Fireplace
J. Master Bedroom
K. Dressing Room
L. Utility
M. Pool
N. Roof Terrace

Kaufmann House

A bird's-eye view of the structure provides a reading of the house as a series of rectangles expanding into the landscape. The form appears to reflect Neutra's thoughts: "The architect who is sensitive to his site is not content with merely digging a foundation as a means of securing adhesion between the building and the ground. As a further means of site-anchorage he may send out tentacles of structure to catch or hook some surrounding feature of the land."[2] Along the "arms" of each wing, outdoor spaces are captured; in some places, the only physical separation between indoors and outdoors is large sheets of glass that slide away. These outdoor spaces were not superfluous areas but, instead, integral to everyday life. Neutra was deliberate about incorporating them into the design rather than merely surrounding the house with greenery and plants. He wrote: "A house surrounded by a garden is one thing, but a house that has an *articulated outer extension of the living area* is another thing for the body and soul."[3]

Extending into the landscape achieves Neutra's aesthetic, which aligns with the dictates and vernacular of the International Style. With its long, taut lines, thin columns, and abundant use of glass, a sense of weightlessness is realized while providing beautifully framed views of nature in nearly every space. However, his design rationale—providing comfort while living in a climate such as southern California—demonstrates his deep admiration for the traditional architecture of Spain and Latin America. Deep overhangs and covered walkways provide relief from the unrelenting sun, as do shading louvers along the west side of the guest wing. Also, his palette of materials includes textured stone, recalling the color of the desert, and wood, providing warmth and visual relief from the steel and glazing used throughout the house.

Although local ordinances did not allow for second stories on residences, Neutra's creative interpretation permitted a small, semi-enclosed terrace or "gloriette," as he labeled it. It was not uncommon to see open, roof-top spaces used for sleeping quarters during the hottest evenings. Formally, the roof terrace gives a stronger profile to a structure that is predominately flat. Experientially, the use of vertical louvers to regulate the sun's intensity along the west and north façades provide beautiful and striking patterns of light and shadow that move across the walls and floor. Neutra described the various elements of the house as "reflect[ing] the dynamic changes [in] . . . the moods of the landscape."[4] Over fifty years later, when speaking about his late father's work, Dion Neutra (also an architect) would echo his late father's sentiment about movements and variation within the Kaufmann house: "My favorite series of slides shows how the building responds to changes in the light."[5]

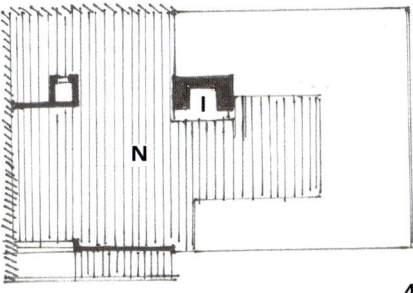

1

Extending Rectangles

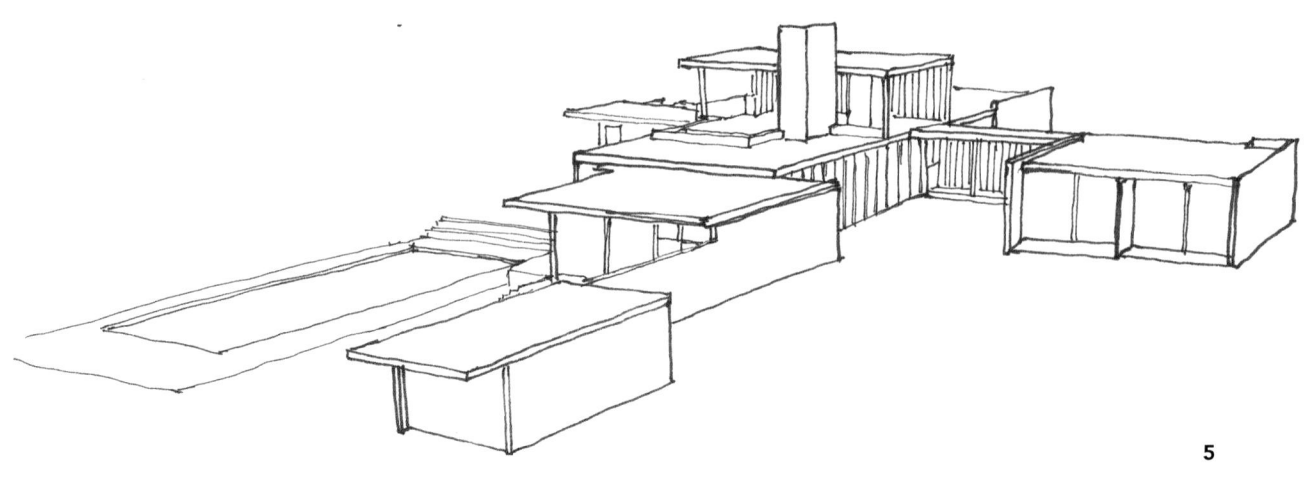

5

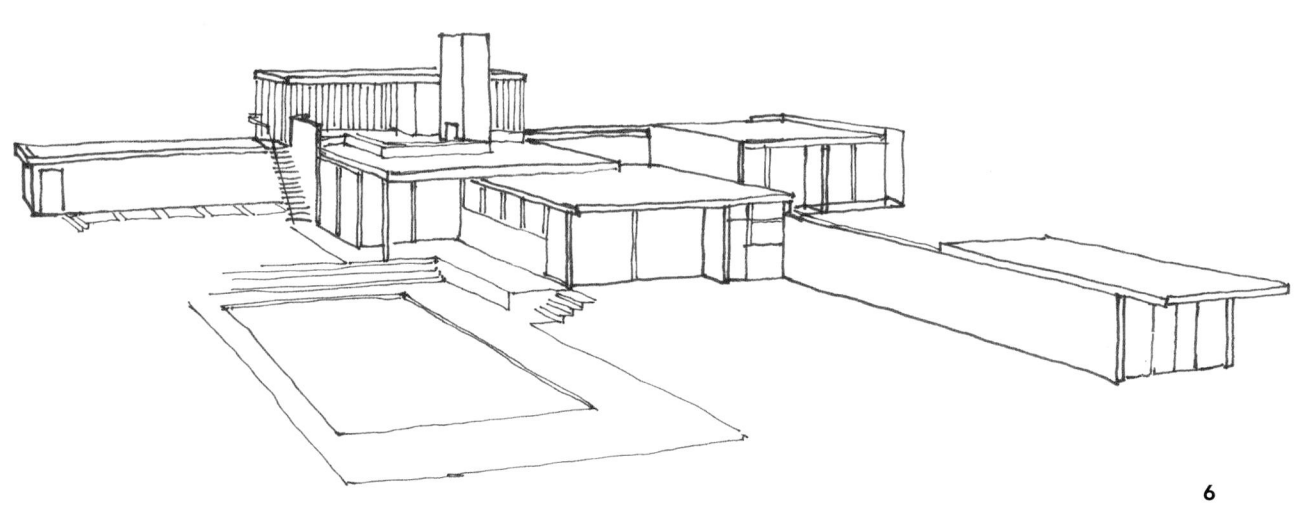

6

Kaufmann House

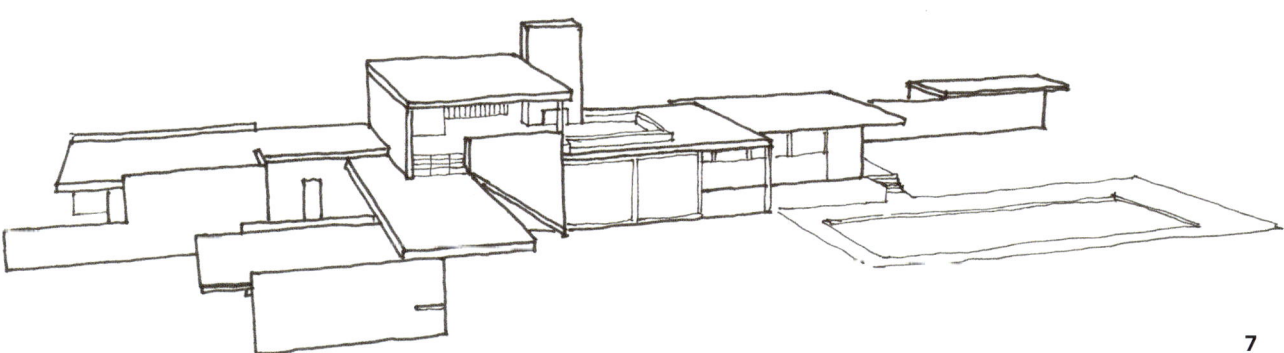

7

Diagrams 5, 6, 7. Shown in various perspectives from above (Diagram 5 is looking from the northeast; Diagram 6 is a view from the southeast; Diagram 7 is looking northward), the house's sprawling rectangular volumes reach out towards the cardinal points. In each instance, an area of land adjacent to the house becomes an integral part of the interior experience.

Extending Rectangles

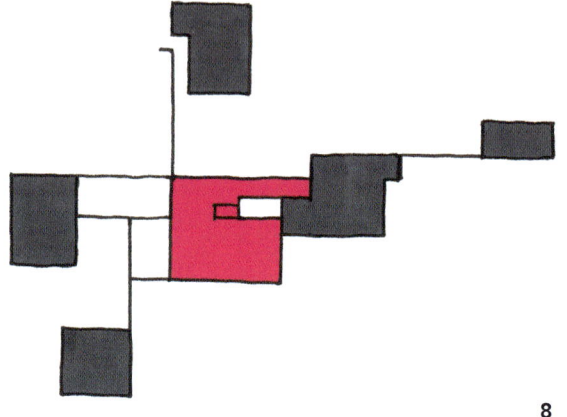

Diagram 8. The heart of the house, in pink, is the living and dining room. The gray areas are private and semi-private components: master bedroom, guest rooms, carport, storage, and study rooms.

Diagram 9. Forming a cross, two axes come together with the majority of the spaces clustered along the east-west line.

Diagram 10. In this diagram, private spaces are shown in dark gray. The living and dining area, the most public, are colored light gray with the semi-private spaces in medium gray.

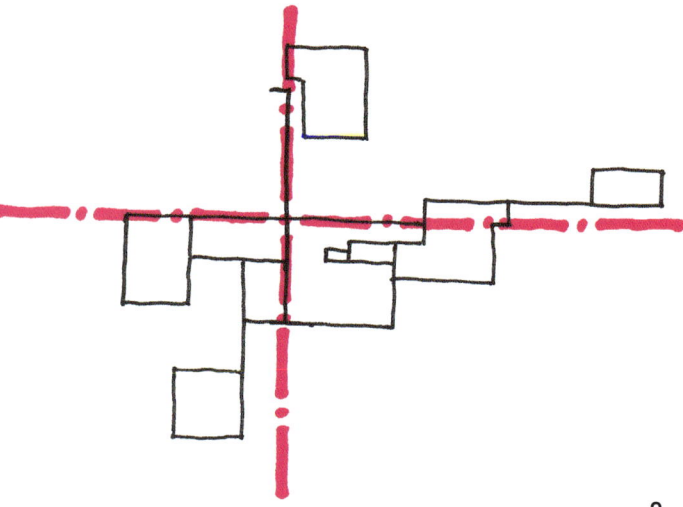

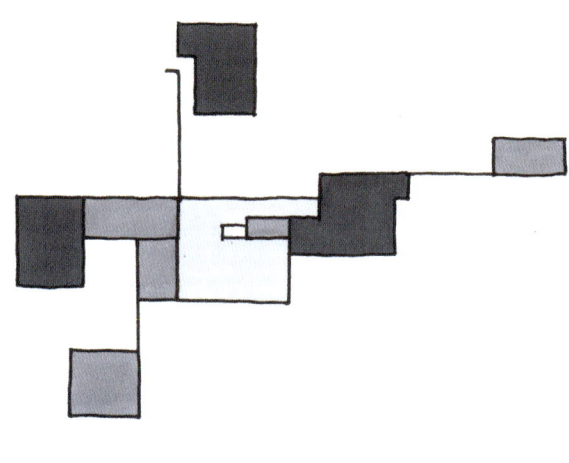

Kaufmann House

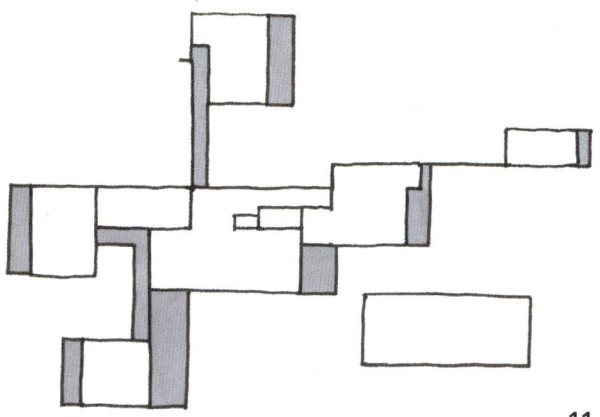

11

Diagram 11. Exterior spaces incorporated in the architecture that protect the users from the sun's rays—through overhangs or covered walkways—are in gray, a constant reminder of Neutra's sensitivities of the dwelling in a desert climate.

Diagram 12. It is as though Neutra conceived of this floor plan from a large rectangle, integrating the landscape within this box. He felt strongly about the context of the residence, noting: "While not grown there or rooted there, the building nevertheless fuses with its setting, partakes in its events, emphasizes its character."[7] The darkest area would be used mostly by guests while the medium gray zone served the Kaufmanns. The most public area, in the light gray, would be accessible to everyone.

12

9 SPLITTING ZONES
Eames House

To seamlessly circulate between living and working spaces, even as these zones are physically split but in close proximity, is the ultimate way to harmonize such aspects of life.

Eames House

Case Study House No. 8, known more colloquially as the Eames House, served as the residence for Charles (an architect) and Ray (a painter) from 1949 until the time of their deaths in 1977 and 1987, respectively. As two iconic figures in American Modernism, it would be highly appropriate for the prolific designers to fashion their own residence to reflect their lifestyle. The opportunity to design their dwelling, flawlessly combining work and living spaces, materialized through their fortuitous friendship with the editor of *Arts & Architecture* magazine, John Entenza. Sponsorship of an experiment called the Case Study House Program afforded Entenza an opportunity to advance an agenda—introduce modern architecture to Post-War America. He was able to curate the architects that would design these homes and establish "some direction to the creative thinking on housing being done by good architects and good manufacturers whose joint objective is good housing."[1] He would even live in one of these—Case Study House No. 9—in close proximity to the Eames House. Prefabricated and off-the-shelf elements, unorthodox for residential use at the time, were utilized to highlight the ease and speed with which the Case Houses could be constructed.

Separating work and living was antithetical to the way the couple approached their lives. Both were endlessly fascinated with their world around them; this sense of wonder pervaded the objects they designed. They embraced working where they lived; even in their first residence, an apartment in the Westwood area of Los Angeles, a spare room became an impromptu work area. By the time they had moved into Case Study House No. 8, they had established their office in Venice, California, so it was not imperative for them to create a secondary studio or office space. However, the idea to continue their design pursuits at home would greatly influence the layout of their house.

The initial design of the Eames House, tucked away within the hills of the Pacific Palisades, resembled a disconnected L, with the elongated leg protruding into a sloping meadow. This living component, as a partially cantilevered volume that hovered over the field, afforded a commanding view of the Pacific Ocean beyond the grove of eucalyptus trees, while the shorter appendage (the studio or work segment) was set more modestly against an existing hill.

Diagram 1. An exterior view from the southeast corner of the site.

73

Splitting Zones

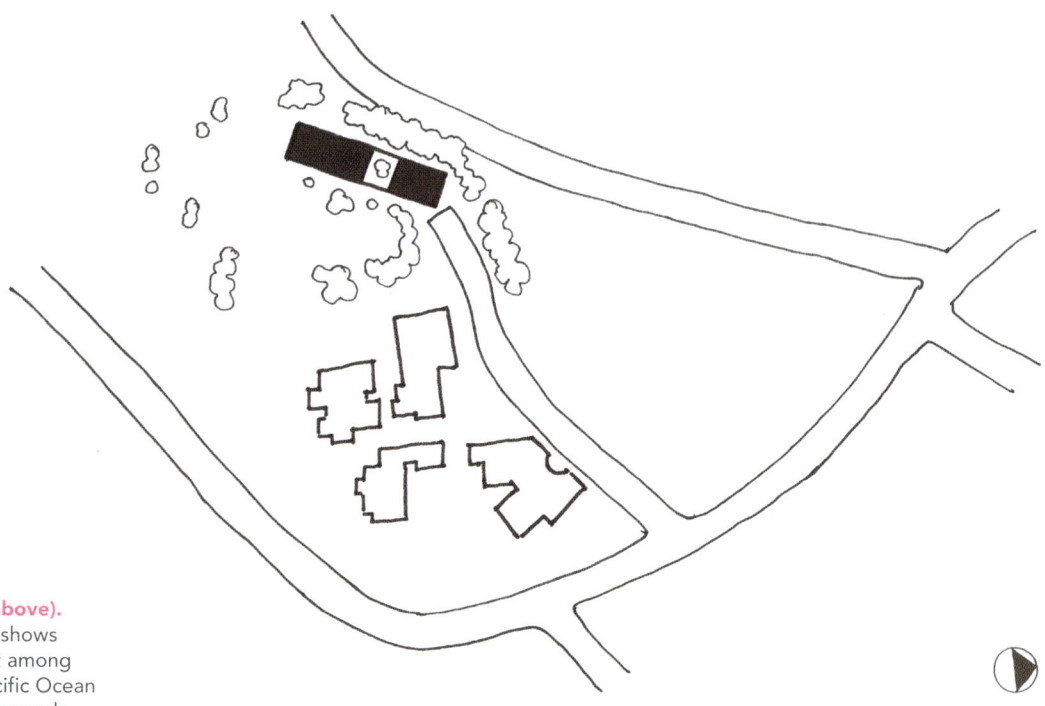

Diagram 2 (above). The site plan shows the house set among trees; the Pacific Ocean can be seen towards the southeast.

Diagram 3 (below). This illustrates the progression from the public street (shown in dark gray) to a semi-public street (shown in light gray) to an open, private meadow within the dashed lines.

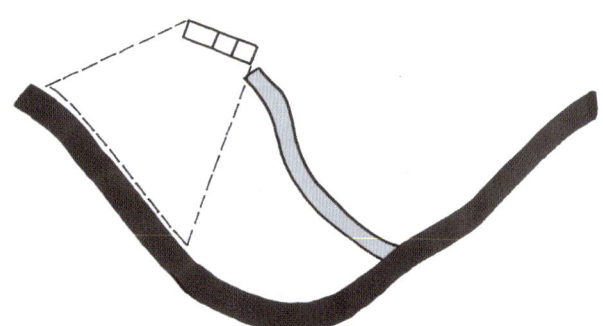

Eames House

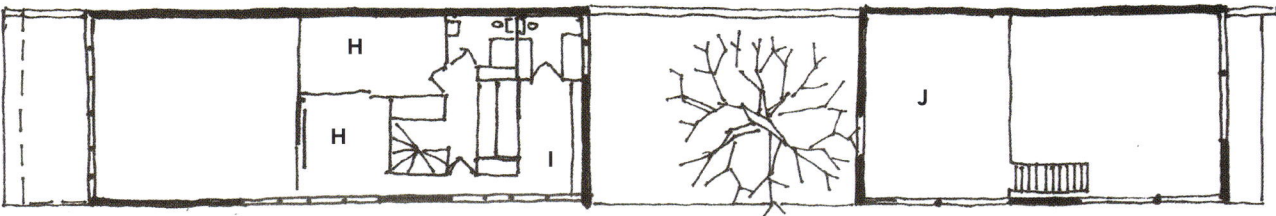

Diagram 4. The second floor illustrates a spacious two-story living room and studio at either end of the house.

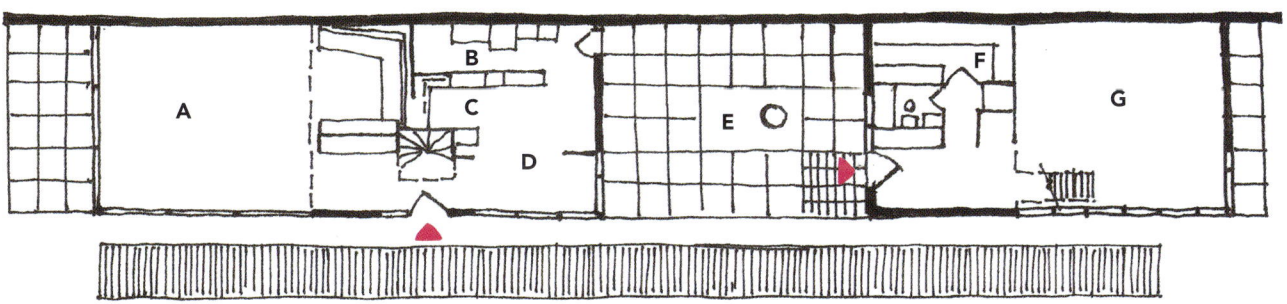

Diagram 5. Viewing the ground floor, one can see how the living and working spaces contain both private (closed) and public (open) space.

A. Living
B. Utility
C. Kitchen
D. Dining
E. Courtyard
F. Darkroom
G. Studio
H. Bedroom
I. Dressing
J. Workroom

Splitting Zones

Over time, the final iteration of the design was simplified into a rectangle with two **zones**—living and working—**split** apart by a generous outdoor space. Relocated to the back edge of the site, the Eameses had greater use and view of the meadow, a part of the landscape that "they had fallen in love with,"[2] as Ray noted.

The temperate climate and the nearly endless days of sun in Southern California invites people to expand their living (and even working) domain into the outdoors. This is exploited in the design of the house. The small, intimate courtyard accommodates the dual purpose of a passage between the residence and the studio while providing respite or a place to pause.

With the physical separation of the two functions, it is apparent how the Eameses could rapidly and conveniently transition from the studio to their home. The work area, consisting of a two-story space, darkroom and storage area, provides a buffer from the most public domain of their property (the driveway and the road leading up to it) as it is the initial portion of the residence that greets the visitor. The second, larger volume is the heart of their home; living room, dining room, kitchen, bedrooms, and other spaces that fulfill quotidian needs occupy this private area. At the south end, an overhang defines an outdoor area that is both a visual and physical continuation of the expansive living room. Interior spaces and exterior areas are artfully blurred as only changes in floor material and the use of glass physically separate the inhabitant from the elements.

While the use of steel and glass might have rendered the volumes of the house austere and restrained, the interior is filled with personal memorabilia, art, potted plants, cut flowers, trinkets—a sense of memories permeates throughout. Indeed, it challenges the notion that modern architecture is bereft of the warmth of humanity. The residence, with its modular black steel delineating a grid pattern on the façades, reminds the visitor of a Mondrian painting. A rich kaleidoscope of materials—panels of white, blue, red, and yellow, along with wire-embedded, clear, and opaque glass—exudes playfulness, not unlike their influential work, which helped to define mid-century Modernism in America.

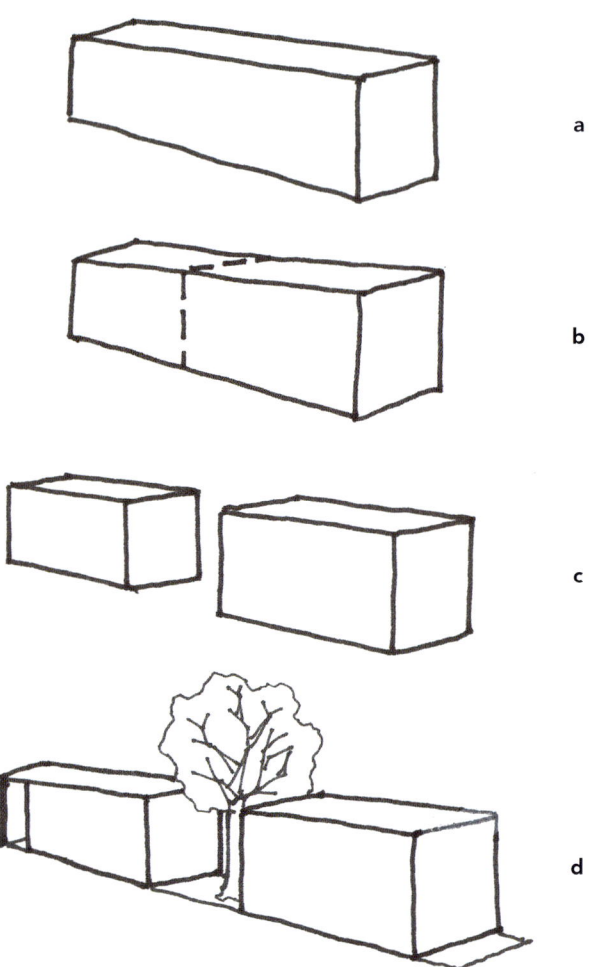

Diagram 6. Imagine a large, rectangular volume (a) . . . split in two (b) . . . which creates an intimate courtyard (c). Small outdoor areas bookend the entire house (d).

Eames House

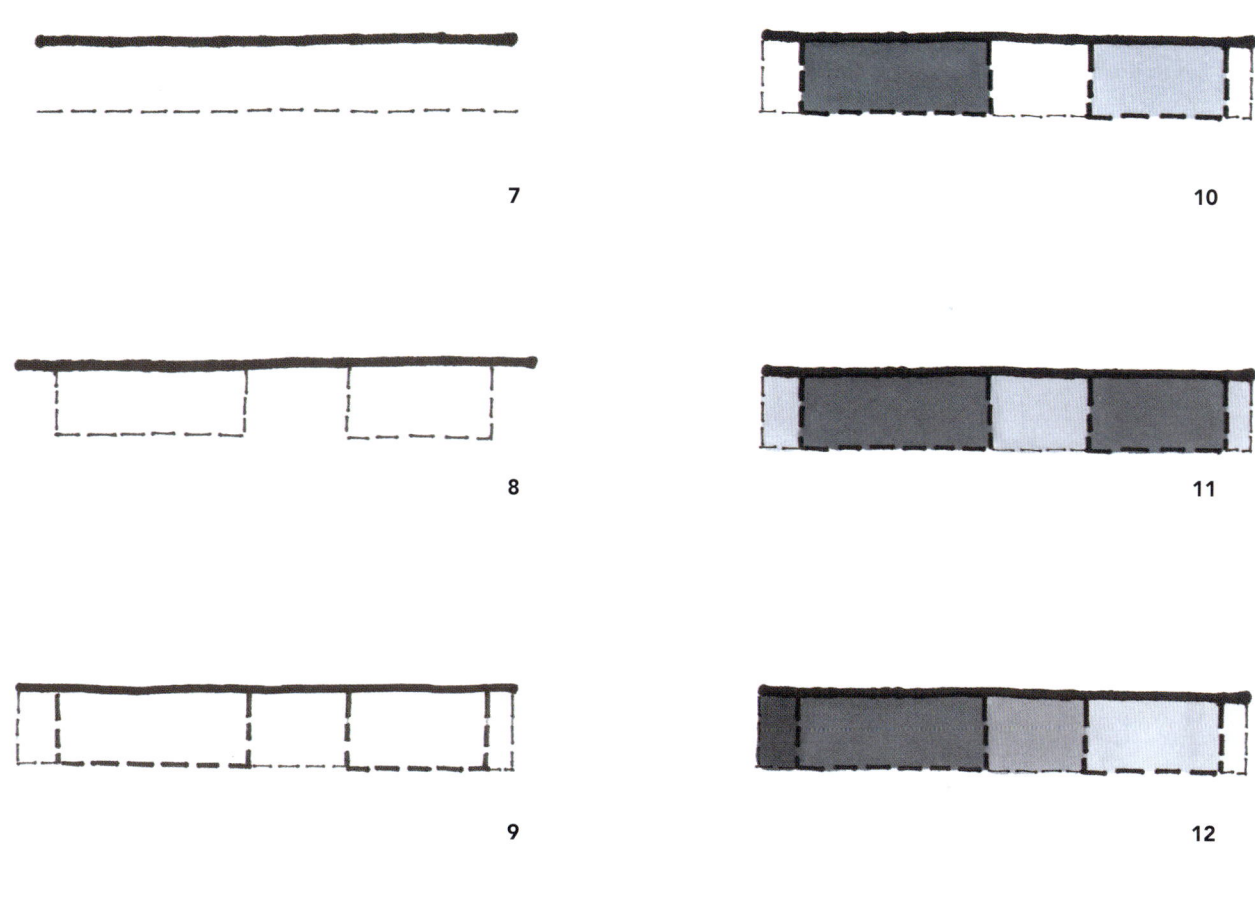

Diagram 7. A thick line represents a heavy, poured concrete wall, contrasting a predominately light glass façade, shown as a dashed line.

Diagram 8. The concrete wall literally and visually anchors the two volumes.

Diagram 9. Exterior spaces, an integral part of the house, are defined with pavers and extend the living and work spaces.

Diagram 10. The light gray area represents the public "work" volume; the dark gray is the private "live" space.

Diagram 11. Three zones in light gray are exterior spaces; the darker gray spaces are enclosed.

Diagram 12. This diagram represents the gradation of public spaces (lightest) to private zones (darkest).

Splitting Zones

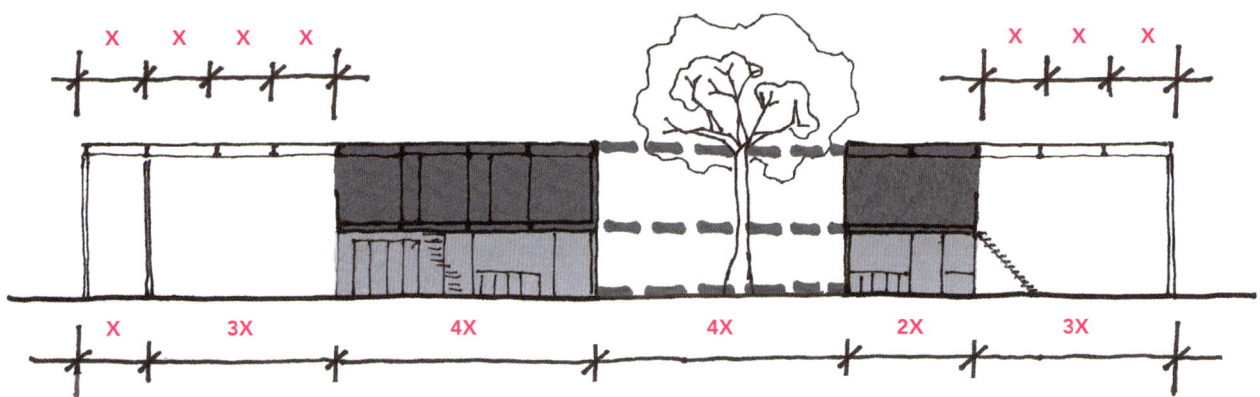

Diagram 13. A section illustrates the use of a 7'4" wide module (as indicated by "x") that creates the rhythm and length of each box.

Eames House

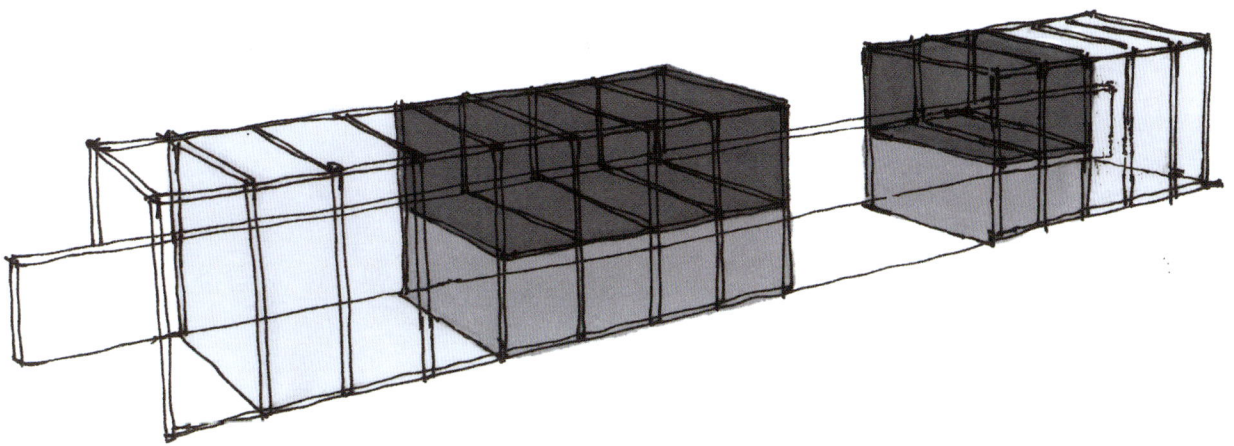

Diagram 14. This perspective shows the volumes with varying degrees of public and private activities. Dark gray zones are the most private; medium gray areas are semi-public; lightest gray color represents the most public.

10 OFFSETTING INTERIOR/EXTERIOR
Glass House

By eschewing alignments or offsetting the approach towards an entrance and creating asymmetrical compositions within an interior, elements do not appear static.

Glass House

Arguably one of the most iconic modern houses of the twentieth century, the Glass House, built in 1949, sits upon the site as a pristine, serene box surrounded by a beautiful landscape. When Philip Johnson purchased the property in New Canaan, Connecticut, he surmised within "the first five minutes" the location of a future house, he once wrote, but its design went through many iterations that would take over two years to complete. Each scheme, identified with Roman numerals by Johnson, included construction drawings, while other ideas were executed with only a floor plan.[1]

He decided upon the final design in November of 1947; it includes a large brick cylinder, which houses a bathroom and accommodates a fireplace that faces a living area. Spaces for sleeping, seating, and dining are loosely defined by cabinetry, an area rug, furniture (as designed by Mies van der Rohe for the German National Pavilion, colloquially known as the Barcelona Pavilion), and the **offset** cylinder—a singular element that engages the ceiling plane within a 54-foot by 32-foot glass rectangle. Two pieces of art—a painting, Burial of Phocion, and a sculpture, Two Circus Women—grace the minimally furnished space. The landscape enveloping the house reflects off the glass inside, providing what Johnson referred to as his very expensive "wallpaper."[2] At the same time, ambiguity between inside and outside is heighted as the surrounding trees and terrain can be viewed through the glass; they are part of the interior.

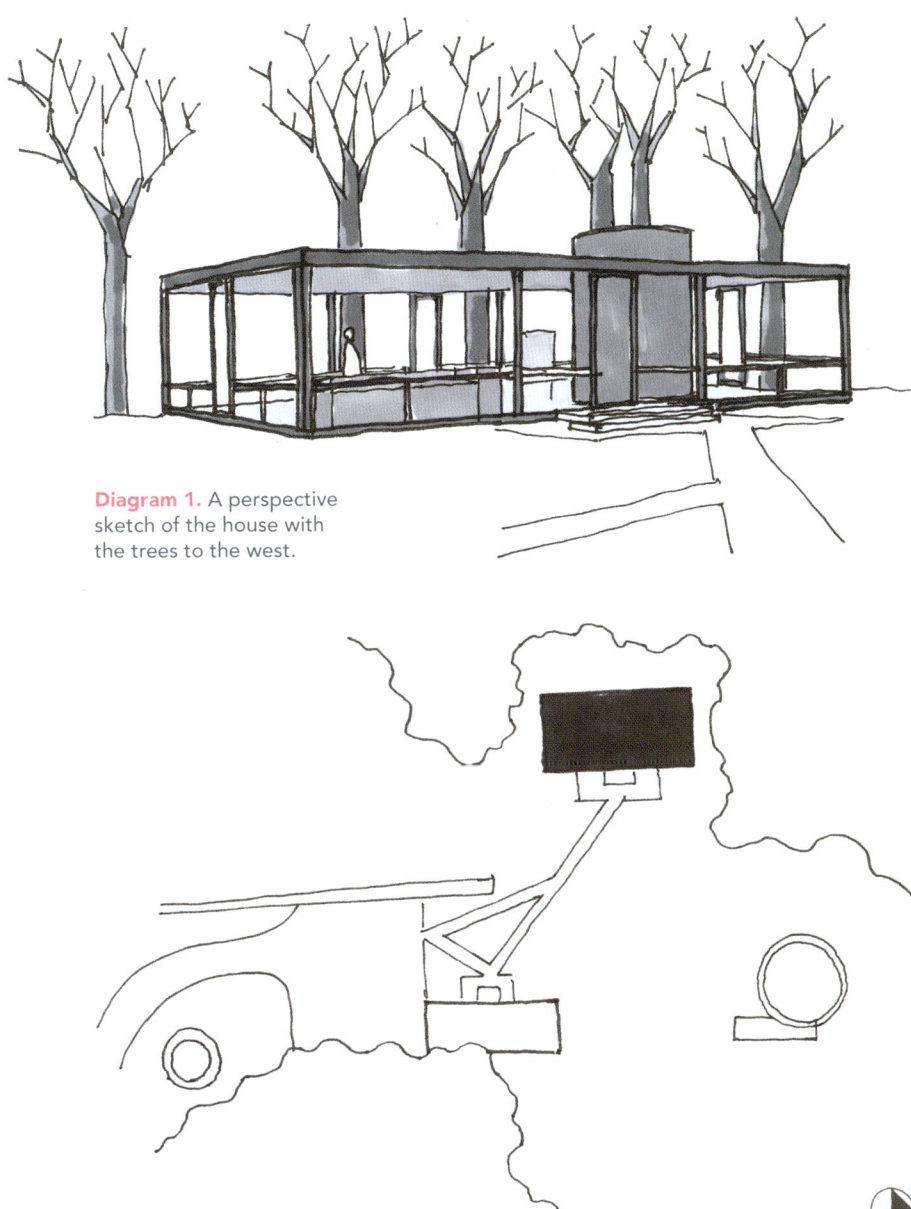

Diagram 1. A perspective sketch of the house with the trees to the west.

Diagram 2. The site plan with the house shows a circular sculpture by Donald Judd to the south, a rectangular guest house to the east and a circular pool to the north.

81

Offsetting Interior/Exterior

Diagram 3. The plan illustrates the open nature of the layout; the only floor-to-ceiling object is the brick cylinder shown near the entrance.

A. Dining
B. Living
C. Bedroom
D. Kitchen
E. Office
F. Bathroom
G. Fireplace

Glass House

Johnson identifies the source of inspiration for his house as the Farnsworth House by Mies, even though the latter was built *after* the Glass House. Initial ideas for a glass house were submitted by Mies in a 1947 exhibition at the Museum of Modern Art in New York City that was curated by Johnson as the Director of the Department of Architecture. Constant comparisons are drawn between the two structures because both are constructed as glass boxes with visible steel frames. The simplistic similarities end there as one begins to scrutinize and experience each within their respective context. Mies elevates the house with its crisp, white steel and the horizontal planes of the roof and floors appear to float above the ground. On a thin, brick plinth that is firmly fixed to the land, Johnson's design uses symmetrically placed black steel, engaging with the introspective, seemingly windowless Guest House and establishing a quiet contrast and balance of the two buildings. They are delicately tethered together by a diagonal footpath that cuts through the neatly manicured lawn. **Offsetting** this walkway to the threshold avoids a static, symmetrical view of the house; instead, the oblique approach creates a dynamic experience.

The Glass House served to host salons discussing art and architecture with professionals and students. While never intended to be utilized as a dwelling in the traditional sense, the house and its idyllic surroundings, which Johnson expanded from the initial five-acre property to approximately forty (now in the hands of the National Trust for Historic Preservation), served as a kind of "diary" for him, as he referred to it.[3] Dotted across the landscape, he explored design ideas through follies such as the Ghost House (constructed with chain link fence, recalling Frank Gehry's use of the same material) and other small structures such as the Painting Gallery, which housed some of his extensive modern art, by preeminent figures such as Andy Warhol and Frank Stella.

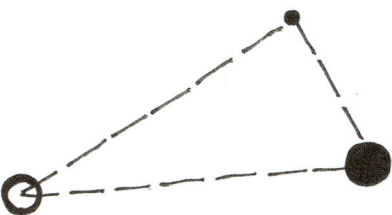

Diagram 4. In analyzing the forms of the house and its context, the circle appears as a shared geometry. This abstracted diagram shows the visual and experiential relationship between the on-site circular elements: a sculpture (to the left), the brick cylinder (at the top), and a pool (to the right).

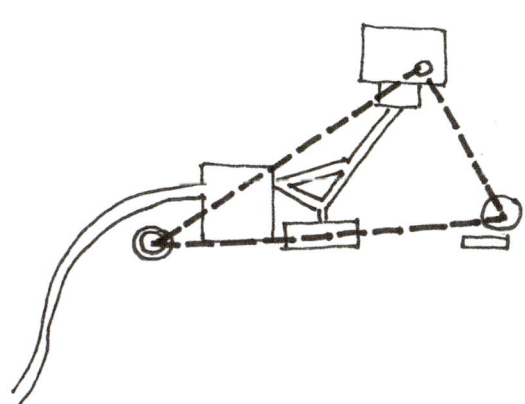

Diagram 5. The circles in this diagram are shown along with the sidewalk, Guest House, and Glass House; these shapes are not easily read but understood gradually as the visitor explores the site.

Offsetting Interior/Exterior

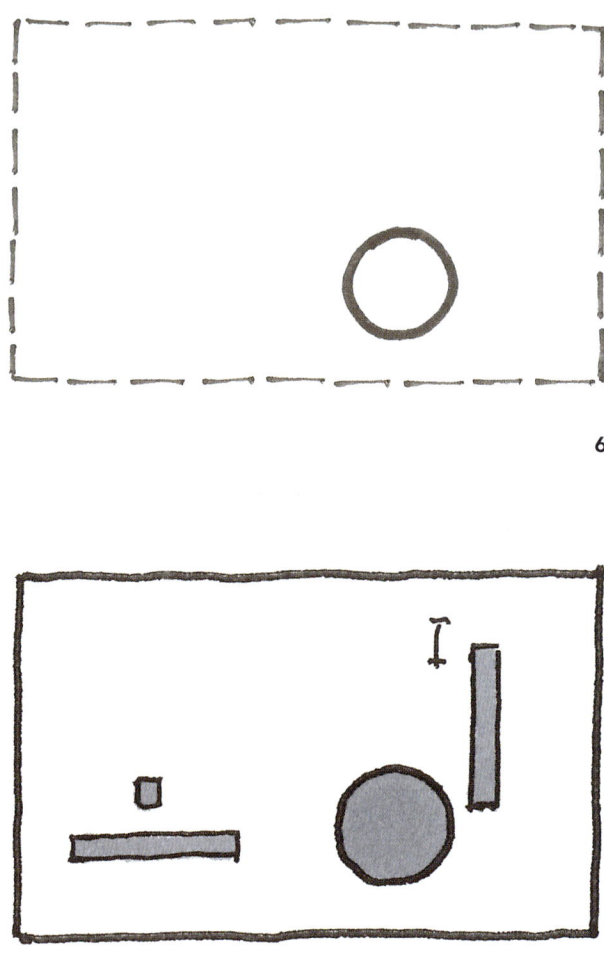

Diagram 6. The heavy, brick cylinder is in sharp contrast with the thin, glass building skin.

Diagram 7. Very few built elements are designed for the space. The kitchen to the east is defined by a cabinet/countertop, and a sculpture, entitled *Two Circus Women* by Elie Nadelman. To the north, a low-height cabinet establishes the sleeping area, while the painting *Burial of Phocion*, by Nicolas Poussin, stands on an easel designed by Johnson.

Glass House

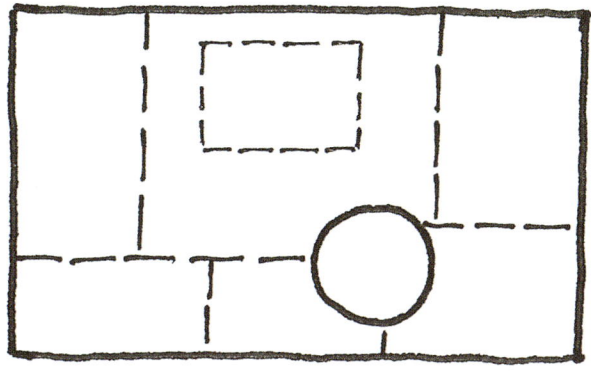

8

9

Diagram 8. This diagram divides the space into specific but implied areas through the use of the elements as shown in Diagram 7. Clockwise from the top left: dining room, living room (the smaller, dashed rectangle represents the area rug where the seating is clustered), bedroom, office, entry, and kitchen.

Diagram 9. Very simply, the left portion of the house—in light gray—is public while the right is private. The brick cylinder provides the suggested dividing line of these two zones.

Offsetting Interior/Exterior

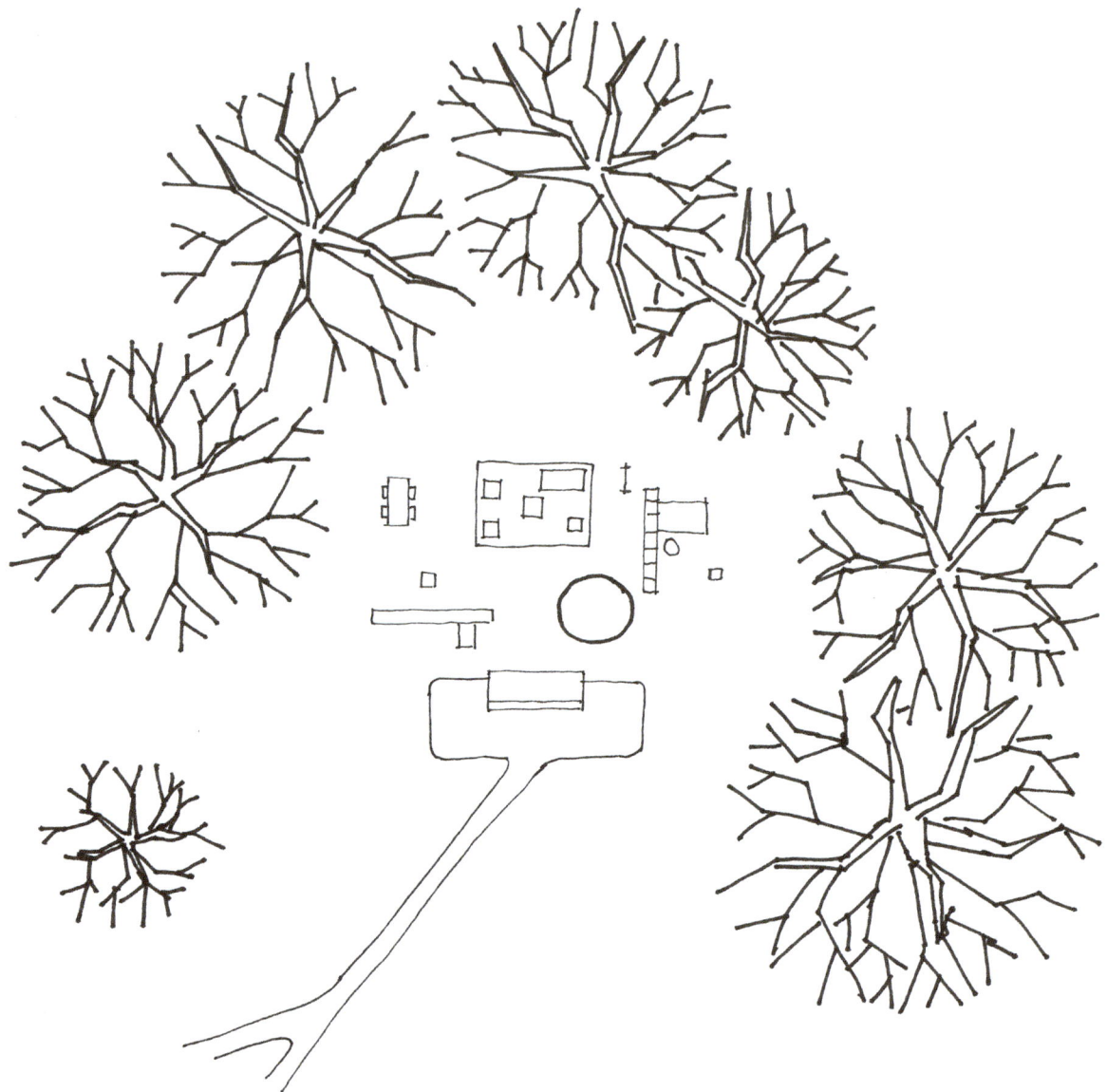

Diagram 10. Transparency enables boundaries to melt away between interior and exterior. The furniture of the Glass House appears to float within the landscape; it is as if the walls do not exist at all. The interior space forms a strong connection with nature.

Glass House

Diagram 11 (above). Investigating the immediate context, one can see the glass walls of the house disappear, while the surrounding trees create a boundary that envelops the solid cylinder.

Diagram 12 (right). Looking at the west elevation emphasizes the trees seen through the house as the glass fades away.

11 LAYERING PLANES
Farnsworth House

Layered planes, suspended over the landscape, define a simple interior space while offering protection from the elements in the most fundamental and elegant manner.

Farnsworth House

Dr. Edith Farnsworth's weekend house, a retreat located approximately sixty miles west of Chicago, stands near the edge of the Fox River as a pristine glass and white, painted steel structure. An accomplished nephrologist, she was also an avid violinist who met the architect, Ludwig Mies van der Rohe, in 1945. A relative unknown in the United States, he had been the director of the Bauhaus in Dessau, Germany, from 1930 to 1933 until, under pressure from the Nazi regime, it was brought to a close. His immigration to Chicago would pave the way for opportunities such as designing the campus of the Illinois Institute of Technology, becoming its director, and designing one of the seminal structures of modern architecture for Dr. Farnsworth in 1951.

The house was to be, in his words, "almost nothing," made manifest through his emphasis of minimal and austere forms, rectilinear geometry, and materials. The identical-sized planes of roof and floor, welded at eight vertical wide-flange columns along the north and south sides, give these horizontal surfaces or **layered planes** the appearance that they float above the grassy clearing. Dr. Farnsworth, in her memoir, writes that the interior was "[a] space to remain undisturbed caught between two horizontal planes."[1]

Interestingly, walls that create separate rooms for living are conspicuously absent. Rather than filling up the house, Mies sought to create a void, a container, or "empty spaces that make the room livable" by *defining* rather than *enclosing* areas.[2] He created interior zones by placing the core strategically within the glass box, enabling the loose delineation of dining, office, living, bedroom, and kitchen. These implied spaces within the open floor plan facilitated freedom of use and movement while affording literal and visual continuity of space. Confined, prescribed rooms, with doors and walls that divided interior spaces in the traditional manner of his day, were not his aesthetic.

At a cursory glance, the straightforwardness of the Farnsworth House appears to require little to no analysis regarding its composition; however, many nuances underscore Mies's fastidiousness and acute attention to details. The reciprocation of symmetry and asymmetry affords relief from rigid, simplistic, and static spaces. Each travertine slab measures 2'9" × 2'0", establishing the proportion and rationale for determining the geometry and location of nearly every constructed element. Rather than terminating the east and west edges of the roof and floor planes at the vertical wide-flange columns, Mies extended beyond them by the width of two slabs on both sides, creating cantilevers that emphasized their horizontality. The east and west glass walls are set apart by twenty rectangles of travertine; columns and the seams of the slabs delineate the line of symmetry. Although this implied line might appear to cleave the interior space, it is negated and obscured by the core, a volume that is itself symmetrical along its north-south axis but located asymmetrically within this living area.

Diagram 1. The Farnsworth House, viewed from the southwest.

Layering Planes

A generous porch amplifying the entrance of the house completes the main platform. This area, mediating between interior and exterior space, becomes the continuation of both zones. Being surrounded by nature while protected from the elements enforces the malleability of the function of this area, which is neither completely inside nor outside. Again, Mies eschewed physical and literal confinement; he attempted to "make the buildings a neutral frame where human beings and works of art may live their own life." His affinity to nature is revealed when he continued by stating, "Nature should also live its own life . . . But we should try to bring nature, houses, and human beings together into a higher unity."[3]

The least defined zone is a simple platform that mediates between the ground and porch. While deceptively simple, Mies asserts the established rules; the width of this terrace is exactly the same number of travertine rectangles inside the glass as noted earlier but not the same depth. The supports for this plane, greatly reduced in height, share alignment with the vertical wide-flange columns located to the north. Cantilevered east and west ends of the terrace measure two widths of travertine slabs past the supports. Positioned asymmetrically with the rest of the house, this plane is another defined space, opened completely to the sky and nature, yet providing a stage for people to connect with the ever-changing landscape.

The sublime design of the Farnsworth House was a crystalline and ideal representation of Mies's intention to "achieve the greatest effect using the meagerest of means."[4] Mies noted that using glass "permit[s] a measure of freedom in spatial composition that we will not relinquish anymore. Only now can we articulate space freely, open it up and connect to the landscape."[5]

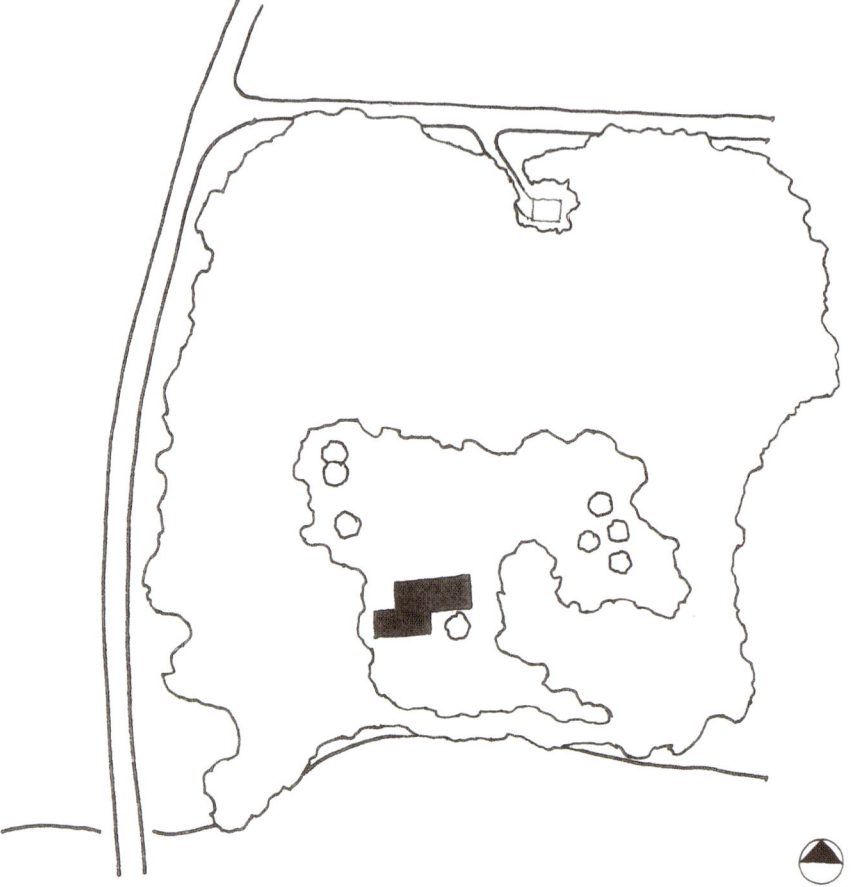

Diagram 2. Dr. Farnsworth had a garage built north of the house, located immediately off River Road. The site is hemmed by the Fox River to the south and Plano Milbrook Road to the west. Because of the house's proximity to the river, it has been subjected to frequent and, at times, damaging floods.

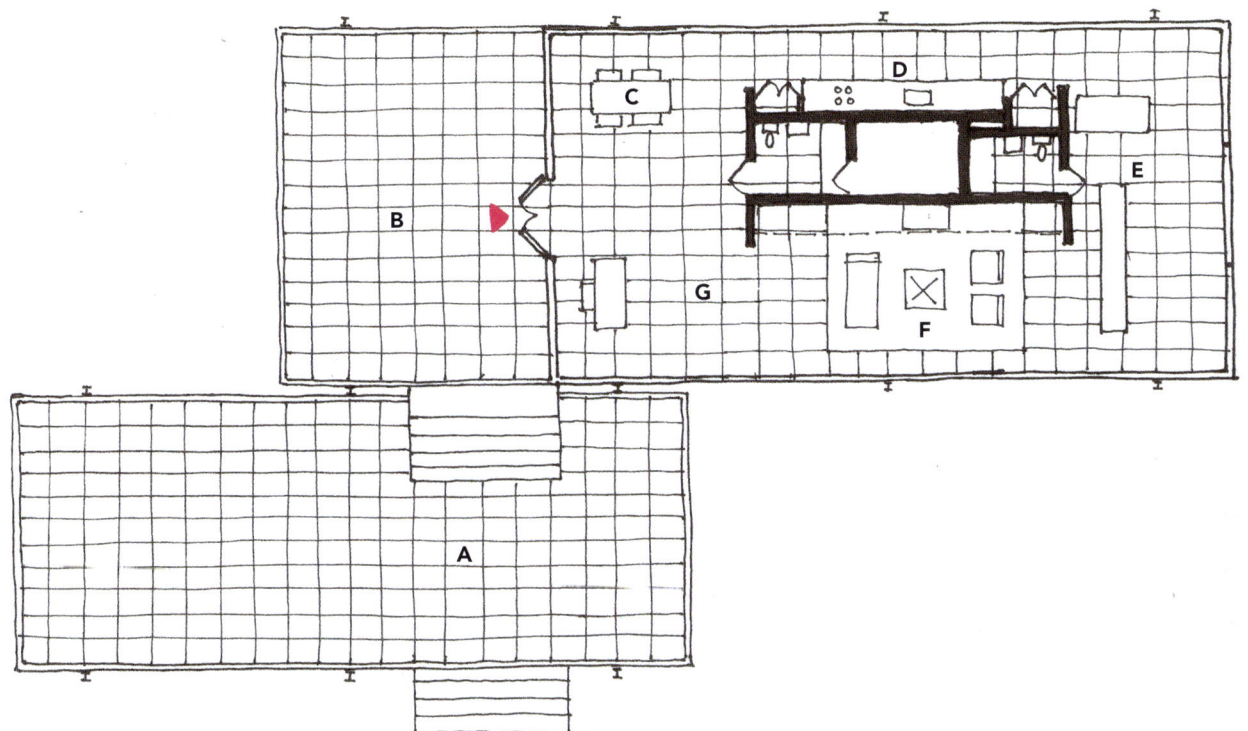

Diagram 3. A floor plan of the Farnsworth House.

A. Raised Plinth
B. Covered Porch
C. Dining
D. Kitchen
E. Bedroom
F. Living
G. Office

Layering Planes

4

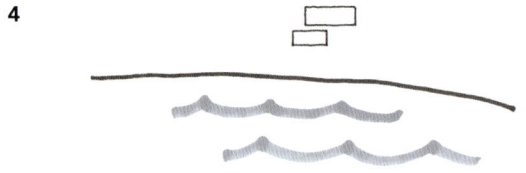

5

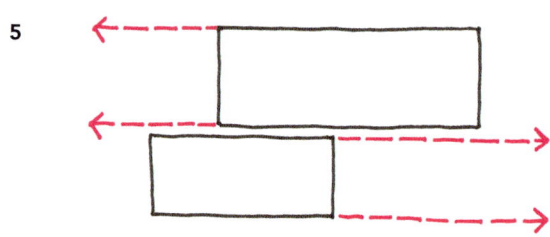

Diagrams 4, 5. The river and the house are inextricably linked. As with every facet of Mies's work, the distance from the river's edge was calculated. The structure is close enough to afford views of the Fox River from inside while maintaining a distance to avoid being subsumed by it (Diagram 4). One could imagine the motion of the river pulling the planes apart as it flows by in Diagram 5.

6

7

Diagrams 6, 7. Pristine, white horizontal planes define the major structural components of the house as shown in Diagram 6. Wide-flange steel vertical members, as seen in Diagram 7, play the secondary visual role, while frames for the glazing are thin to minimize their presence. Practically, Mies raised the platform 5'3" above the ground to mitigate the potential damage of encroaching water when the river periodically flooded; aesthetically, its elegance was highlighted with this simple gesture. The long, pristine, horizontal lines can be viewed unmarred by the uneven line of the ground plane.

Farnsworth House

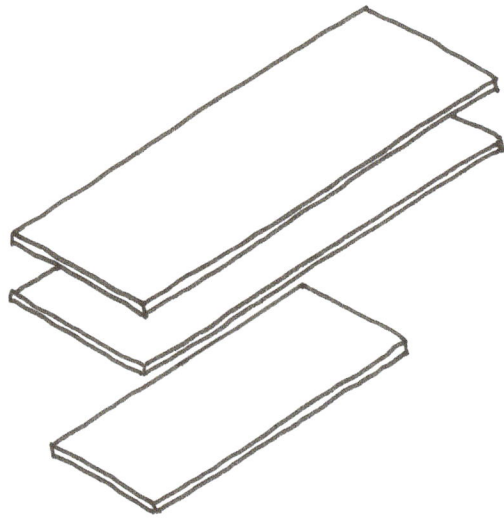

Diagram 8. The basic constituents of the house are the three horizontal planes which appear to be floating.

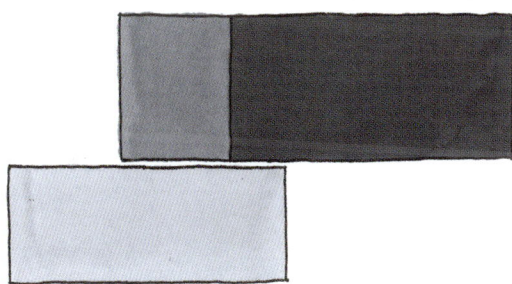

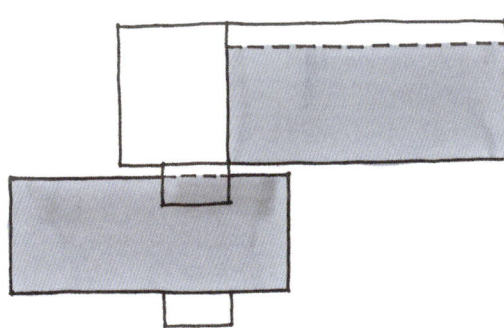

Diagram 9. Progression from the exterior to the interior is defined by an ever-increasing number of vertical planes surrounding the visitor. Although the darkest shaded area is literally enclosed with glass, there is a sense of the exterior coming inside and the view of nature is constant.

Diagram 10. The width of the entry platform and the width of the living area are identical. Experientially, this is not possible to "read" but instead, provides a refined sense of harmony and proportion that is pervasive throughout the house.

Layering Planes

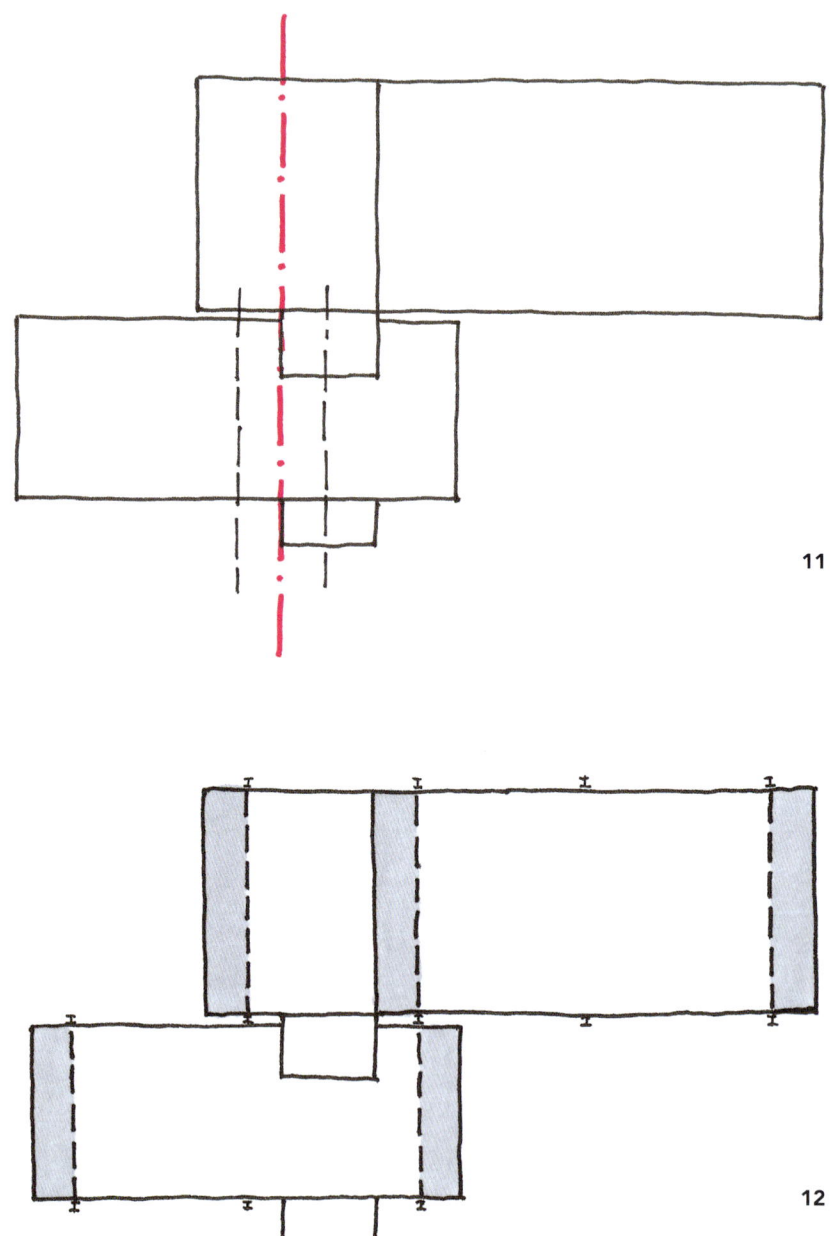

Diagrams 11, 12. The centerline of the porch (in pink, Diagram 11), is also the line of symmetry of the smaller dashed lines on either side. The line to the left represents the centerline of the entire platform while on the right, the midpoint of the stairs' width is shown. Not coincidentally, the distance between the pink line to either minor centerline is two travertine slab widths apart. This exact dimension is repeated in Diagram 12, where the gray areas highlight the overhang or cantilever of the horizontal planes, extending beyond the vertical members. Lastly, the west-facing glass is positioned two slab widths from the nearest steel stanchion.

Farnsworth House

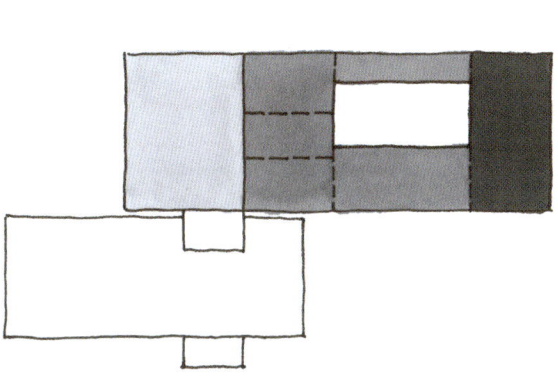

13

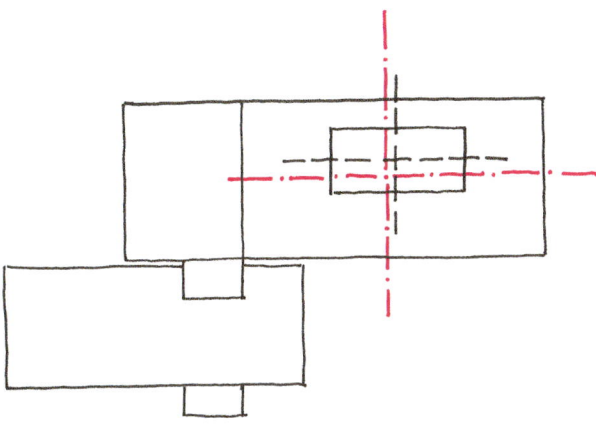

14

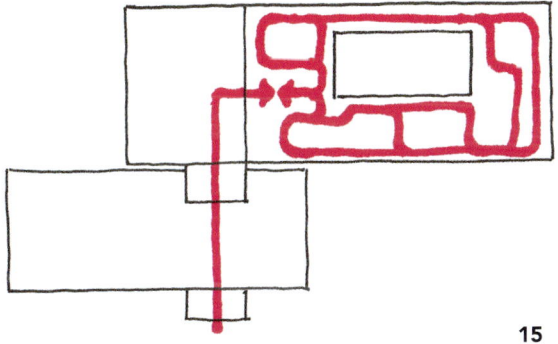

15

Diagram 13. Varying degrees of privacy of implied zones are represented in this diagram. The darker shading suggests the more private aspects of dwelling.

Diagram 14. Within a static, symmetrical box, Mies positioned a core that does not align or comply with its surrounding geometry. By off-centering this volume, the sizes of the spaces are quite varied. Mies believed that the design of this "free space" required "much discipline and understanding from the architect."[6]

Diagram 15. A structured progression into Dr. Farnsworth's house is celebrated with two small sets of stairs, leading to the entrance. Upon entering the living area, the plan allows for freedom of movement around the core.

12 UNDULATING FORMS
Casa das Canoas

Harmonizing supple, undulating forms with rigid vertical and horizontal lines requires mastery of the language of architecture, as all the elements can appear too disparate when viewed.

Casa das Canoas

In the first page of his memoirs, *The Curves of Time*, the Brazilian architect, Oscar Niemeyer, unabashedly writes: "I am not attracted to straight angles or to the straight line, hard and inflexible, created by man. I am attracted to free-flowing, sensual curves. The curves that I find in the mountains of my country, in the sinuousness of its rivers, in the waves of the ocean and on the body of the beloved woman."[1] His residence in the Canoas district of Rio de Janeiro epitomizes this declaration of love for his country and the beauty that inspired him during an illustrious and prodigious career, spanning nearly eight decades. Some of his formative years were spent working with the acclaimed architect, Le Corbusier. Both men collaborated with a team of architects, designing the headquarters of the Ministry of Education and Health in Rio.

Niemeyer was a well-established architect by the time he designed his home in 1953; he was unfettered by the restraints of what he observed as "obsessive concern for architectural purity,"[2] visible in the emotionless, rational architecture of Europe. Nature as inspiration and "not an enemy" gave impetus to "adopting it [the house] to the irregularities of the terrain, without changing it, and making it curved, so as to permit the vegetation to penetrate, without being separated by the straight line."[3]

Despite this admission by Niemeyer, the Swiss designer, Max Bill, disparaged the house by writing, "[the] free-form shapes are purely decorative."[4] Assuredly, the structure does appear to be the sum of these **undulating forms**; its most notable feature is the sinuous roof. In pure elevation, it is only a slab, but it becomes animated with the observer's movement, its soft edges bending and arcing to frame the sky and surrounding verdant landscape.

The site's natural topography and landscape work in concert with the architecture in various ways. Niemeyer designs the house around a massive granite rock, a natural material of the site, that juts out of the smooth surface of the ground plane like a diminutive mountain. This bolder blurs the boundary between inside and outside as it literally occupies both places. A large outcropping of it spills into the adjacent pool; the rough rocks disrupt the curved, man-made edge of the basin. Another portion of this boulder defines one side of the stairs that leads to the lower level of the house. Inside, the presence of the rugged granite is felt as a contrasting element to the smooth, sleek finishes of the white ceiling, glass, and polished dark floor. Niemeyer's architecture dwells comfortably within the natural world; the built environment and nature exists harmoniously.

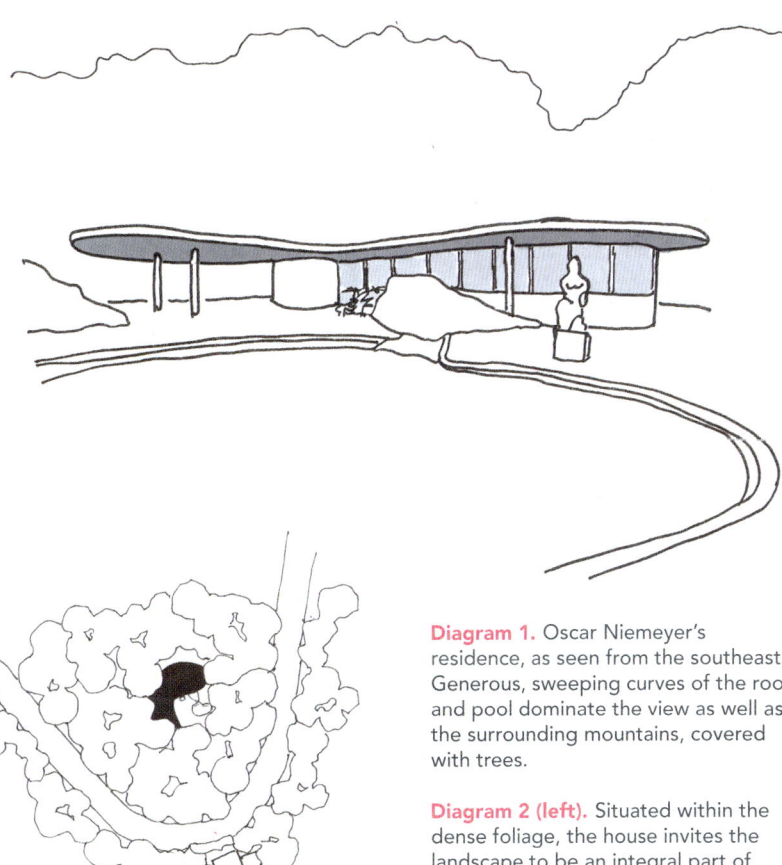

Diagram 1. Oscar Niemeyer's residence, as seen from the southeast. Generous, sweeping curves of the roof and pool dominate the view as well as the surrounding mountains, covered with trees.

Diagram 2 (left). Situated within the dense foliage, the house invites the landscape to be an integral part of the architecture; Niemeyer even notes that he "did not touch the terrain."

Undulating Forms

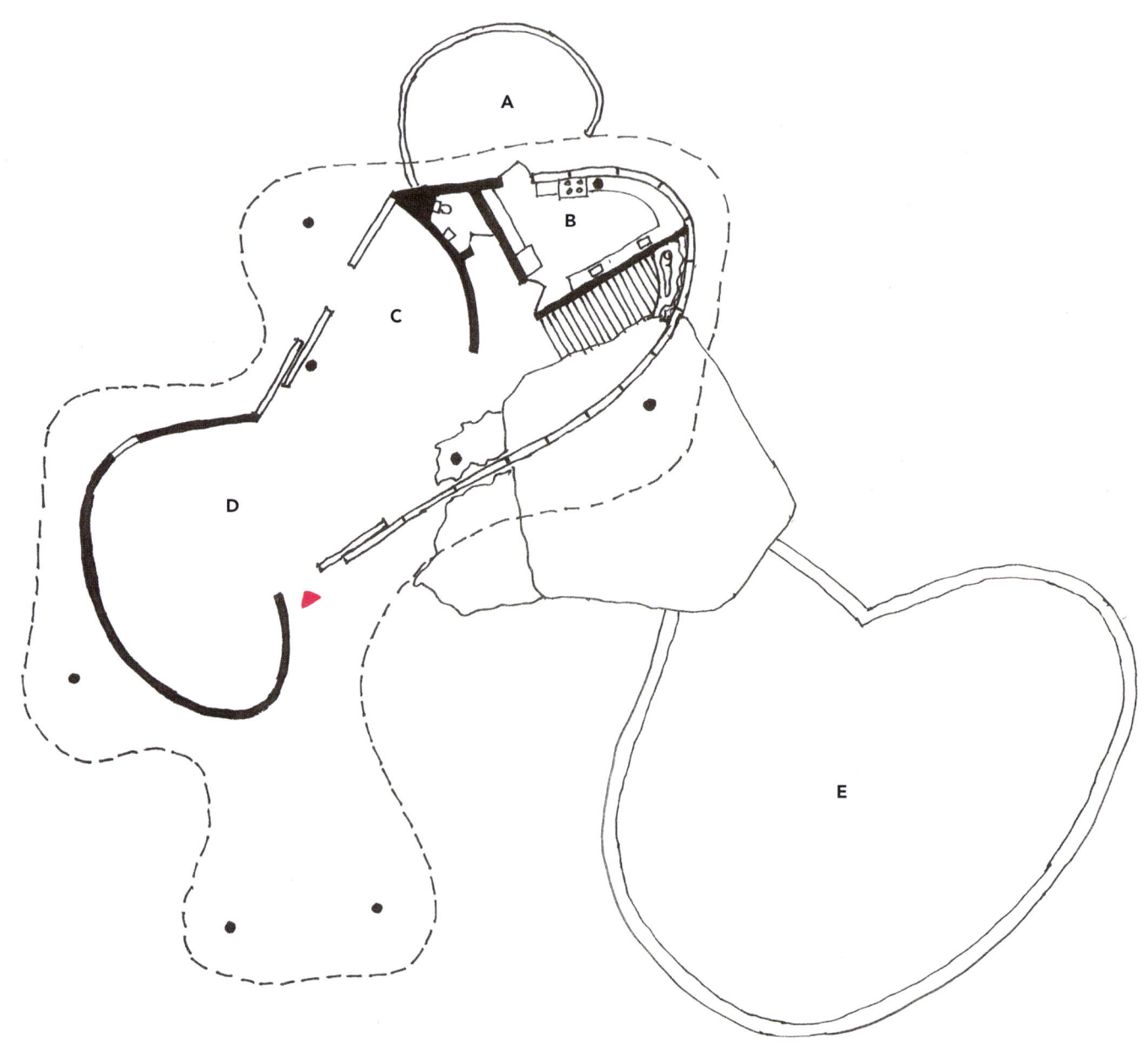

Casa das Canoas

Diagram 3 (opposite). The entry level of the dwelling with its pool and irregular, massive granite boulder is shown. A slender column is embedded within it and the rock's edge abuts to the edge of the stairs, leading to the lower level. A sensuous and free-form roof, shown as dashed, shades the house while creating an alluring shape.

Diagram 4 (right). The intimate and private lower level of the house is not visible at the visitor's initial encounter. Niemeyer uses the steep terrain to conceal a part of this area below ground. Bedrooms along the southeast wall are not completely underground; there are windows, providing natural light and views.

A. Patio
B. Kitchen
C. Dining
D. Living
E. Pool
F. Bedroom
G. Sitting Room

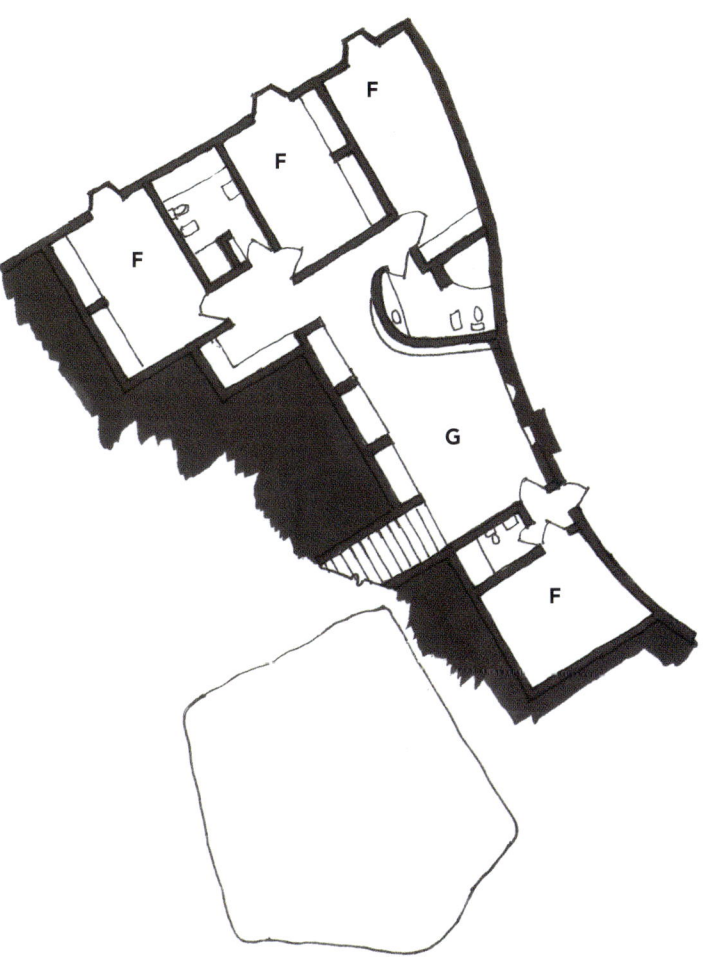

Undulating Forms

Diagram 5 (above). Christ the Redeemer, the iconic statue overlooking Rio de Janeiro atop the Corcovado mountain, is a symbol of Niemeyer's beloved city. The majestic surrounding peaks, with their gentle contours, were always a part of his architectural vocabulary, as observed by Le Corbusier, who declared: "Oscar, you always have the mountains of Rio in your eyes."[6]

Diagram 6 (left). Not only was nature his muse—the soft, fluid, and voluptuous curves of a woman's body captivated the architect. This statue by Niemeyer's friend and sculptor, Alfredo Ceschiatti, is in the viewer's line of sight when walking down the stairs of the house.

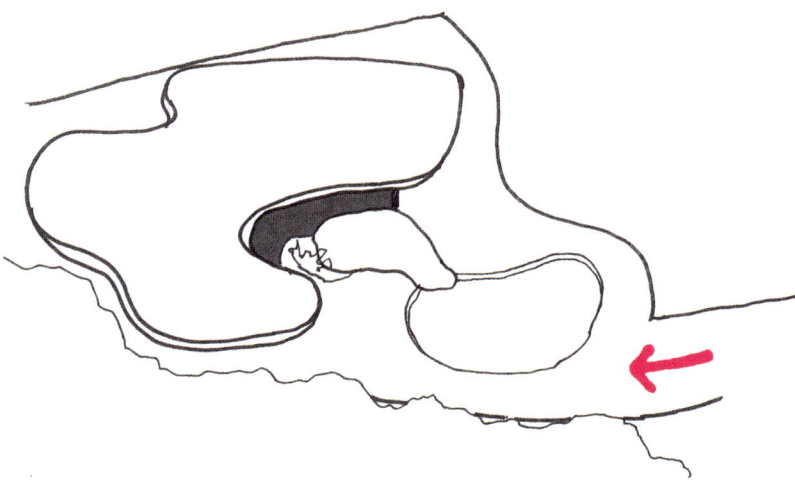

Diagram 7. A visitor's initial introduction to the house is the pool; the procession to the entry is an encounter with nature rather than a formal, axial approach to the front door.

Casa das Canoas

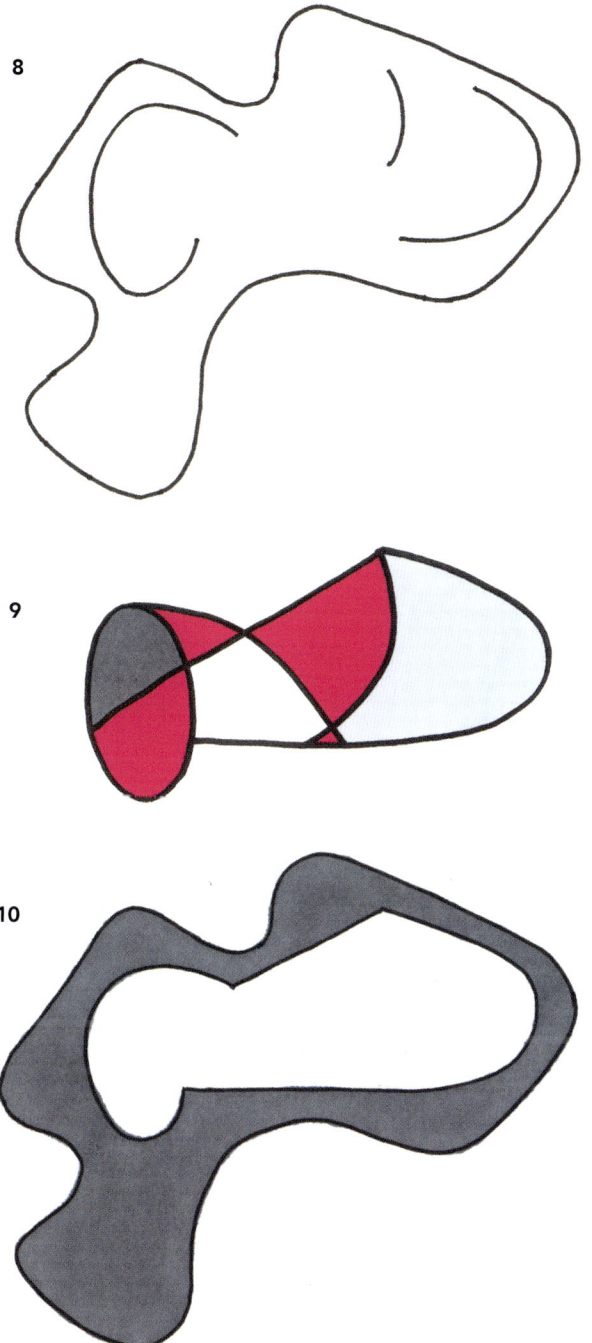

The lush vegetation, teeming with the vibrancy of nature, is celebrated in the design of his residence. With the site densely populated by trees and encircled with mountains, Niemeyer carries this visual feast through and beyond the house to the beautiful Copacabana Beach below. Sightlines are never hindered due to the architecture; instead, they are integral to the experience. As one emerges from the interior to the back of the house, a generous terrace gives space and time for the visitor to be fully immersed in the vast beauty of the Brazilian landscape.

Placid curves bookend the longitudinal ends of the house. The northeast arc, with warm wood vertical narrow strips, protectively curls to form an intimate living area while glass creates an imperfect parabola at the northwest, providing a light-filled kitchen. A smaller, interior crescent of wood, in dialogue with its larger sister in the living space, echoes the shape of a circular dining table. These gestures, while argued as "irrational," were executed with intent. Niemeyer writes: "I deliberately disregarded the celebrated right angle and rationalist architecture designed with ruler and square to boldly enter the world of curves and straight lines offered by reinforced concrete." Private, yet expansive, simple and masterful, this dwelling is the apotheosis of the architect's lyrical statement of his "favorite architecture: beautiful, light, varied, imaginative, and awe-inspiring."[5]

Diagram 8. Curves of the walls and roof are uncommitted to anything rectilinear. The rules of a grid do not apply to these gentle arcs.

Diagram 9. Abstraction of the plan's arcs and lines is one technique to examine the composition of these elements.

Diagram 10. The dark gray roof area subsumes the white area of the floor plan's interior, revealing the supple, organic shapes that behave independent of one another.

Undulating Forms

Diagram 11. The house consists of so few solid walls; it appears as a simple pavilion with glass, conflating the distinction between inside and outside.

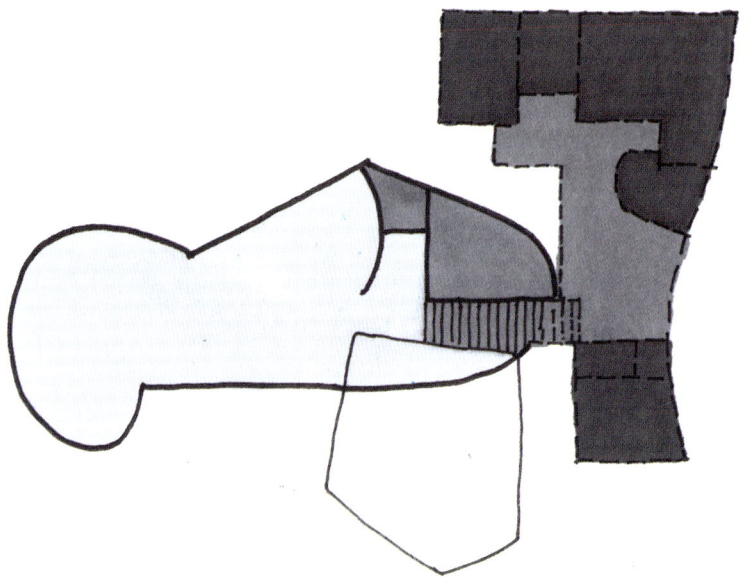

Diagram 12. Both the ground and lower levels are superimposed in this diagram. The stairs and the granite boulder are the only two elements that physically connect the floors. Public areas are shown in a light gray; the darkest areas represent the bedrooms. The medium gray zones are semi-public or semi-private.

Casa das Canoas

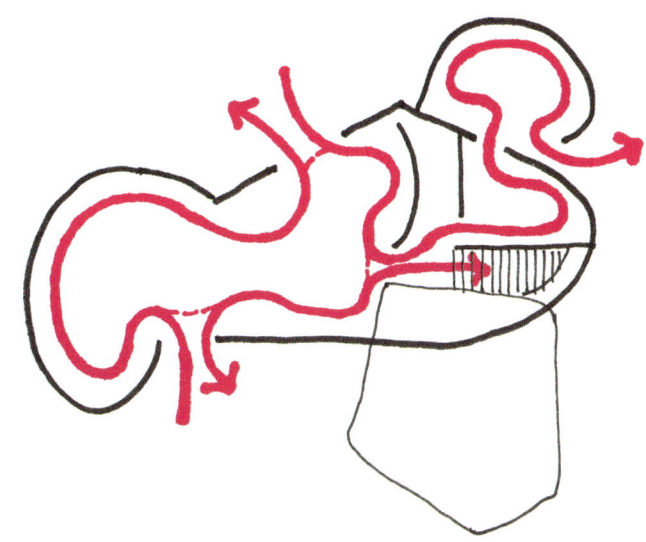

Diagram 13. There are many possible circulation paths to the entry or exit points for a house of this scale. Immediate accessibility to the outdoors is an essential feature of this structure, as shown with three of the four arrows.

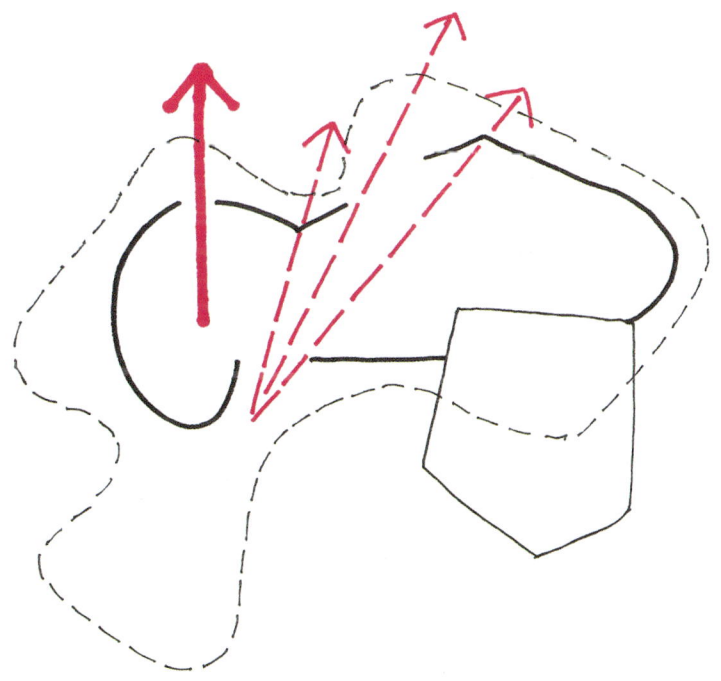

Diagram 14. Stunning, expansive views of nature, shown in the direction of the arrows, are provided even before the visitor reaches the threshold of the house (shown as dashed lines). Once through the house, the spectacular sights are of Rio de Janeiro, below. In contrast, the pink solid line represents a focused, framed view of the outdoors as seen through a small window in the living room.

Undulating Forms

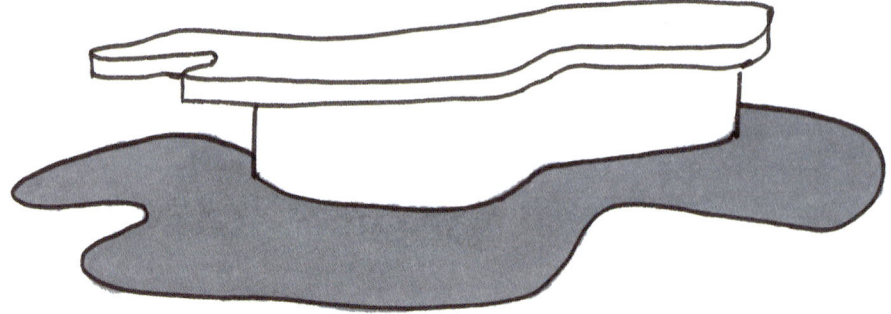

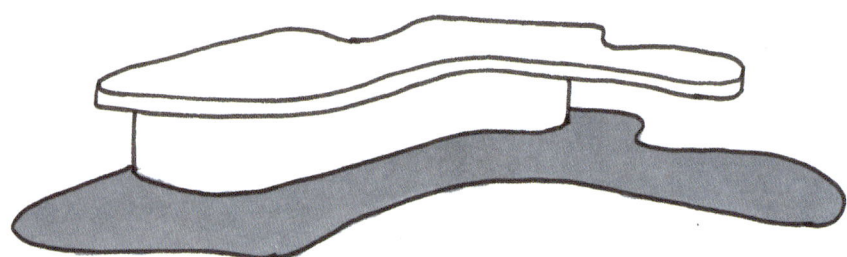

Diagram 15. When viewing the house from nearly any direction, the sweeping arcs and curves of the roof cast similar shadows but in a more pronounced and exaggerated way.

Casa das Canoas

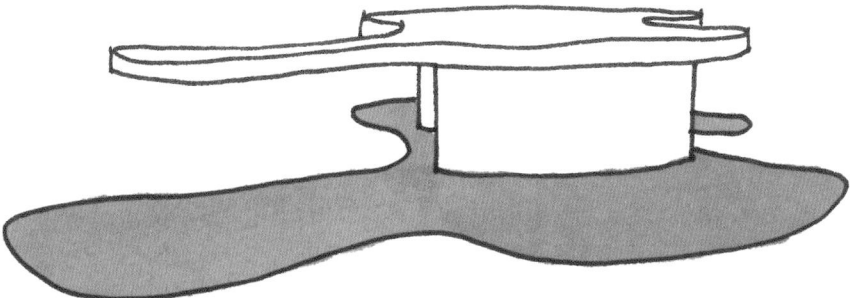

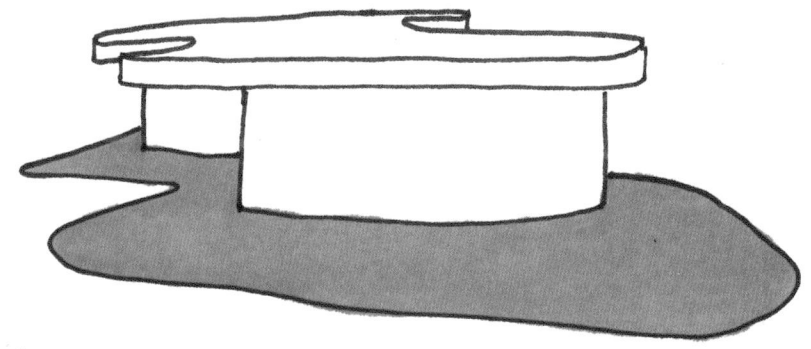

13 MANIPULATING LIGHT
Chapel of Notre-Dame du Haut at Ronchamp

When light is manipulated to achieve the desired effect within a space, the architecture nearly becomes background; the senses are evoked, and emotions are a part of the experience.

Chapel of Notre-Dame du Haut at Ronchamp

One of the most enigmatic and celebrated structures by Le Corbusier, the Chapel of Notre-Dame du Haut at Ronchamp defies categories or singular analysis. Contributing to this mystery is the architect's lack of documentation, despite his penchant for writing, which might have indicated or defined the impetus for such a profound building. Interpretations of the chapel proliferate, likely due to its sculptural, distinctive qualities.

Located in the Vosges, a low mountain range in eastern France, the site commands a view of the verdant landscape atop a hill that was always designated as a place of worship. Beginning in the fourth century, it was once a place of pilgrimage for those devoted to the Virgin Mary. Various structures stood on this sacred ground until the existing church was destroyed in air strikes during World War II. The initial appeal to commission Le Corbusier to design the new structure was rejected by the architect himself. Perhaps through entreaties and a promise that he would be granted creative autonomy, Le Corbusier acquiesced and accepted the project in 1953.

The approach to the chapel is from the southeast, where the visitor encounters this remarkable structure slowly emerging into view as one traverses to the top of the hill. A voluminous, dark concrete roof, inspired by a crab's shell, is supported by dense, tilting, white walls, positioned independent of the roof's placement and geometry. Inside, this heavy covering is lifted nearly four inches above the walls, allowing a thin line of light to define the seam where vertical and horizontal elements would be expected to intersect. This void—the light—creates an aura of holiness, a mystical presence of the sacred. The unexpected illumination defies the presumption of gravity as the immense roof appears to be draped and floating overhead.

Multiple apertures of various sizes pierce the southern wall in a seemingly haphazard manner. These openings, cut through an immense wall (in some places, nearly six feet thick), seem to produce diminutive windows when seen from the exterior. However, the light appears magnified from the interior. Here, Le Corbusier incorporates color—red, green, yellow, blue—with clear panes of glass, creating a luminous, prismatic effect. The wall dissolves into an array of varying intensities of light, piercing the darkness within the chapel. Nearly thirty years before, in his book *Towards a New Architecture*, he had written: "Architecture is the masterly, correct, and magnificent play of masses brought together in light. Our eyes are made to see forms in light; light and shade reveal these forms."[1] Light imbues the structure with a sense of beauty, poetics, and mystery; it is the catalyst that enables the visitor to feel the sacredness and serenity of the space.

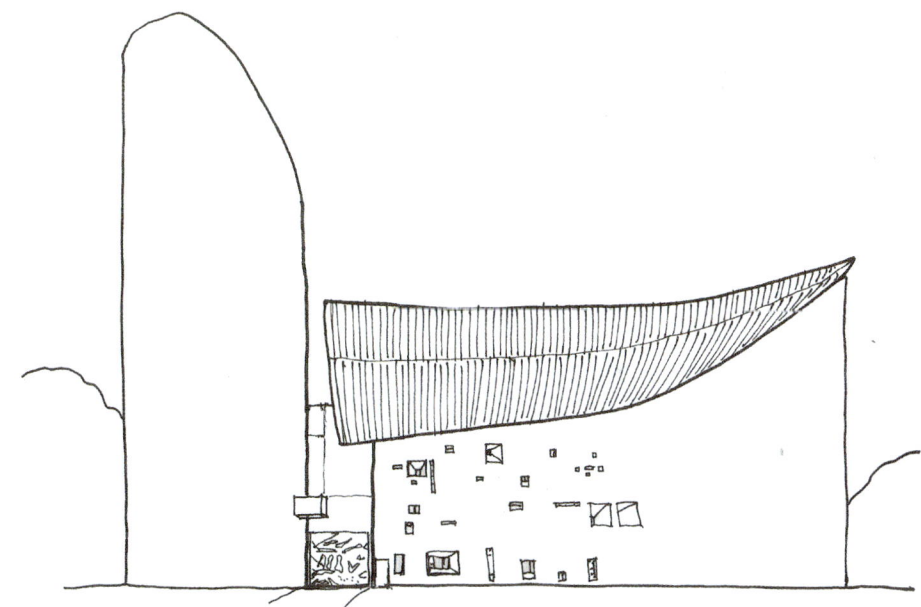

Diagram 1. The view of the chapel, looking north. To the left, a tower-like figure containing a tiny chapel looms above, seemingly detached from this south façade. The main entrance is located just to the right of the tall structure.

Manipulating Light

Diagram 2. The site plan reveals the path of approach. A humble pilgrims' house is situated to the southeast; the Pyramid of Peace, at the northeast, was designed by Le Corbusier to commemorate the soldiers who died during the defense of Ronchamp during World War II. Immediate west and adjacent to the chapel, an oval cistern is placed to catch the rainwater from the roof.

Chapel of Notre-Dame du Haut at Ronchamp

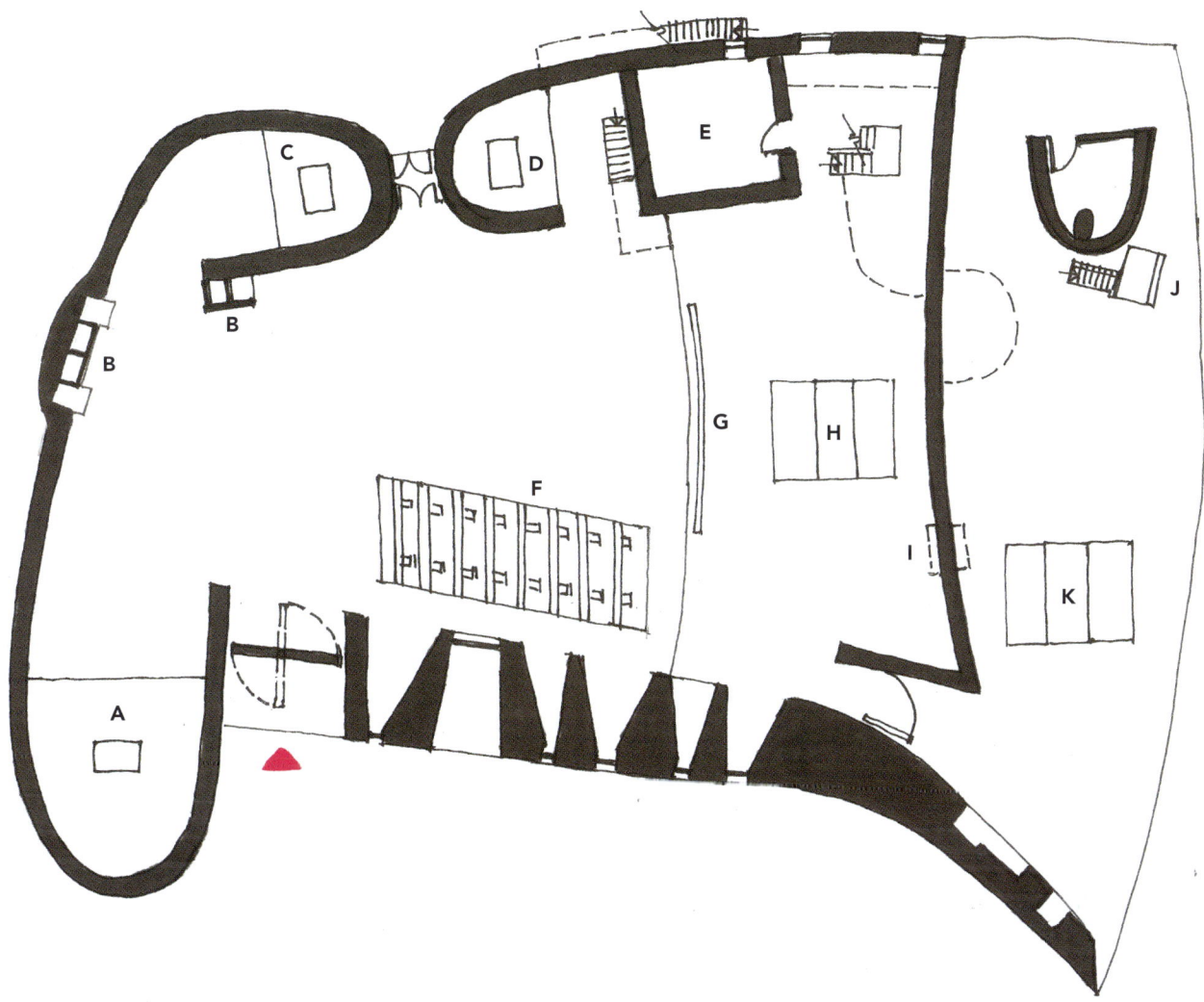

Diagram 3. The floor plan of the Chapel of Notre-Dame du Haut, completed in 1955.

A. South Chapel
B. Confessionals
C. North Chapel
D. Chapel of Peace
E. Sacristy
F. Pews
G. Sanctuary
H. Interior Altar
I. Niche with statue
J. Lectern
K. Exterior Altar

Manipulating Light

Diagram 4. Areas shown in light gray are of significance; Le Corbusier uses materials to differentiate the various functions of the chapel.

Chapel of Notre-Dame du Haut at Ronchamp

Diagram 5. Three organic and independent forms enclose and define the interior space. Even in plan, they are idiosyncratic and sculptural; when experienced, the entire effect is intimate and remarkable. Spaces between the walls signify entry points.

Diagram 6. Some walls curl inward, ensconcing the visitor within introspective spaces. The black wall, nearly six feet wide at its thickest point, creates a dramatic gesture, pulling away and thinning out like a knife's edge.

Diagram 7. The rectangles represent altars, some of which are used during Mass by the priest, located both inside and outside. Even within the small chapels, Le Corbusier placed altars, signifying their roles as sacred spaces.

111

Manipulating Light

Diagram 8. Poetic and sculptural, the arcs on the exterior south and east walls bend to follow their own circumference, not relating to each other but never in conflict.

Diagram 9. Thin, dashed pink lines complete the forms inside, creating womb-like pods around each altar. Larger gestures, shown as thick, dashed pink lines, are more extroverted in nature, appearing like open arms to welcome the congregation to the celebration of Mass.

Diagram 10. Three diminutive chapels, shown in light gray, appear simple in plan; however, these enigmatic forms capture light in the most sublime way.

Diagram 11. The lightest gray depicts the open-air sanctuary to the east; the medium gray zone represents the main area of the chapel. Recesses, shown in dark gray, curl protectively around the solitary pilgrim in these semi-private zones.

Diagram 12. Unperceivable from the exterior, lines converge at a point west of the chapel. Le Corbusier articulates the centerline in the pavement with a thin line of dark concrete, terminating at the arc of the steel balustrade. This line of axis, corresponding with the center of the altar, bisects the pink area.

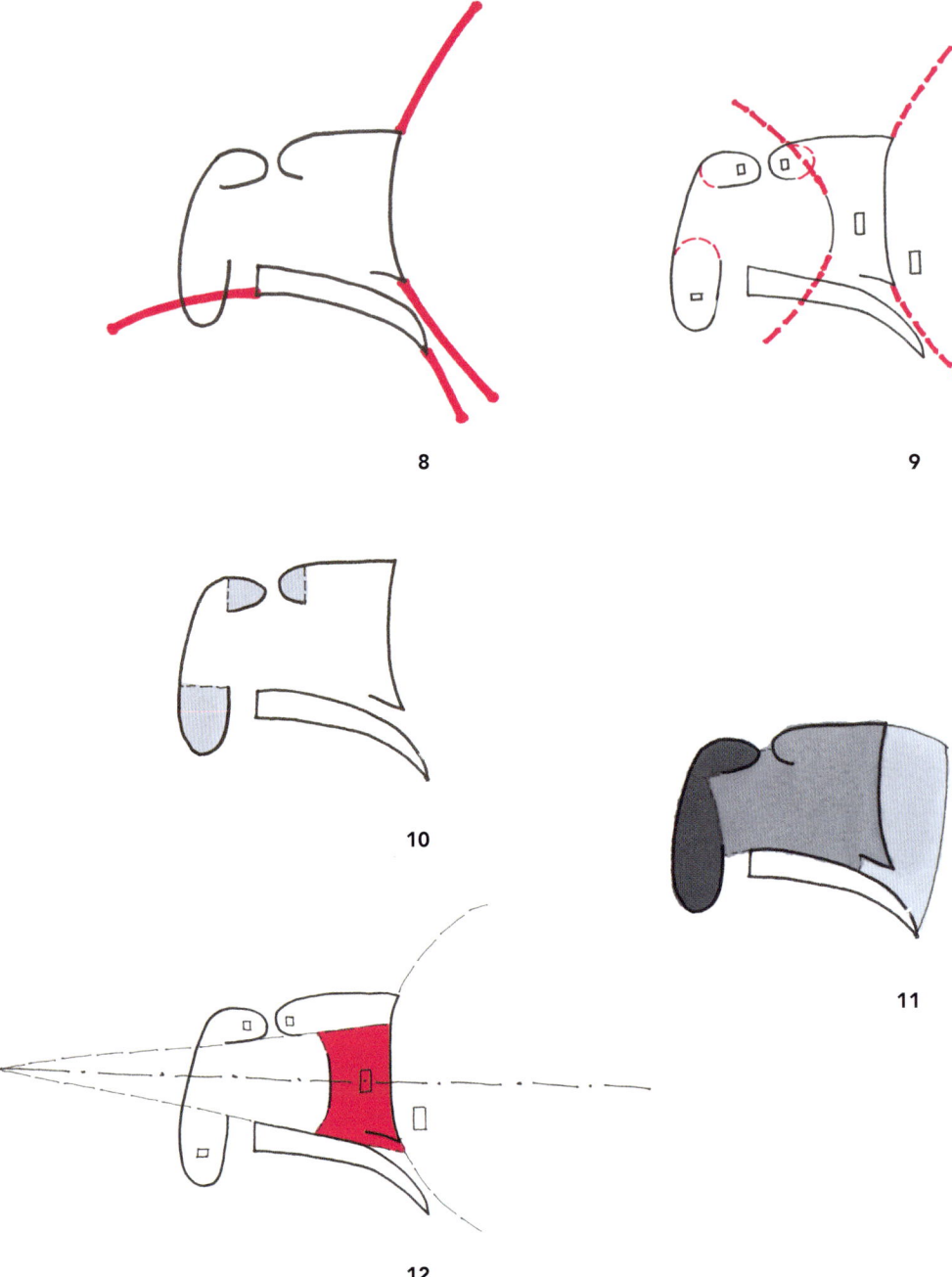

Chapel of Notre-Dame du Haut at Ronchamp

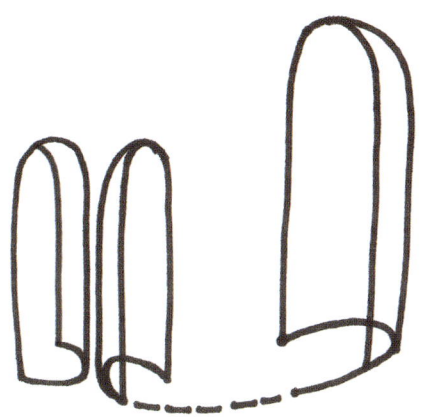

Diagram 13. The minor chapels are vertical elements that stand like hooded figures or sentinels.

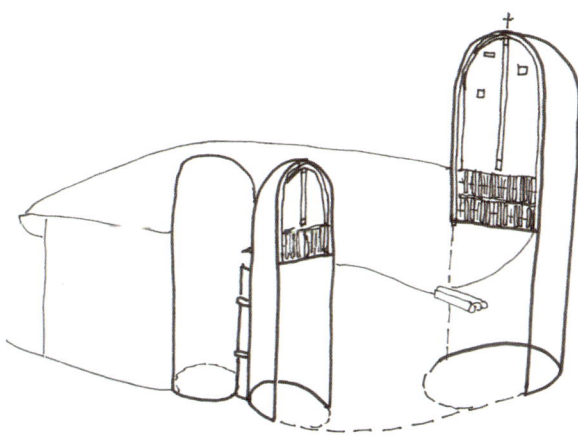

Diagram 14. At the north façade, the two chapels face east and west, capturing the sun's rays at the beginning and end of the day. They are not perceived from the path as the pilgrim approaches from the south, unlike the larger chapel that looms large with its softly rounded top. Each has a thin, vertical opening, allowing the light to fill these introspective spaces with an otherworldly glow. Louvers bring in additional illumination, creating a sense of wonder for the visitor as the source of the light is not apparent. The intensity of the light dissipates and is muted as it grazes the roughly textured walls of these chapels.

Although the main entrance door—resplendent and colorful—is located at the southern wall, the architecture is so unique that the form invites the visitor to explore it from all sides, as one would view a sculpture. Moving counterclockwise from the south, the dynamic façade simultaneously bends forward and soars up to nearly converge with what appears to be a tip of a horn but, actually, is where the roof tapers to its apex. Turning the corner, the wall's edge peels away, revealing another entrance at the east façade. This slightly concave plane forms the backdrop to an exterior sanctuary, complete with an altar and lectern. Seen from this perspective, the building takes on a very different quality. A solitary box, surrounded by pin-like perforations, juts slightly away from the surface of the east-facing wall. Le Corbusier frames a statue of the Virgin Mary that is able to rotate 180 degrees within this aperture, enabling her to turn her gaze on either the interior or exterior altar.

Inside, the view of the east wall is sober and dim, with the exception of the opening at the southeast corner. What is seen as a simple frame from the exterior that houses the statue is the source of an intense burst of illumination, heightened by the enveloping darkness. The Virgin Mary is also surrounded by subtle specks of light, a constellation of stars that come to life and reveal themselves with the sun. Ironically, these tiny openings on the exterior appear like black dots on the pale wall; it is only from within that the purpose of these gestures can be wholly appreciated.

Le Corbusier's acute understanding of space prompts him to observe, "Architecture is like a vase . . . it is from the interior that it lives. It is in the interior that the essential takes place." Here, in this chapel, the "essential" is the presence of the sacred, made manifest through the wondrous manner in which **light** is **manipulated** and fractures the darkness. Experiencing the solemnity and tranquility of this atmosphere, the visitor feels the significance of the words that Le Corbusier penned in his book, *Ronchamp*: "The key is light/and light illuminates shapes/and shapes have an emotional power."[2]

14 INTERLOCKING CUBES
Trenton Bath House

The cube—one of the most fundamental geometric volumes—when overlapped and interlocked, creates a spatially varied structure that derives its complexity through simple manipulations.

Trenton Bath House

There is little doubt that such a stark and humble structure, Louis Kahn's Trenton Bath House, would greatly impact and actuate the architect's philosophy and approach to architecture. So influential was this project that, in later years, he reminisced, "I discovered myself after designing that little concrete-block bathhouse in Trenton."[1]

Initially, Kahn's responsibilities were much broader than the design of this single structure. Approached in 1954 by the Trenton Jewish Community Center in New Jersey, Kahn produced no less than five master plans for the campus of this complex, including a main community building and recreational spaces. Architecture and landscape were conceived together; Kahn believed that they fully complemented each other as exterior spaces wove the procession from building to building and also supported outdoor activities, such as archery. In time, the relationship between the client and Kahn deteriorated, leaving only two structures that he designed to be fully realized: the Bath House, finished in 1955, connected to the outdoor pool, and a cluster of pavilions identified as the Day Camp.

With this understated yet seminal work, his articulation of "servant" and "served" spaces—the notion that, as he stated, "certain spaces are very unimportant and some spaces are the real *raison d'etre* for doing what you're doing"—came into being.[2] In the Bath House, this hierarchical separation allows for the secondary areas to house such mundane but essential services such as storage and restrooms. Some of these eight-foot square servant spaces are U-shaped "hollow columns,"[3] as Kahn identified them; they also create entry and exit points for the men's and women's dressing rooms without relying on the use of doors for privacy and separation. The "served" spaces—basket room, atrium, dressing rooms, and pavilion leading to the pool—are uncluttered and liberated to support these primary activities. The design was executed with such economy, without forsaking elegance and simplicity, that Kahn would later recall that, "It was solved with absolute purity. Every space is accounted for, there is no redundancy."[4] When viewed in plan, the combination of the "servant" and "served" areas create a layout of **interlocking cubes**.

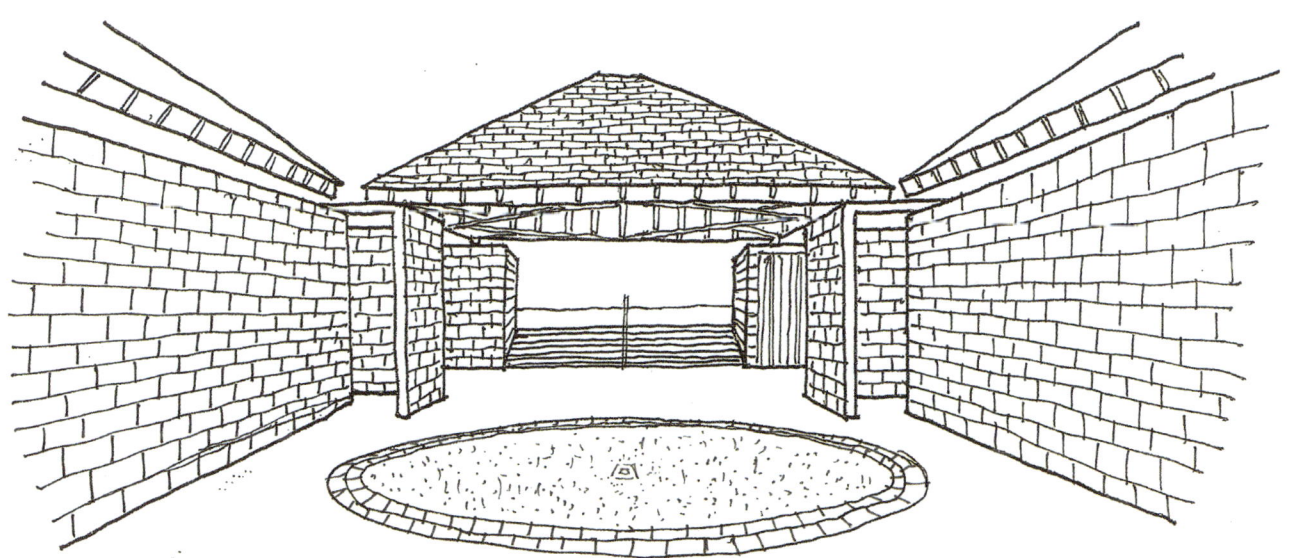

Diagram 1. This perspective shows the view within the structure, looking towards the stairs that lead to the pool. By elevating the area beyond, it feels nearly ceremonial as one approaches it. The circle inside the atrium or courtyard reinforces the building's organizational layout of a central plan.

Interlocking Cubes

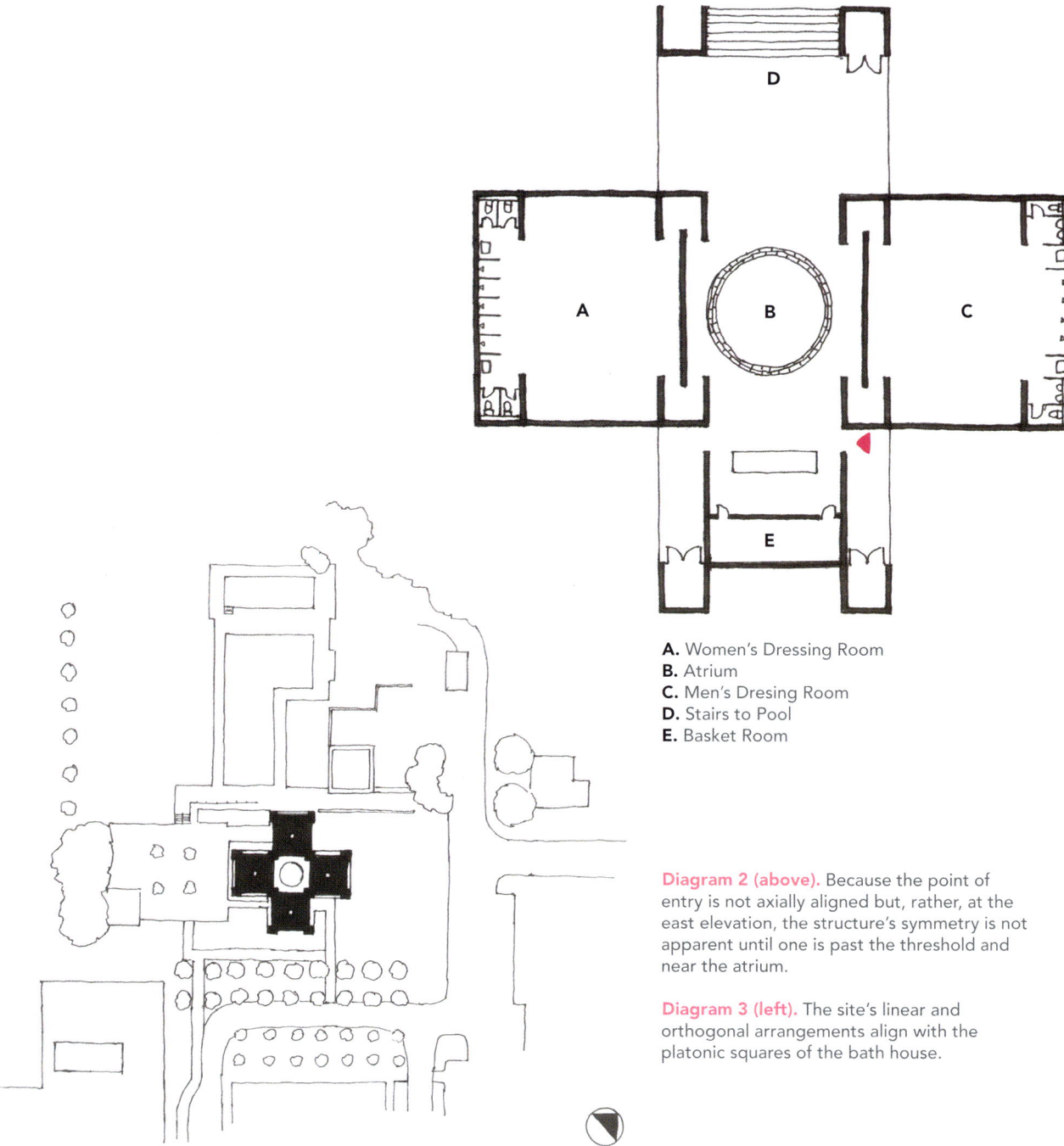

A. Women's Dressing Room
B. Atrium
C. Men's Dresing Room
D. Stairs to Pool
E. Basket Room

Diagram 2 (above). Because the point of entry is not axially aligned but, rather, at the east elevation, the structure's symmetry is not apparent until one is past the threshold and near the atrium.

Diagram 3 (left). The site's linear and orthogonal arrangements align with the platonic squares of the bath house.

Trenton Bath House

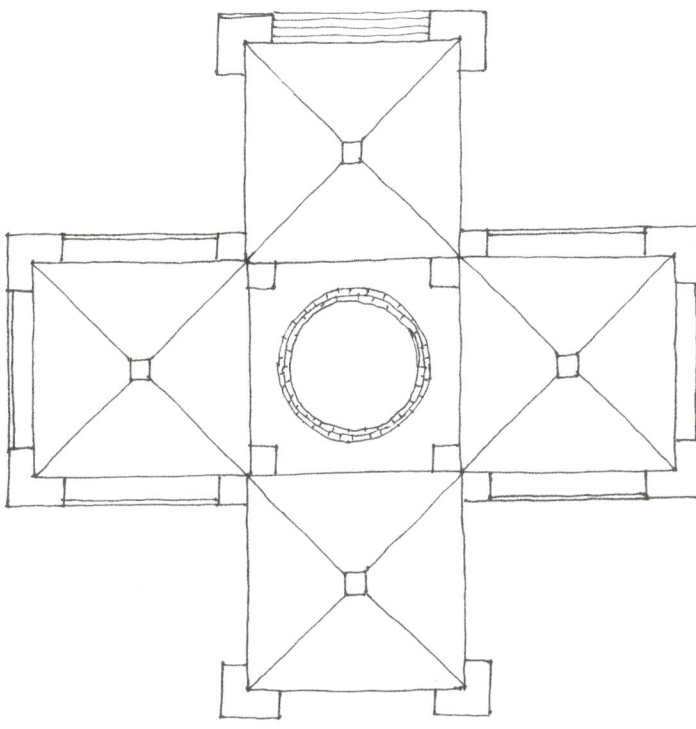

Diagram 4. Although the roof plan is never seen in this manner, Kahn's beautiful and elegant solution of creating individual pyramid-shapes over four spaces, whose ridges meet to create a rotated square, appears to frame the interior courtyard space.

By late April of 1955, the last iteration of the Bath House plan was complete. However, the design of the roof was not at all to Kahn's satisfaction; construction of it was conspicuously struck from the contract. Kahn was still ruminating over it during the summer months, evidenced by the roofless Bath House that opened with the pool on July 31. Any doubts that he had neglected completion of the structure were assuaged when the roof drawings were provided to the client by October. The design of four pyramids—one on top of each square, with the exception of the center atrium—reiterates and emphasizes this geometry or "room-space," as the architect called it. The cruciform floor plan had already separated each area as a discrete entity or room; it made sense to provide four distinctive pyramid roofs to further emphasize the individualities. Kahn, in later years, would write that "the most inspirational point from which we might try to understand architecture is to regard the room . . . as the beginning of architecture . . . I think the plan is a society of rooms."[5]

Because the corners of every roof rest upon a concrete cap at the top of the eight by eight "hollow columns" and not directly on any walls, the pyramids appear to be floating. Aesthetically, this gesture is worth noting, but, practically, Kahn achieves so much more with this elementary but masterful design. In the dressing rooms, a four-foot separation between the walls and the edges of the roofs provides the visitor with an ample view of the sky and trees above, eliminating the need for windows. A square oculus open to the above, at every pyramid provides some light but the primary source of lt in the dressing rooms is from the opening between the roof and walls. The periphery walls, bathed with natural light, mostly exclude the use of artificial lighting. Lastly, this design alleviates the requirement for an artificial ventilating system since air flows naturally through this large divide.

Vincent Scully, the distinguished Yale art history professor and a friend of Kahn, reflected on the work of the great architect: "From the very beginning, he was after symmetry, order, geometric clarity, primitive power . . . he wanted to make everything right . . . he's in some way communicating with this fundamental thing, that God is in the work. So it has to be perfect, you see. It has to be perfect. It can't be impatient. It's timeless."[6]

Interlocking Cubes

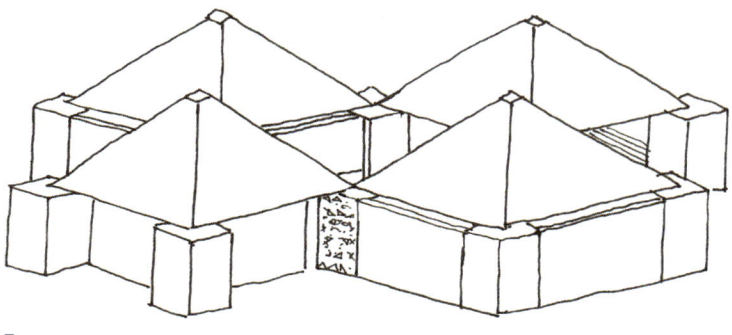

5

Diagrams 5, 6. The four roofs appear to be floating above their respective spaces, due in part to the strategy of never aligning the top edge of a wall to meet with the eaves of a roof. This unique edge condition of the wall and roof provides plenty of daylight and views, lending a sense of airiness to the entire structure.

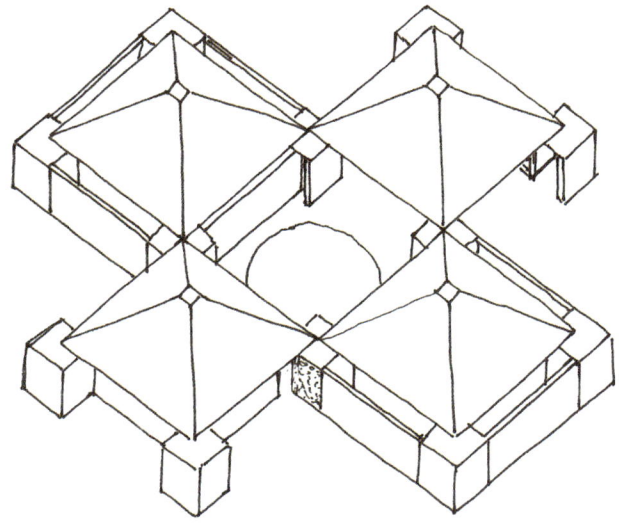

6

Trenton Bath House

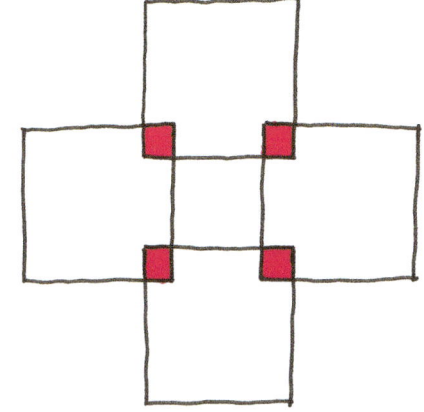

7

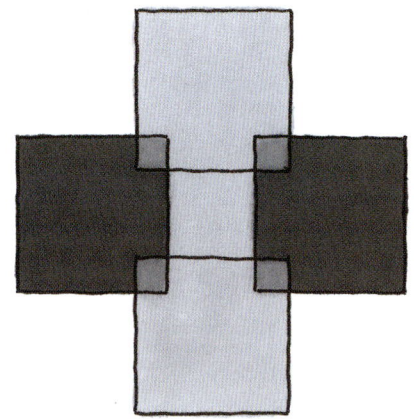

8

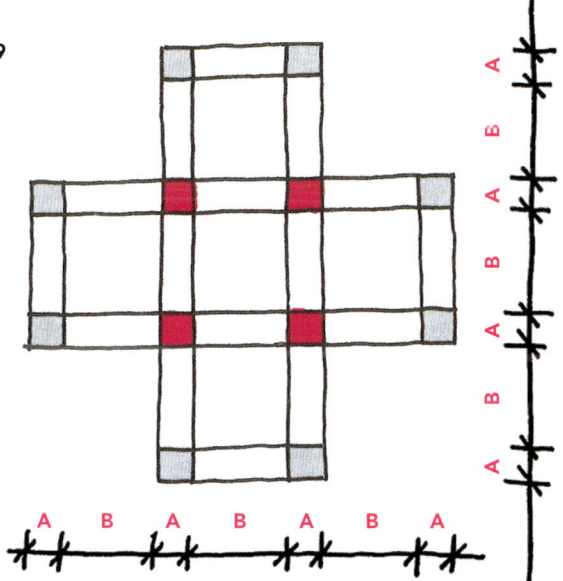

9

Diagram 7. All four squares overlap, creating an additional four smaller squares, shown in pink. Each large square overlaps to form the negative space—the medium-sized cube in the center, which is the heart of the pavilion.

Diagram 8. The darkest gray represents the most private areas; the light gray are public areas with the greatest amount of circulation. The entry and exit points of the dressing rooms are medium gray.

Diagram 9. Lines derived from the four small pink squares generate other small squares, shown in light gray, identified by Kahn as "servant" spaces. Despite the seemingly minor role of these areas, he recognized that they were not merely leftover spaces, but, in fact, they were part of the very fabric of the A-B-A grid, widely implemented by Renaissance architects.

Interlocking Cubes

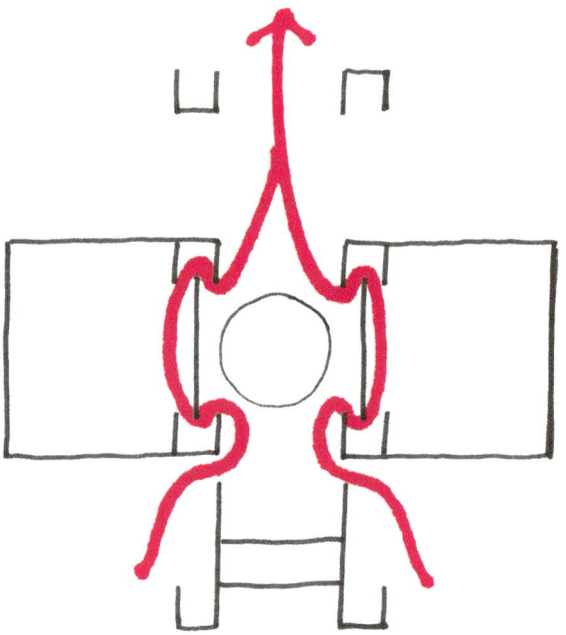

Diagram 10 (above). A grid, formed by the major centerlines (in the heavy, black lines), begins to emerge. When connected diagonally, the diagram recalls the lines created by the ridges of the roofs. In pink, a secondary, minor grid bisects the one in black, reaching beyond the confines of the structure.

Diagram 11 (right). Kahn provides very few doors; their absence is unusual, especially for dressing rooms. He was able to use the small, cube-like "servant" spaces and strategic placement of walls to create an extremely efficient method of entry and exit.

Trenton Bath House

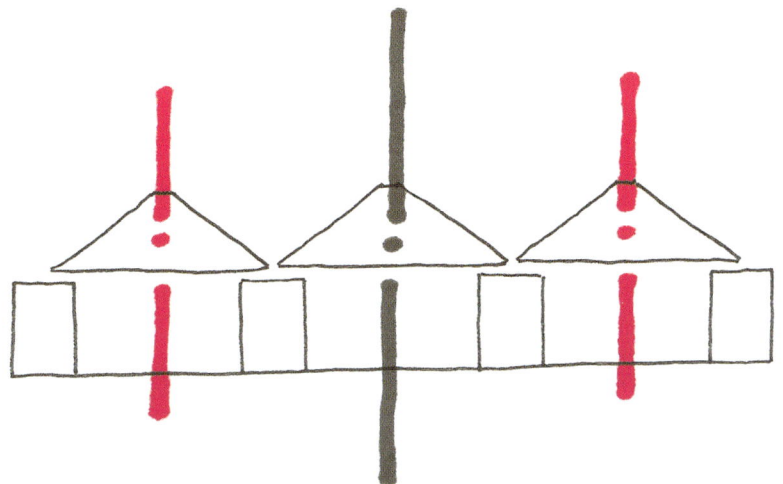

Diagram 12 (above). Each volume of the Bath House has its own distinct centerline. The major axis, in black, links the entry, atrium, and the space leading to the swimming area; the enclosed spaces of the dressing rooms have less pronounced axes (in pink).

Diagram 13 (below). The section of the building looking towards the pool belies its cruciform layout; rather, it appears to be a series of small pavilions linked together.

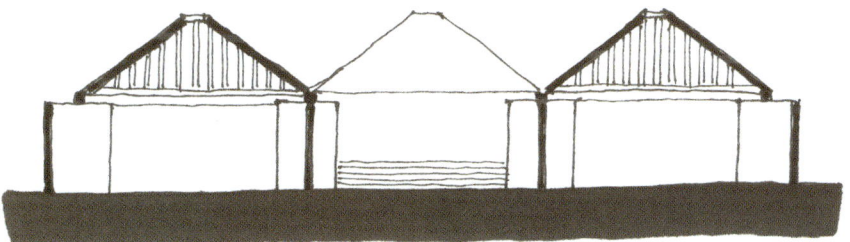

15 CONNECTING FORMS
Miller House

Forms that are connected in a loosely clustered manner provide open, interstitial spaces that can act as public or communal areas in an exterior or interior setting.

Miller House

Existing between Eero Saarinen and J. Irwin Miller was a deep and abiding admiration and friendship, rarely seen between architect and client. The latter, CEO of Cummins Engine Company, a Fortune 500 company, commissioned Saarinen to design four projects; among them was a main residence for his family in Columbus, Indiana, that was finished in 1957. In a letter from Saarinen to Alexander Girard, the textile and interior designer who collaborated on the project, this fondness for the client is palpable as he writes that he was, "enthusiastic about their [the Millers'] response because I feel there is a genuine feeling on their part that it [the house] is for them, and I have a feeling also that nothing is 'put over' on them, but simply right for them."[1]

The site, a thirteen-acre parcel of land that is defined by the Flatrock River to the west and a busy street to the east, was large enough to allow the house to be set back on the property, providing adequate privacy but stopping short of appearing aloof and withdrawn from its neighbors. An ostentatious residence would have been an affront to the Millers' humble sensibilities. As the head of a large company, J. Irwin Miller needed a home formal enough to entertain business guests, and yet casual enough to meet the demands of a household that included five of his children.

Sixteen columns, commodiously spaced apart, are arranged in a rectangular grid, forming nine boxes that are outlined by linear skylights. Ingeniously, this affords the deepest portions of the interior to be bathed in natural light, creating a beautiful, diffused glow on the walls and within the space. Although the grid's regularity establishes order and symmetry, any assumptions of predictability end here as Saarinen places four rectangular volumes of varying sizes, each housing the most private functions of the home, at the corners of the floor plan. They are arranged in a pin-wheel effect, creating varying widths between them. Despite the fact that the grid is respected, the remaining negative space in the center and in between the solids is an irregular shape, which would appear to play a lesser role. However, Saarinen deftly positions public areas of the home within these pockets of negative space, which **connect** the **forms** and provide cohesion.

Each public zone provides a view of the sweeping landscape, through floor-to-ceiling glass panels, which also act as counterpoints to the substantial, marble-encased rectangular volumes. Equally, the exterior is framed throughout the house, acting as the background to the events occurring inside. The leftover space—or a sort of interior courtyard—contains one of the most memorable elements of the Miller house: the conversation pit. A perfect square nestled literally within the ground, this area provides unobstructed views towards the expansive west lawn that eventually terminates at the banks of the Flatrock River.

Diagram 1. A view of the west elevation of the Miller House.

123

Connecting Forms

Saarinen stated, "Great architecture is both universal and individual . . . The individuality comes through . . . as a result of a special quality."[2] Alexander Girard brought that "special quality" by contrasting the formal, white, pristine architecture with joyful and exuberant colors, textiles, and an appreciation for personal effects and collectables that were an integral expression of the Millers' interests and their love of art. His intention of circulating various fabrics (such as pillows and curtains), figurines, indoor plants, etc., throughout the year was promoted enthusiastically by Mrs. Miller. His influence is exhibited everywhere in the home, underscoring the importance of creating a warm yet urbane dwelling. Girard works within the confines of the order established by the architecture: panels of color dot the floor-to-ceiling wooden bookcase; the gridded, custom-made carpets for the dining room and informal sitting area adhere to the area delineated by the adjacent white, marble walls; pink, red, and orange pillows enliven the conversation pit.

With such a broad expanse of land, Saarinen collaborated with landscape architect Dan Kiley to amplify the concept of the house to the surrounding gardens. Strict adherence to the grid is evident but it does not become heavy-handed or monotonous. The geometry of the architecture is emulated in the landscape through a series of defined open spaces, tree-lined axes, and hedges manicured into low, rectangular boxes. In order to counterbalance these lines and those of the house, Kiley included elements such as weeping beeches, trees characterized by draping branches. The neutral exterior materials that Saarinen selected act as the background to the multitude of colors that the changing seasons bring forth from the myriad varieties of flowers and trees.

Saarinen's father, Eliel, who was also an architect, wrote: "Always design a thing by considering it in its next larger context—a chair in a room, a room in a house, a house in an environment, an environment in a city plan."[3] Eero heeded his father's words and collaborated to create a masterpiece that amalgamated the interiors, architecture, and landscape into a residence that is one of his finest works.

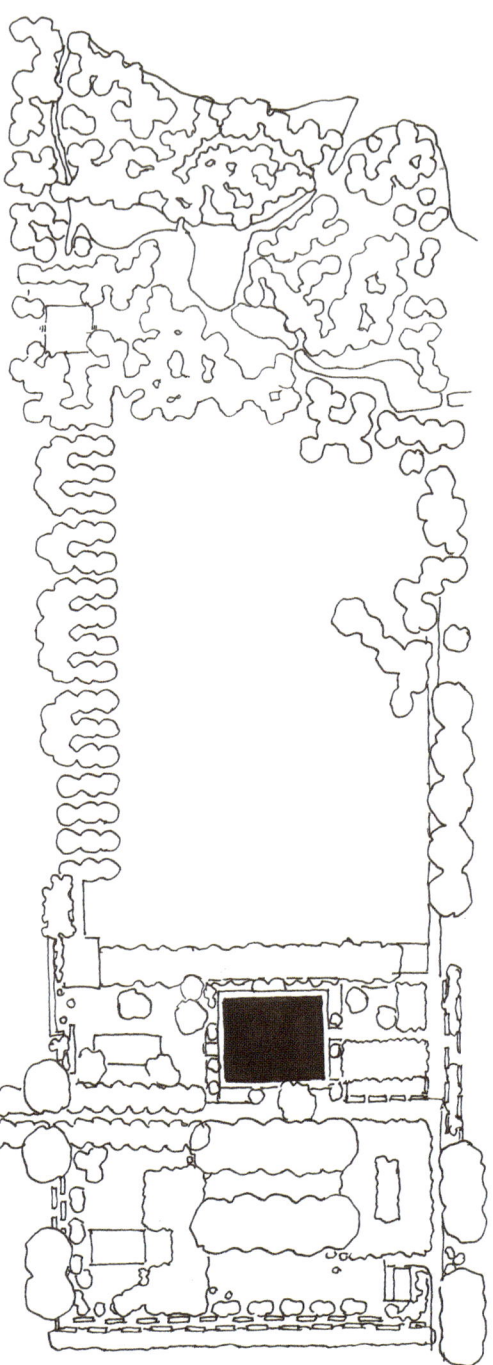

Diagram 2. To the west of the house, the manicured lawn gently slopes down to the Flatrock River. Dan Kiley, the landscape architect, designed the surrounding gardens as a seamless extension of the orthogonal and grid-like architecture as expressed by Saarinen.

Miller House

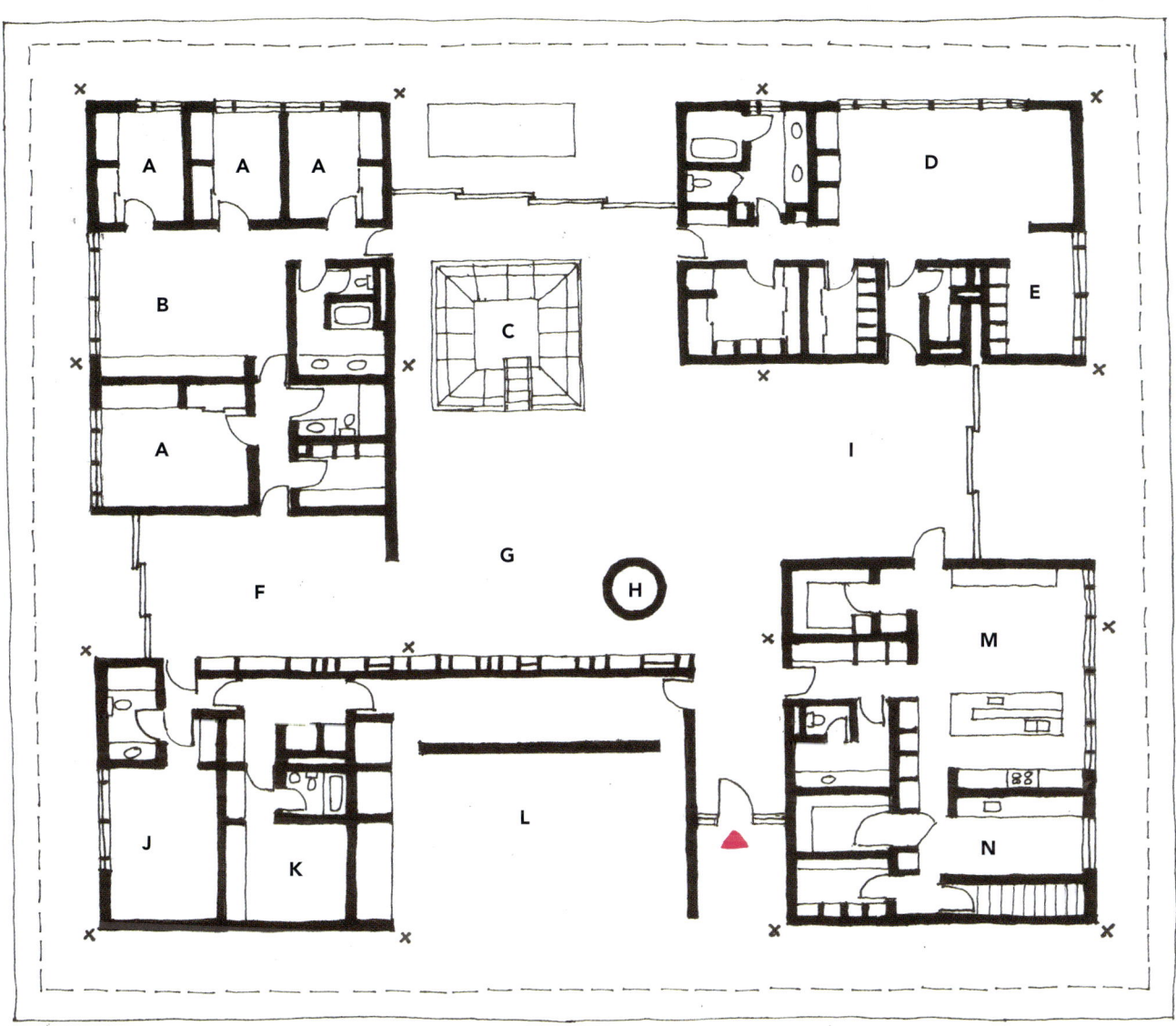

Diagram 3. The plan of the Miller House. Spacing between the rectangular volumes varies; this allows for all the communal activities to occur comfortably within these areas.

A. Bedroom
B. Play Area
C. Conversation Pit
D. Master Bedroom
E. Office
F. TV / Sitting Area
G. Formal Living
H. Fireplace
I. Dining
J. Guest Bedroom
K. Maid Bedroom
L. Carport
M. Kitchen
N. Laundry

Connecting Forms

4

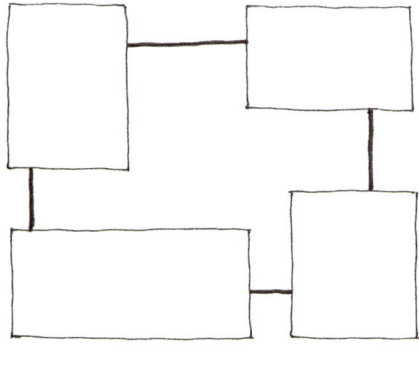

5

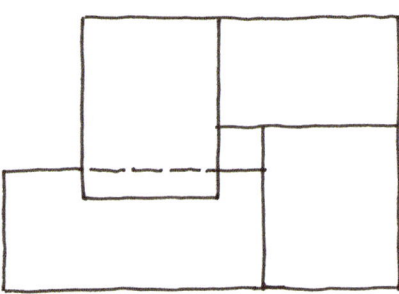

6

Diagram 4. Four rectangular volumes house the most private and utilitarian areas of this home, such as bedrooms, kitchen, and carport. None are the same size; however, the outer edges all align to maintain an orderly façade.

Diagram 5. Each volume is connected to its neighbor through a series of floor-to-ceiling glass panels that afford views to the beautiful landscape.

Diagram 6. If joined together, the rectangles would still maintain an open space in the center. This void is seemingly protected by the masses and it is, in fact, the main gathering area and heart of the home.

Miller House

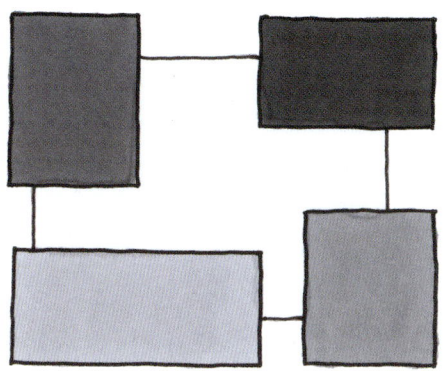

7

8

Diagram 7. The darker gray boxes represent the most private areas: the master bedroom and the bedrooms of the Miller's children. These face west to capture the view towards the river. Less private spaces—the kitchen, carport, guest bedroom—are shown in lighter gray boxes. Lastly, the very light gray zone in the center is the most open and public part of the house.

Diagram 8. The contrast between the dark and light gray zones highlights the pinwheel-like void that remains. Although some of the spaces in between the volumes might be perceived as narrow due to their adjacency to solid walls, they feel more expansive because of their unobstructed views to the outdoors.

Connecting Forms

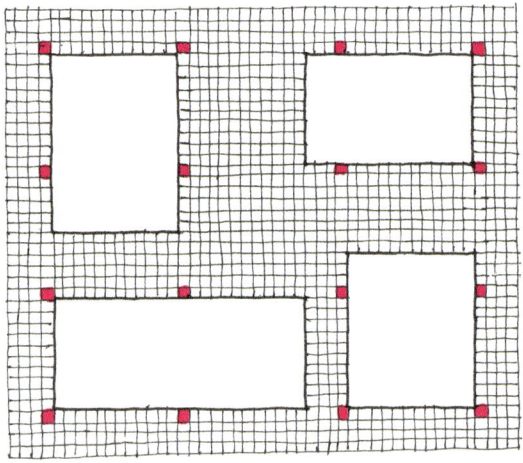

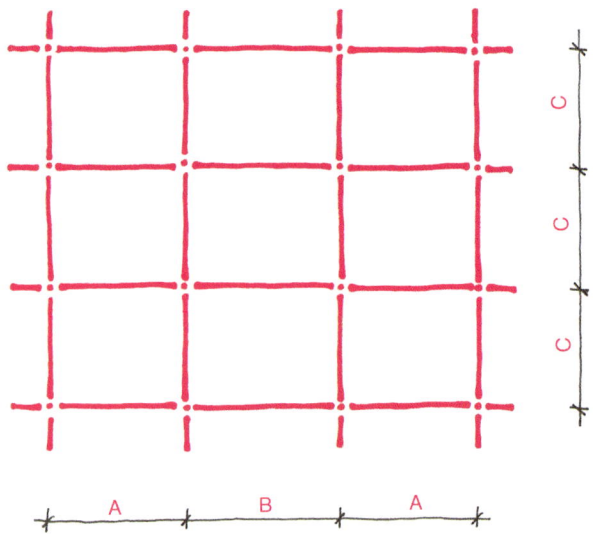

Diagram 9. Saarinen establishes a 2′6″ × 2′6″ grid and places the sixteen columns and volumes within this rigid arrangement; however, experientially, the entire effect achieves a remarkable degree of variation.

Diagram 10. Sixteen pink dots represent the placement of the cruciform-shaped columns. Easing the monotony of the grid is the variation of spacing shown here: the A, B, and C spacing of the structure.

Miller House

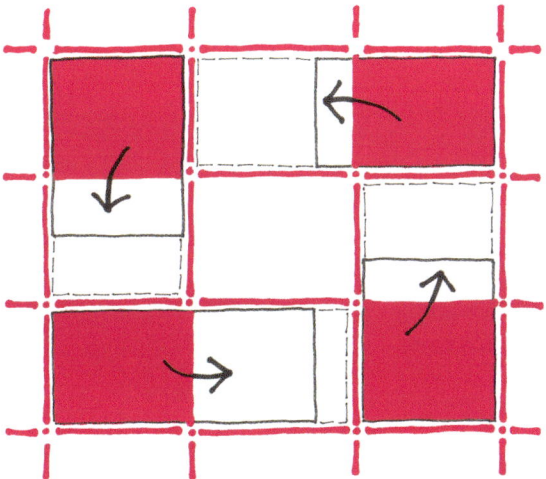

Diagram 11. This diagram studies the checkerboard effect of solids and voids of the plan. The black solid lines indicate the simple and subtle modification of each rectangular volume that anchors the house. One could imagine the forms protruding into the adjacent spaces, or retreating away from the gridlines delineated by the dashed lines.

16 LENGTHENING VIEWS
Stahl House

Lengthening views expand the interior beyond the envelope, integrating the landscape with the spatial experience.

Immortalized by the architectural photographer Julius Shulman, who captured an image of the gravity-defying Stahl House, the residence appears to hover above the street grid of the Los Angeles landscape below. Pierre Koenig, its architect, advocated the use of steel and glass to their utmost potential in order to capitalize the views of the city and surrounding mountains. Carlotta and Buck Stahl purchased the narrow site at the edge of a precipice in 1954 but their search to find an architect who was willing to design a house on such a challenging location yielded little until three years later, when they contacted Koenig. Undeterred by the formidable demands of the property, he modified Buck's vision into a residence on the sliver of land, which he identified as "essentially as a contextual problem because of the unusual and challenging site."[1]

Also known as Case Study House #22, the home was part of the ambitious plan by John Entenza, the editor of *Arts and Architecture* magazine, to introduce modern architecture to the masses through the Case Study House Program, which included the Eames House. Reflecting on his work and the attitudes of some architects during the post-war years, Koenig stated, "The idea was to be able to provide better housing for the common man at a better price . . . We wanted to produce something in a new idiom that was cheaper and mass produced."[2] Using readily available materials not only facilitated the efficient construction (the entire frame of the Stahl house was constructed in one day) but the homes were envisioned to be affordable and accessible during a post-war era that experienced a shortage of housing.

Koenig designed a simple L-shaped floor plan, which affords nearly every room in the house with a view of the pool and the city. Floor to ceiling glass seamlessly blends inside and outside, capitalizing the beautiful, sunny, and temperate weather of southern California that enables the exterior to be an integral facet of daily living. He would later recollect that during the design process, he "couldn't see anything other than to create an interior space that was an extension of the exterior" due to the severe limitations of the site.[3] To illustrate this point, the house and the pool's edge abut; entry into the house is not on *terra firma* but rather, it is a pathway that is surrounded by water and extends over it. A deep, eight-foot roof overhang creates a porch-like zone that mediates between inside and outside while protecting the interior from the sun's glare during the afternoon hours. Primary circulation from one leg of the house to the other is located between the zone of space around the pool, which can only be defined as "inside" or "outside" relative to the large, glass sliding doors. In fact, when the doors are open, there is no clear delineation between the spaces, further underscoring the ambiguity where architecture ends and nature begins.

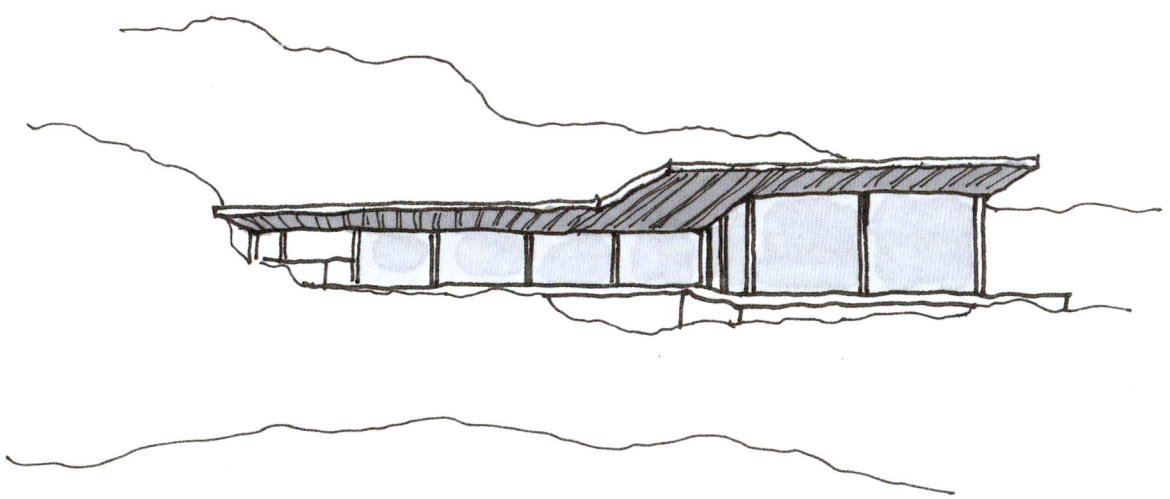

Diagram 1. A view of the southern façade of the Stahl house.

Lengthening Views

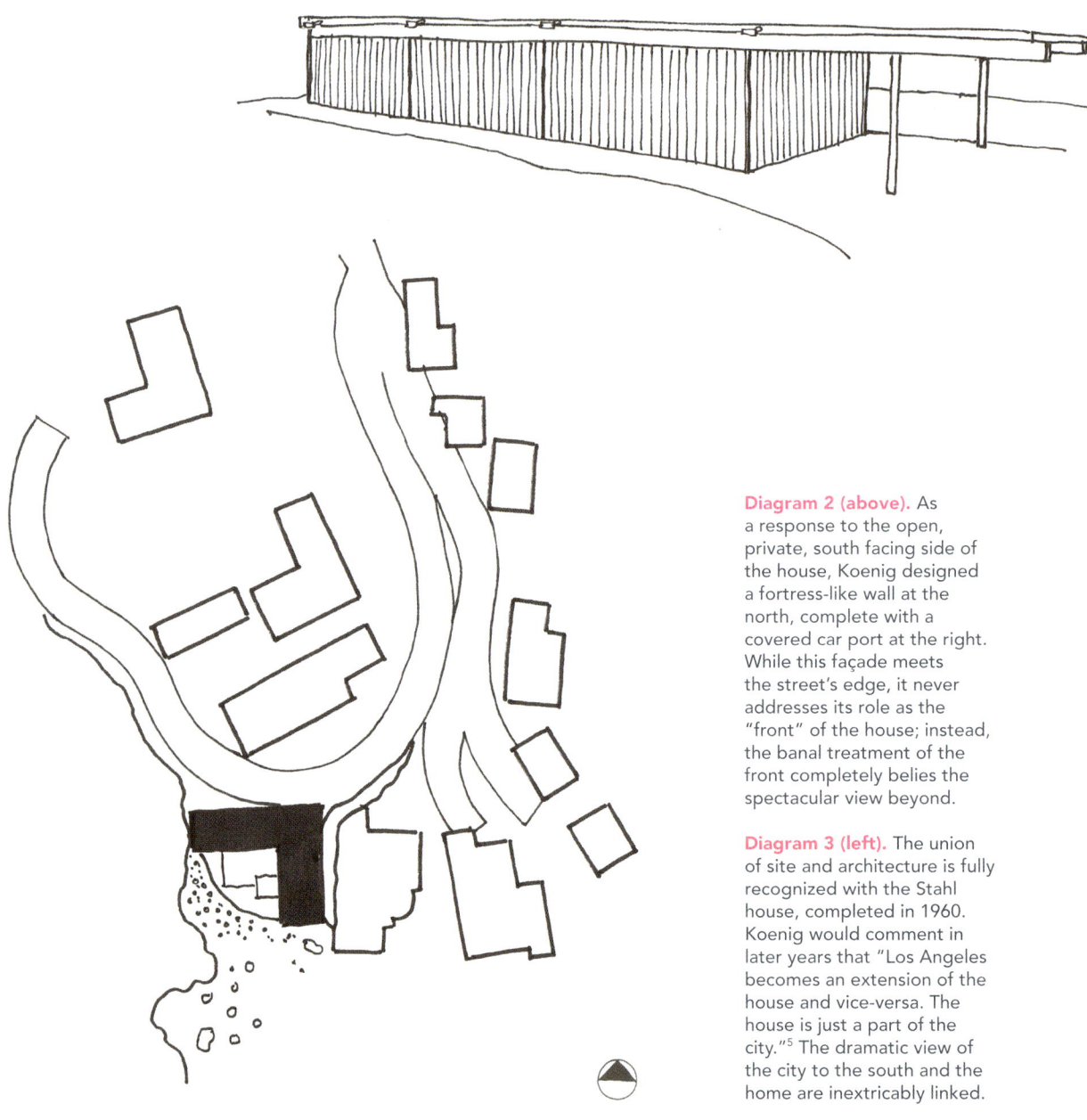

Diagram 2 (above). As a response to the open, private, south facing side of the house, Koenig designed a fortress-like wall at the north, complete with a covered car port at the right. While this façade meets the street's edge, it never addresses its role as the "front" of the house; instead, the banal treatment of the front completely belies the spectacular view beyond.

Diagram 3 (left). The union of site and architecture is fully recognized with the Stahl house, completed in 1960. Koenig would comment in later years that "Los Angeles becomes an extension of the house and vice-versa. The house is just a part of the city."[5] The dramatic view of the city to the south and the home are inextricably linked.

Stahl House

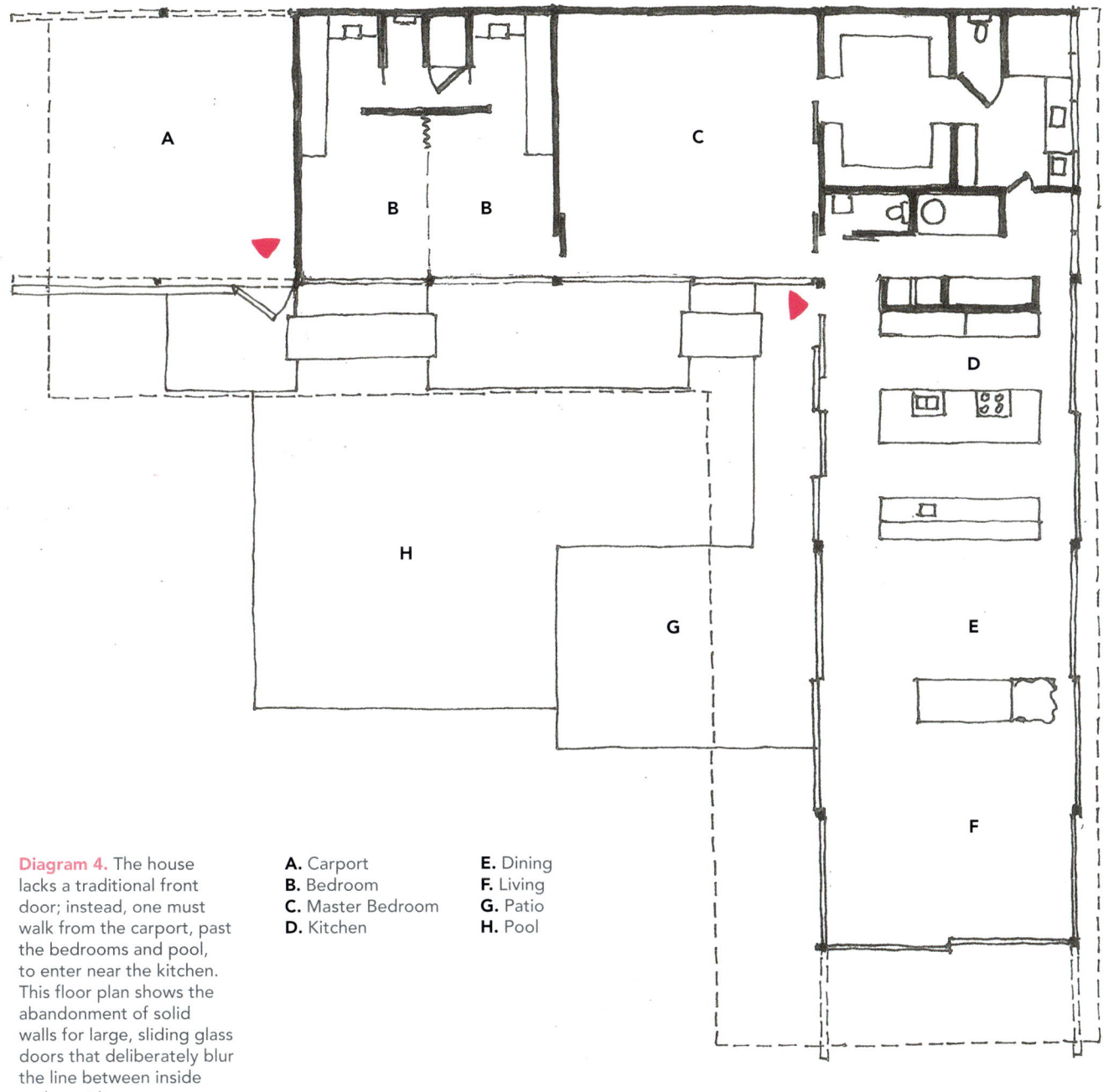

Diagram 4. The house lacks a traditional front door; instead, one must walk from the carport, past the bedrooms and pool, to enter near the kitchen. This floor plan shows the abandonment of solid walls for large, sliding glass doors that deliberately blur the line between inside and outside.

A. Carport
B. Bedroom
C. Master Bedroom
D. Kitchen
E. Dining
F. Living
G. Patio
H. Pool

Lengthening Views

Similarly, the pool's edge and the horizon beyond appear to converge, creating a memorable experience between the built environment and site. One leg of the house cantilevers beyond the precipice of the slope, giving the house the appearance that it floats effortlessly yet impossibly above the landscape. From the interior, the panoramic views of the city reinforce the notion that the dwelling is suspended and is not rooted to the ground. Perhaps inspired by others such as Mies van der Rohe's Farnsworth House, a residence that is the epitome of a "free flow of space," full-height walls are scarcely present; this provides uninterrupted and **lengthened views** while discarding the traditional way of designing houses with partitions.

Another example of Koenig's intention to use exterior spaces as extensions of the interior is the large, concrete pad that is surrounded by water, immediately adjacent to the dining room. Frequently pictured with a table and chairs, this poolside area invited the casual meal to be enjoyed in the mild, southern California weather. Koenig noted that his design enhanced a communal lifestyle and "allowed interaction between family members at the highest level, especially during mealtimes. Eating, playing, and homework were done in one space rather than in individual rooms."[4]

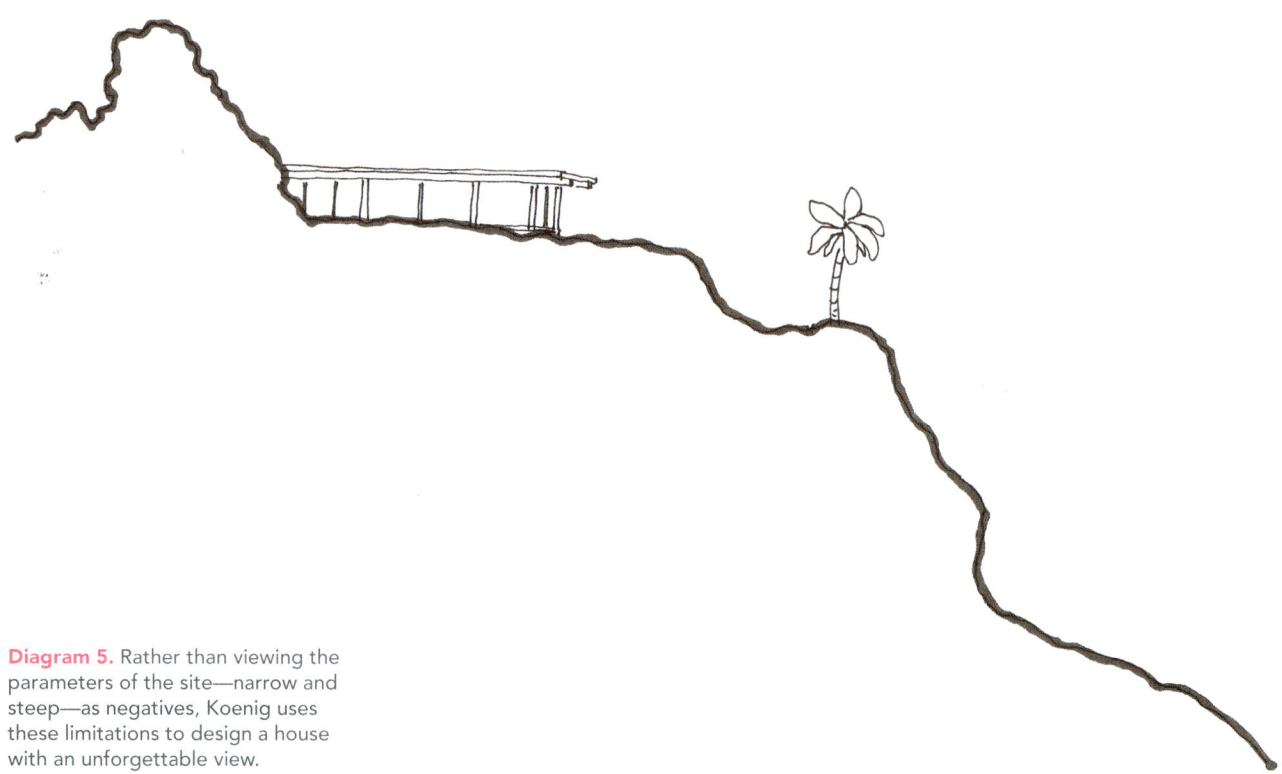

Diagram 5. Rather than viewing the parameters of the site—narrow and steep—as negatives, Koenig uses these limitations to design a house with an unforgettable view.

Stahl House

Diagram 6. A simple L-shaped floor plan neatly divides private areas along the solid wall from the public zone that extends to the south. This impenetrable line is in stark contrast to the dashed lines, which represent glass, providing a light, airy quality to the house.

Diagram 7. The private (dark gray) and public (light gray) zones are very simply divided in the house. The area in white represents the carport.

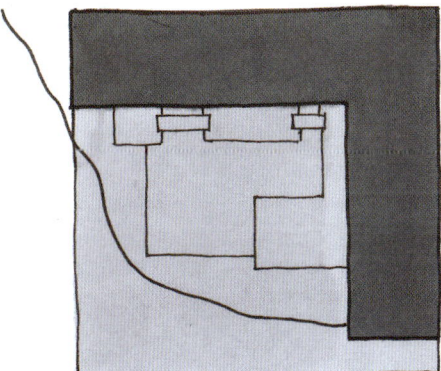

Diagram 8. Although the actual footprint of the house is shown in the darker, shaded area, Koenig's vision to expand the house beyond its immediate boundaries can be felt because of the extensive use of glass. The area with the lighter shading is the exterior; the ease with which literal and visual access is granted to the exterior gives the home a much larger presence.

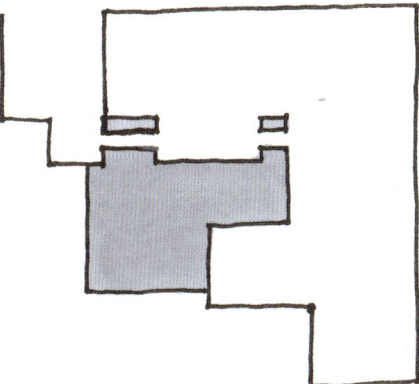

Diagram 9. The shaded areas represent the extent of the pool, as it is an integral physical and experiential part of the Stahl house.

17 OVERLAPPING CIRCLES
Pre-Columbian Gallery

Using the circle as a module creates a sense of harmony and symmetry; the circles' subtle overlaps organize the space into a compact and seamless composition.

Pre-Columbian Gallery

Dumbarton Oaks, one of the most beautiful gardens in the Georgetown neighborhood of Washington, DC, conceals a singularly small but outstanding structure. As described by the notable architectural critic Ada Louise Huxtable, this "delicate duet"[1] between art and architecture, designed by Philip Johnson and completed in 1963, housed a collection of pre-Columbian artifacts, acquired and donated by Robert and Mildred Bliss. They were the former owners of the lush and exquisite sixteen-acre estate and surrounding gardens that were later gifted to Harvard University and became Dumbarton Oaks, a museum and research center. Undoubtedly, this modern museum does not appear to have any relationship to its adjacent Georgian-style mansion nor the larger, historical context of Georgetown. Rather than being defiant in its milieu, the building is most restrained; it is hidden, nestled amongst the trees as Johnson intended. In fact, as he noted, he "wanted the garden to march right up the museum displays and become part of them."[2] The height of the structure does not compete with its neighbors nor with the enveloping foliage; this is also in deference to the scale of the museum's artifacts.

Using a 25-foot-diameter circle as a module, Johnson arranged eight to fit the periphery of an imaginary square. The gentle, fluid arcs of glass provide unimpeded views while the edge of the roof undulates softly, loosely delineating the floor plan. Each **circle**, positioned close together, creates an undiscernible **overlap**. The proximity of the modules, rather than causing a collision of geometries, establishes a point of connection where the circulation forms a continuous loop around the entire building. In addition, this strategy allows the abutting circles to share two 3'1" diameter columns that demarcate the nexus between the modules. Since the pavilion is enveloped by trees and each side is identical, its non-directional design cultivates a quiet, introverted atmosphere, inviting the visitor to observe nature from within, unobstructed by the surrounding glass.

The ninth circle stands within the absolute center of the pavilion. It deviates from the other modules due to the absence of a roof, and it is not physically—only visually—accessible. Astutely, Johnson encircled this completely private "outside" module with interior spaces that, due to the use of glass, become one with the exterior. The fountain at the center engages the viewer, visually and audibly, promoting an acute awareness of an introspective, internal space. As he stated, "[t]he museum that we built is not an 'outside' building. It is to be seen from the inside."[3] He deftly accomplishes this by blurring the delineation between the interior and exterior.

Another anomaly of this central module is its geometry, which differs slightly from the surrounding eight circles. It is assembled with eight *convex* glass arcs—the inverse of the concave segments that define the others. The columns, layout, and close adjacency of the circles naturally generate four, square-shaped residual spaces, each housing a very large plant. An arc of glass from these spaces help to give shape to the inverted circle. While this central area is not physically accessible, visually, the contained fountain and plants are integral to reinforcing the juncture of architecture and landscape.

Diagram 1. The roundness of the columns and the arcs of glass create a softness that is reinforced by the gentle waves of the pavilion's base and roof.

Overlapping Circles

Although understated in stature, Johnson was able to spare no expense for the sumptuous materials that present a stately and serene aura in the pavilion. Since he was unfettered by a budget, he was able to indulge his desire to create something of great beauty, all the while exercising restraint. One of the most lavish details is the teak floor, with its precise, radiating slivers encircled with rich, green Vermont marble. The light-colored columns are also clad in marble (quarried from Illinois) with contrasting bronze rings, mediating the juncture between the stone and ceiling. Often, the pavilion has been identified as a "modern jewel box," words that Huxtable wrote to describe it, also noting that there was "restrained use of the richest and most luxurious materials for maximum impact without ostentation."[4] Indeed, Johnson himself, when asked what building he was most proud of, noted, "the owner and I worked together and it was pure delight from beginning to end and it came out very well."[5]

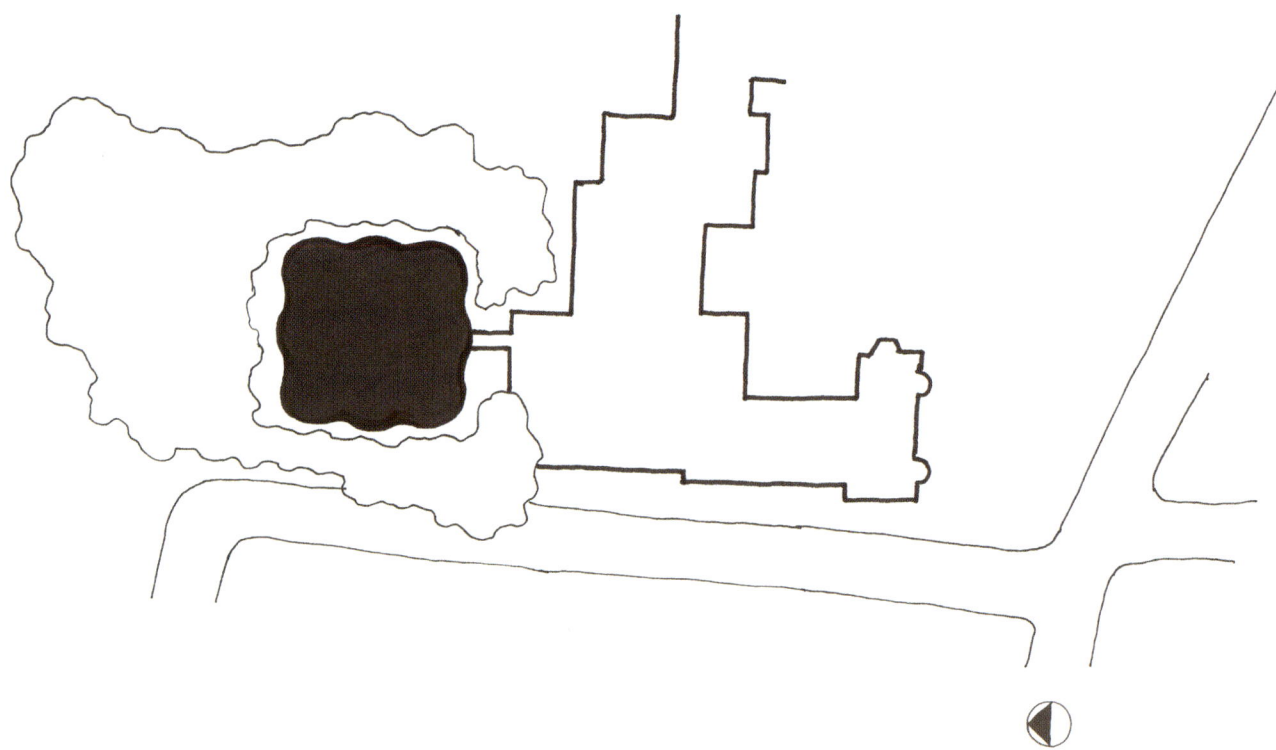

Diagram 2. The surrounding trees are an integral component of the architecture. Philip Johnson would note "the way I built it, all you see is the outdoors when you are inside the museum."[6]

Pre-Columbian Gallery

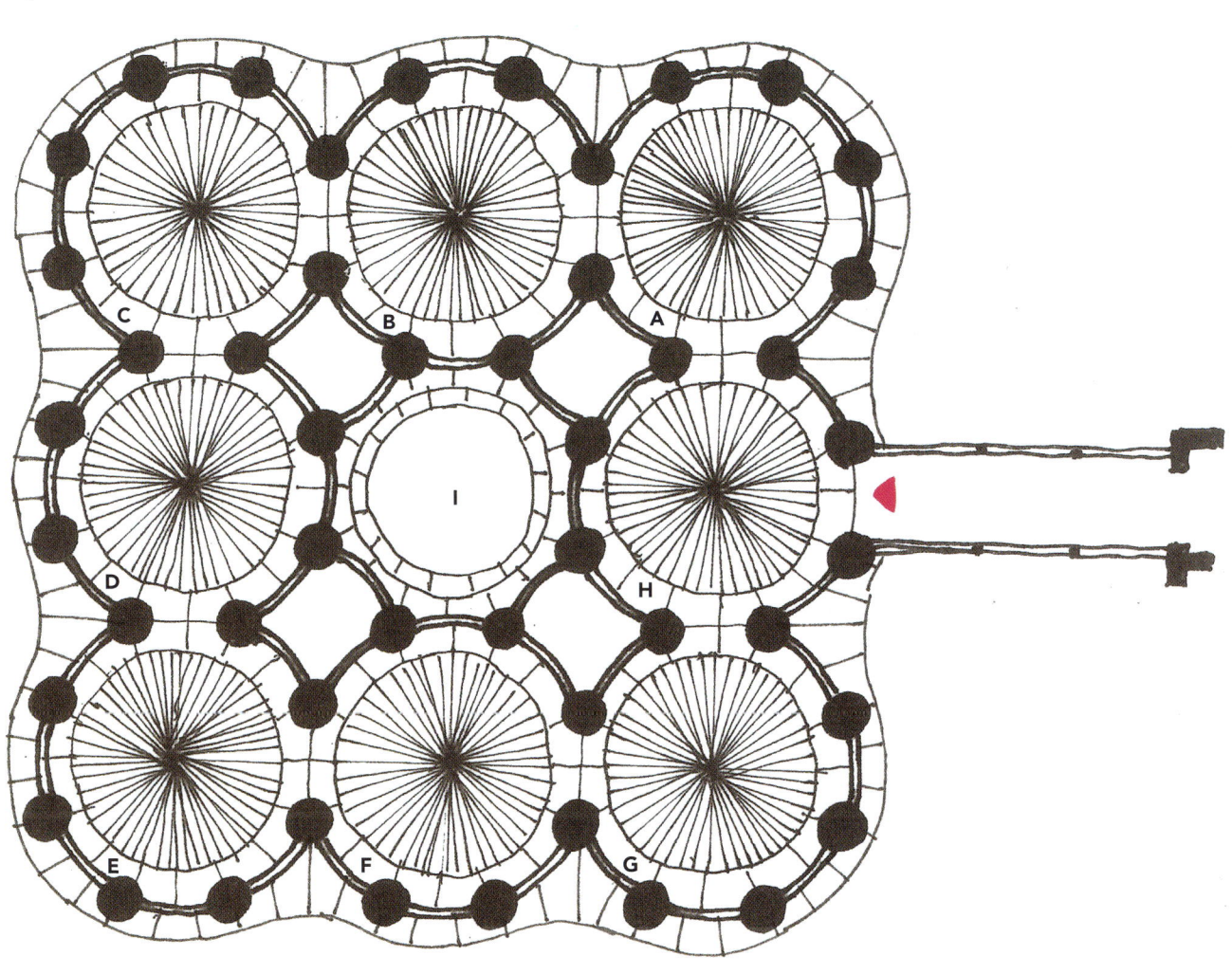

Diagram 3. The floor plan illustrates the fine details of the teak and marble floor. To the right, a glass-enclosed walkway connects the galleries to the Dumbarton Oaks Museum.

A. Gallery 1
B. Gallery 2
C. Gallery 3
D. Gallery 4
E. Gallery 5
F. Gallery 6
G. Gallery 7
H. Gallery 8
I. Courtyard

Overlapping Circles

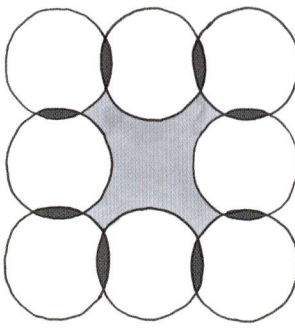

4

Diagram 4. The overlaps connect the eight circles. Experientially, the dark gray almond-shaped areas are undetectable. The light gray zone in the diagram appears to be left over space but actually functions as a zone to house nature.

Diagrams 5, 6. Like beads precisely placed in an intricate pattern, the 3'1" diameter columns generate the circles. Every module shares these columns with the adjacent one, creating a fluid continuity of forms and circulation.

5

6

Pre-Columbian Gallery

Diagram 7. In the light gray zones, the visitor is welcomed to experience the architecture and the Pre-Columbian artifacts, presented in acrylic displays. The darkest gray areas are residual spaces, and the white, center circle houses the fountain.

Diagrams 8, 9. Gentle, glass arcs link the "beads" of columns, allowing a clear view outward and inward (Diagram 8). The high degree of transparency permits the viewer to see through the entire pavilion along its diagonal and orthogonal axes (Diagram 9).

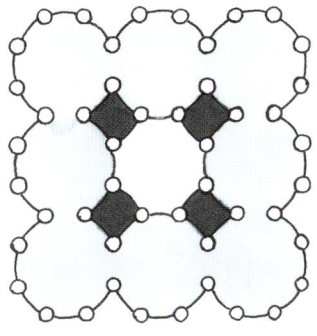

7

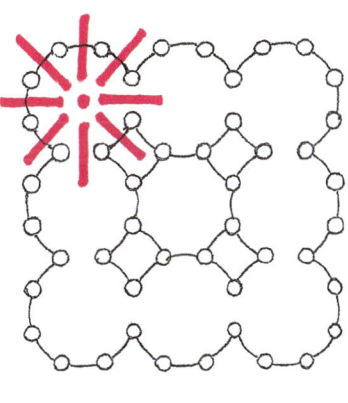

8

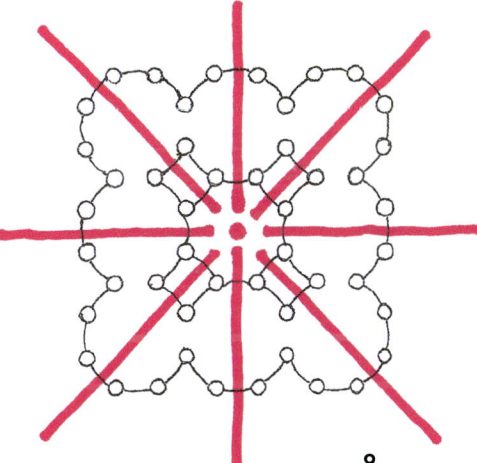

9

Overlapping Circles

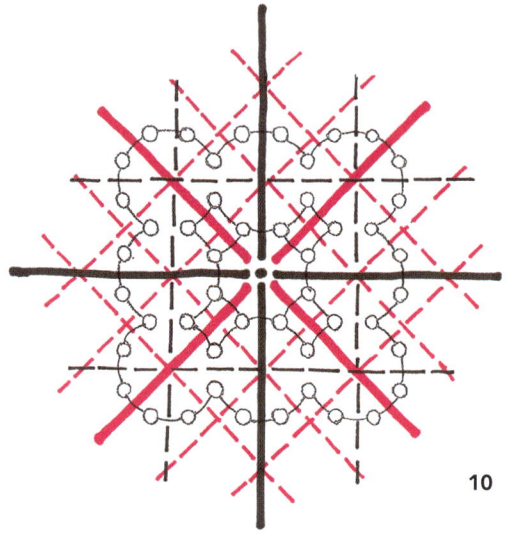

10

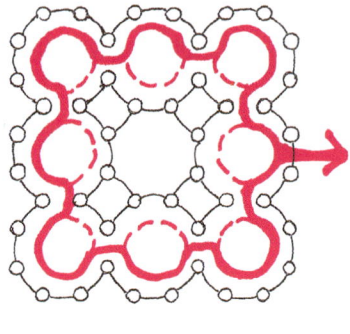

11

12

Diagram 10. Each circle possesses a strong focal point in the center. When they are connected, the diagonal pink lines and orthogonal black lines construct a starburst-like pattern of axes that is inherent in the layout. Secondary axes are shown in thinner dashed pink and black lines.

Diagram 11. The majority of the circulation, as shown in a heavy pink line, occurs between and along the periphery of each circle, where most of the displays are located. Visitors viewing the inaccessible interior spaces in the center from any of the eight modules would tread along the dashed lines.

Diagram 12. The floor of each module is exquisitely composed of radiating slivers of teak (shown as white), surrounded by green Vermont marble (represented by the gray shading).

Pre-Columbian Gallery

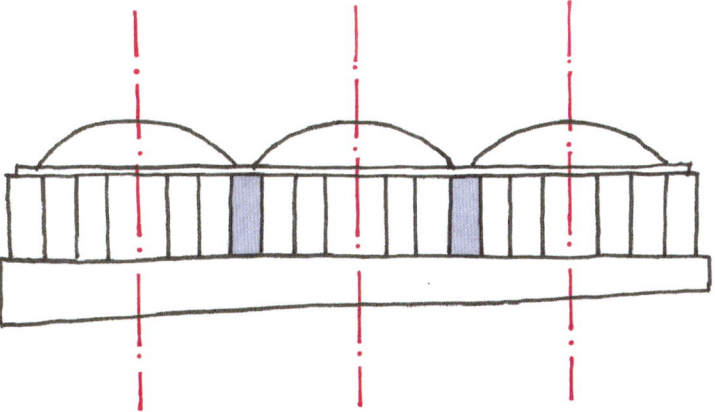

Diagram 13. The pink lines represent the center of each module; the gray vertical zones are the 3'1" diameter columns that are shared between the circles.

18 ROTATING BLOCKS
Fisher House

Rotating blocks give the appearance of complexity from the exterior, while views from the simple, square-plan interior of each volume vary, due to the multiple orientations of the façades.

When Dr. and Mrs. Fisher commissioned Louis Kahn in the summer of 1960 to build a house for them in Hatboro, Pennsylvania, little did they envision a nearly seven-year process to see their home designed and built. This was partly due to the architect's penchant for completely redesigning the house with each adjustment or modification. However, concurrently, his practice was engaged in very large-scale projects such as the Salk Institute for Biological Studies in La Jolla, California, and the Indian Institute of Management in Ahmedabad, India. The Fishers, ever patient, were exceptional clients who intuited Kahn's genius; they accepted the fact that progress on their house was stymied by these prodigious commissions. During these years and even after the completion of the house, an enduring respect and friendship was sustained; later, the Fishers would recall Kahn's "intellect, energy, humor and warmth."[1]

Looking at the house, Kahn's insight into his design approach appears obvious: "I always start with a square, no matter what the problem is."[2] The plan appears simple and straightforward—two squares or **blocks**, one **rotated** 45 degrees—but it belies the long duration of evolution, and to some degree, his own frustration with the endless search for an architecture that would ultimately please him. This even taxed the tolerant Fishers: "If we were not satisfied with a set of plans, he would not modify them but insisted on starting over."[3] Eventually, the form coalesced and condensed from a linear organization to two boxes, "living" and "sleeping," as coined by Kahn, clad with cypress siding. The latter cube is a two-story volume with its elevations precisely facing the cardinal points. Entry is located at the west, with the master's and children's bedrooms facing east. Knowing how intensely the morning sun could fill the rooms, Kahn was exceedingly sensitive about controlling the light, as he explained to the Fishers: "in the bedroom, you tend to reduce the fenestration but never reduce it to the point where walls cannot receive mood of the time of the day and the seasons of the year. And still when you get up you want to feel that you are hugged by the room."[4]

Many factors influenced the output of multiple design schemes and iterations by Kahn; however, what persisted throughout all the plans was the living area as its own discrete volume that was separate from the space that contained the bedrooms. It was his deeply held conviction that, since "the living room is a place where everyone gathers,"[5] this would be the heart of the home, animated by the interactions of family members. Oriented at 45 degrees, the "living" cube—with its dining, kitchen, and living spaces—connects to the other volume at one of its corners. Featured in this room is a large, semicircular, stone fireplace, set slightly askew; it "is what makes the house divide itself into various rooms" as Kahn noted.[6] Perhaps the most striking composition of the entire home is the beautifully detailed wooden bench at the northeast corner of the living room. From floor to ceiling, seven windows of varying sizes as well as four finely

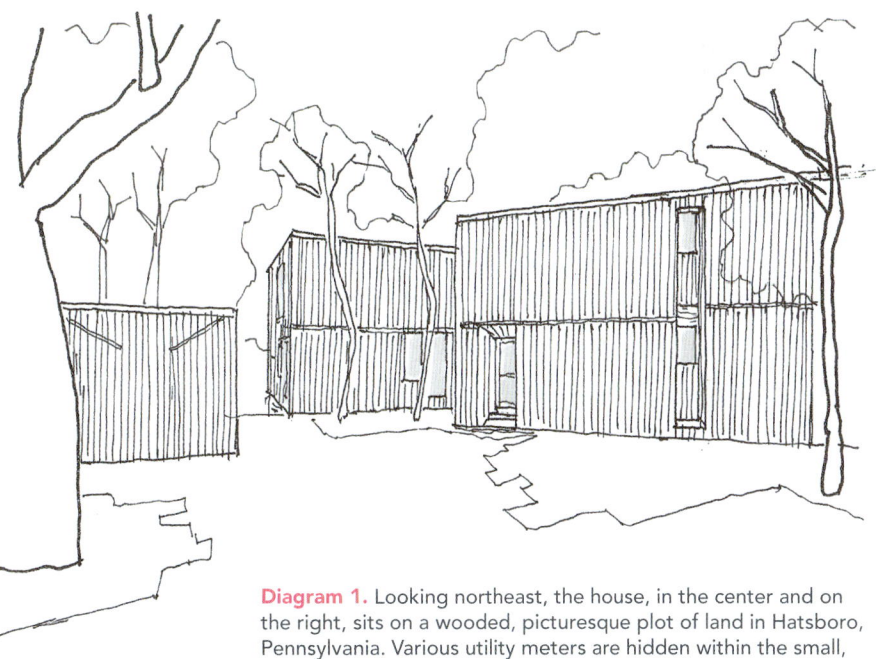

Diagram 1. Looking northeast, the house, in the center and on the right, sits on a wooded, picturesque plot of land in Hatsboro, Pennsylvania. Various utility meters are hidden within the small, free-standing shed to the left. At one point during the design phase, Kahn intended to have one cube clad in wood and the other in Montgomeryville stone from local quarries. Due to budgetary constraints, he revised the materials to create "a wood house on a stone plinth."[10]

Rotating Blocks

crafted wooden panels, like the stiles and rails of a door, surround the seat, which cantilevers above the floor. Some of these windows and panels protrude into the space, creating spatial variation inside as well as dark recesses at the exterior façade.

By rotating one of the volumes, this provided more surface area, enabling every room on the ground and second level access to natural light. For Kahn, this was not a luxury but rather, one of the precepts of his architecture: daylight was a prerequisite for creation of space. He was so adamant about this rule that he initially denied the Fishers' request for a basement since an "aesthetically pleasing way of bringing in natural light"[7] was not feasible; however, he eventually complied and made the necessary changes to the drawings. The architect's profound description of light is poignant and poetic: "We are born out of light and every space we live in is thought of in the choreography, you might say, in the making of a plan which is in search of light and that the structure is the maker of light . . . So, my consciousness of light comes from that source—that without light you don't have space, or, you might say, a room."[8] This hardly went unnoticed by the Fishers or one of their daughters, Nina; years later, she reflected on the extraordinary effects of the architecture. She noted that she "could take the lessons of my childhood home with me: a house that honors light, encouraging it to enter, playing with it, and changing mood as the character of the light shifts."[9]

Diagram 2. In the late 1950s, the Fishers purchased the plot of land, enticed by the creek that ran through the lot. They turned to Kahn in later years to design a bridge for their daughter's wedding, held at the property.

Fisher House

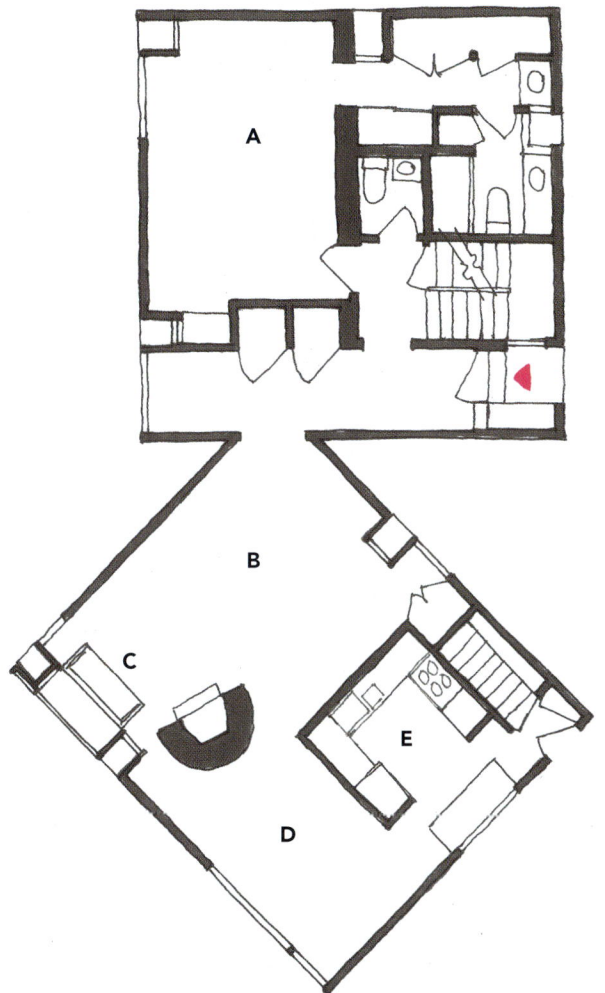

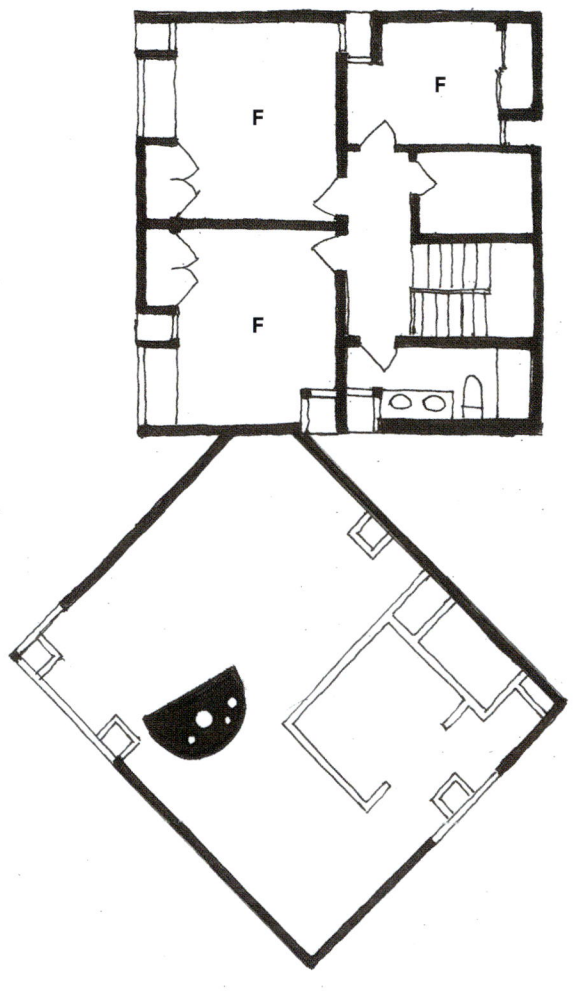

Diagram 3. The first floor of the house shows the near-perfect square plans of the "living" and "sleeping" cubes at the north and south, respectively. With this final iteration of the design, Kahn found some degree of satisfaction. In later years, he would reflect on this: "It is a happy moment when a geometry is found which tends to make spaces naturally, so that the composition of geometry in the plan serves to construct, to give light, and to make spaces."[11]

Diagram 4. The second floor consists of the children's and maid's bedrooms; in the "living" volume, the ceiling is 18 feet tall. This creates a spectacular light-filled atmosphere with views to nature and where the stone fireplace is the only interior architectural element that extends from floor to ceiling.

A. Master Bedroom   **D.** Dining
B. Living   **E.** Kitchen
C. Built-In Seat   **F.** Bedroom

Rotating Blocks

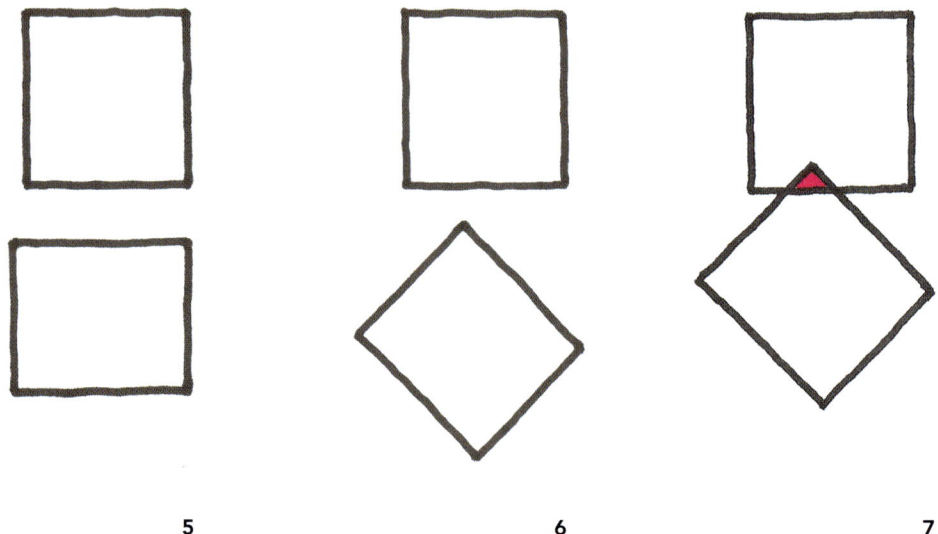

5   6   7

Diagrams 5, 6, 7. Initially, Kahn conceived a "living" and "sleeping" cube to be side-by-side (Diagram 5). He then rotated the "living" volume (Diagram 6). The area of the pink triangle in Diagram 7 does not exist in plan but provides an opening and connection between the two spaces.

Fisher House

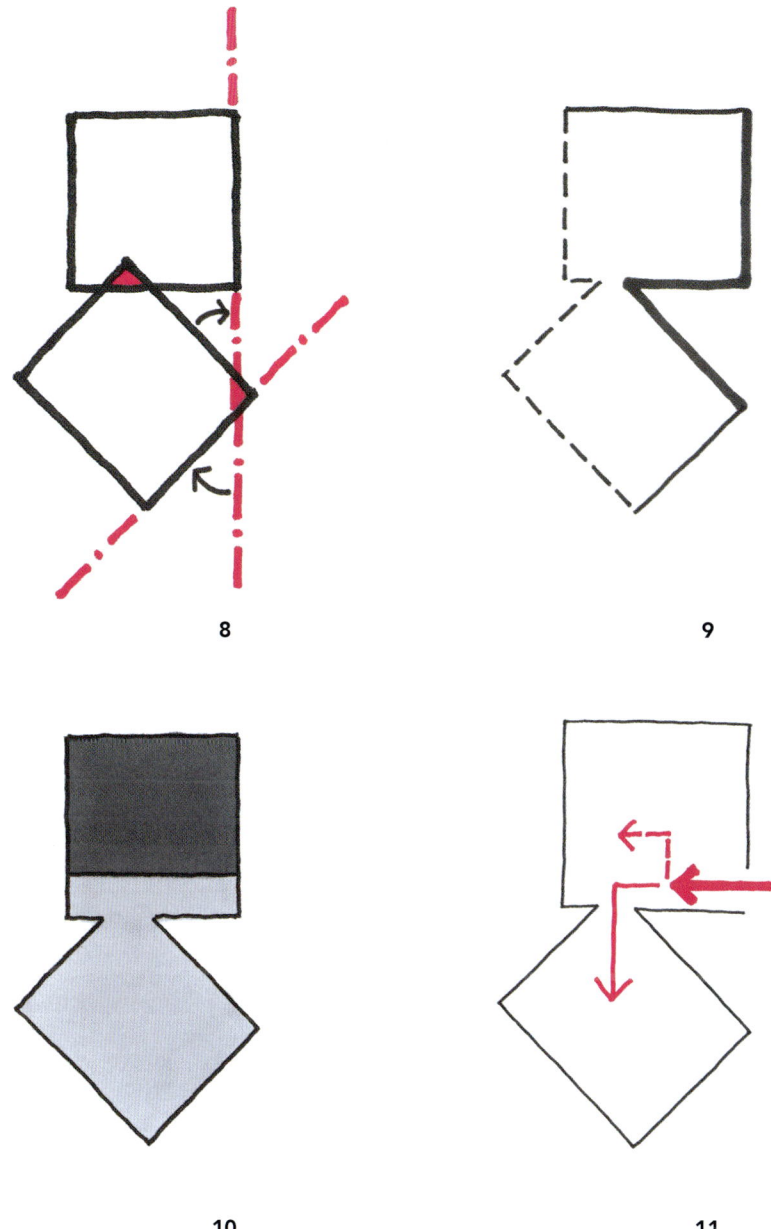

Diagram 8. A simple analysis reveals that the current placement of the 45-degree rotated cube generates two triangles when a vertical line is drawn from edge of the orthogonal box.

Diagram 9. Although windows adorn nearly every façade of the house, the walls that face west—shown in heavy lines—have less openings than the ones facing the creek, shown as dashed lines.

Diagram 10. The areas in light gray represent the public areas. The bedrooms are located in the dark gray box; a hallway (in light gray), used by guests and the Fishers, mediate between the two zones.

Diagram 11. Circulation at the main entry, as shown in a thick, solid, pink line splits immediately after passing the threshold. Access to a staircase and the master bedroom is depicted with a dashed, pink line, while entry to the living room is to the left and shown as a solid, pink line.

Rotating Blocks

Diagrams 12, 13. Kahn notes: "Each space must be defined by its structure and the character of its natural light . . . structure is synonymous with light and which gives image to that space."[12] Voids indicate window locations for the ground (Diagram 12) and second floor (Diagram 13).

Diagrams 14, 15. Narrow, deep-set windows shown in gray provide "a lot of little exciting vistas" that Kahn preferred, as remembered by Dr. Fisher.[13] Some of these openings are designed with wood sides and top, creating a tall, finely-detailed millwork box, framing a window. Nina Fisher, the youngest of the two daughters, recalls with great fondness the unique fenestration: "I would clamber onto the top of an inset window box with book in hand to read. Perched some 18 feet above the ground . . . I felt as Lou had built a soaring treehouse perch just for me."[14]

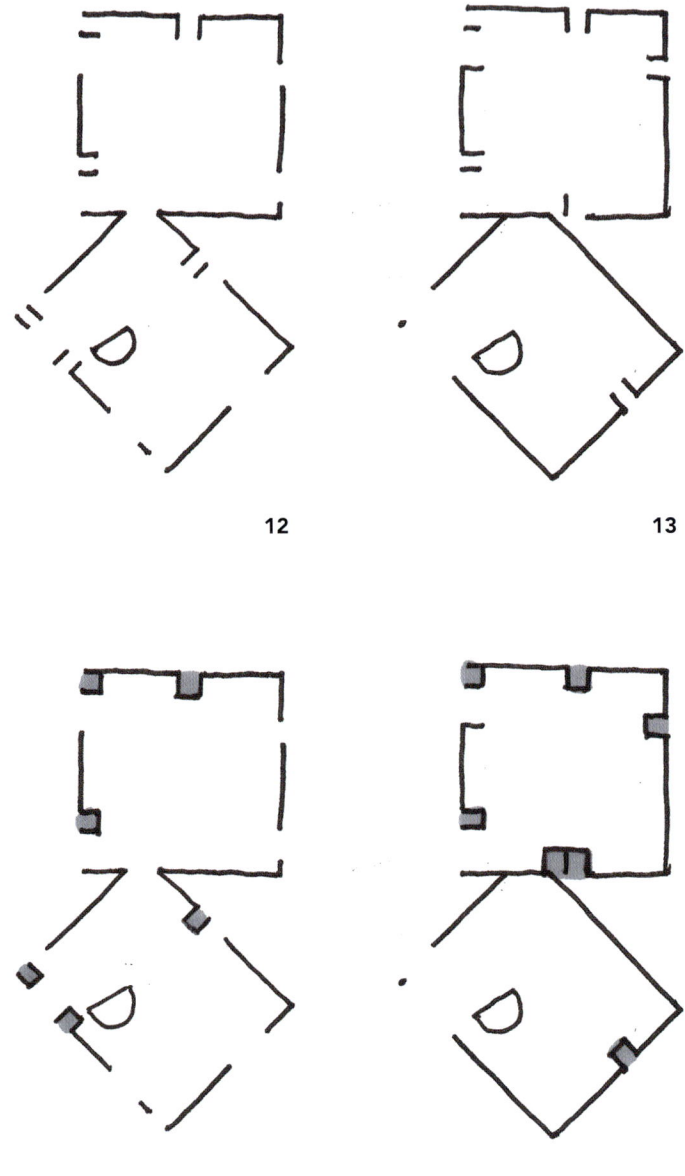

Fisher House

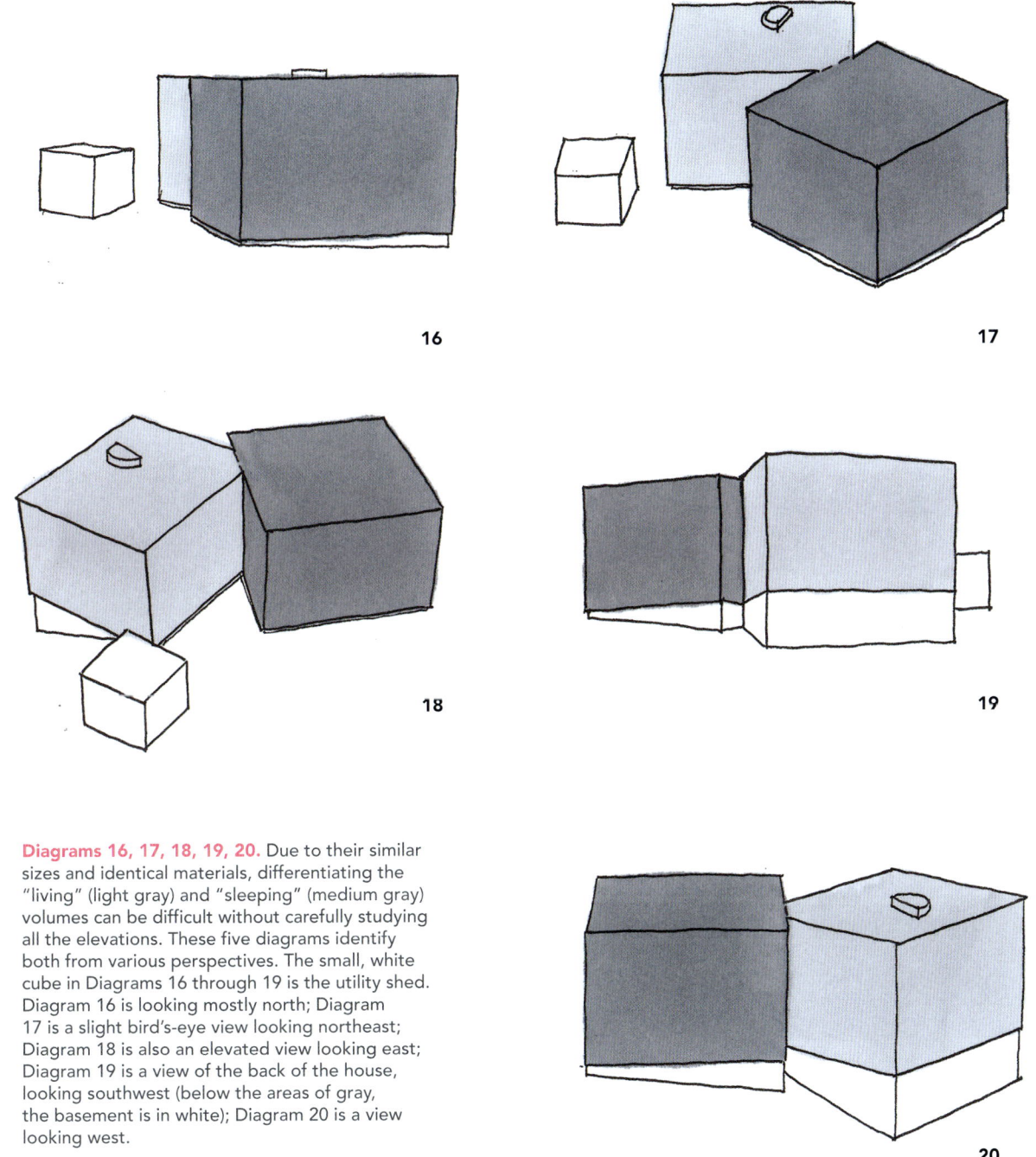

Diagrams 16, 17, 18, 19, 20. Due to their similar sizes and identical materials, differentiating the "living" (light gray) and "sleeping" (medium gray) volumes can be difficult without carefully studying all the elevations. These five diagrams identify both from various perspectives. The small, white cube in Diagrams 16 through 19 is the utility shed. Diagram 16 is looking mostly north; Diagram 17 is a slight bird's-eye view looking northeast; Diagram 18 is also an elevated view looking east; Diagram 19 is a view of the back of the house, looking southwest (below the areas of gray, the basement is in white); Diagram 20 is a view looking west.

19 EMBEDDING COMPONENTS
Koshino House

Embedding architecture into the landscape provides a larger interior footprint while lessening the physical impact the components have on the environment.

Koshino House

In the city of Ashiya, located in the Hyogo Prefecture, Japan, a wooded parcel of land is the site of the acclaimed Koshino House by the Japanese professional boxer turned architect, Tadao Ando. When he accepted the commission in 1979 from Junko Koshino, the notable fashion designer, his decade-long practice had developed a robust portfolio of residences. Reflecting back on his illustrious career over forty years later, he discloses that, despite his fame and the capacity to engage in large scale projects, he persists in designing "two or three houses each year,"[1] as this brings his architectural acumen into sharper focus. Designing residences is a source of vitalization for Ando. He describes how "[t]he more intense the conflict during the creative process, the more vivid and robust the architecture becomes. The house, the smallest building type born from this struggle, is the origin of my architecture."[2]

The site has many trees, and safeguarding the vast majority of them was paramount, but preservation had to be balanced with the excessive shade that would reduce the house's exposure to natural light. His sensitivities and profound respect for the treatment of the site is evident with the architecture, which works in concert with the topography. He writes, "A house must respond to the functional demands necessary for the everyday life . . . At the same time, it is expected to relate intimately to the site's layered context, which is defined by nature, climate, local history, and the communal spirit of the land."[3] With the site sloping down toward the southwest, Ando **embeds** or gently inserts **components** of the architecture into the hillside, producing the effect that the house seems to be emerging from (or submerging into) the landscape. Only the upper portion of the two-story volume is immediately apparent as the architecture does not overwhelm the trees surrounding the site. Instead, the unusual views of the roof tops of the studio to the left and the wing with bedrooms on the right is seen upon entering the second floor of the house.

When initially conceived, the house consisted of two concrete rectangles parallel to each other. Between them, dark gray stairs follow the sloping topography as they gently cascade down to meet an outdoor patio, an extension of the living spaces within. With the addition of the studio completed in 1984, the resulting composition is a sweeping arc that contrasts and provides relief from the rigid rectilinear lines of the original house. Such austere and unencumbered geometries are hallmarks of Ando's work, but he explains the desired effect with his approach: "The breath of nature can be felt more strongly and vivaciously the more reticent the space providing its backdrop. This is what drives my pursuit to find geometries formed by simpler and fewer elements."[4]

The entry sequence begins with the exterior stairs that lead down to a dark recess, located on the southwest façade of the two-story volume. As visitors approach the door, the land slopes away to the right, in the southeast direction. The outer form appears straightforward, but the meditative interiors only reveal themselves after the visitor passes through the threshold. Inside, past the office and master bedroom to the right, more stairs lead down to a spacious, double-height living room, dining area, and kitchen. Because the ceiling plane is detached from the walls, light pours into the dim interiors through this narrow aperture; supporting beams above cast beautiful diagonal shadows across the concrete walls. They are so finely constructed that they appear to be made of fabric, every ripple of the slightly undulating wood forms that molded the concrete can be "felt" with the eyes. Inside, the scenery of the surrounding trees and the swelling slope of the land is ever-present as it can be seen falling away from the openings of the living space.

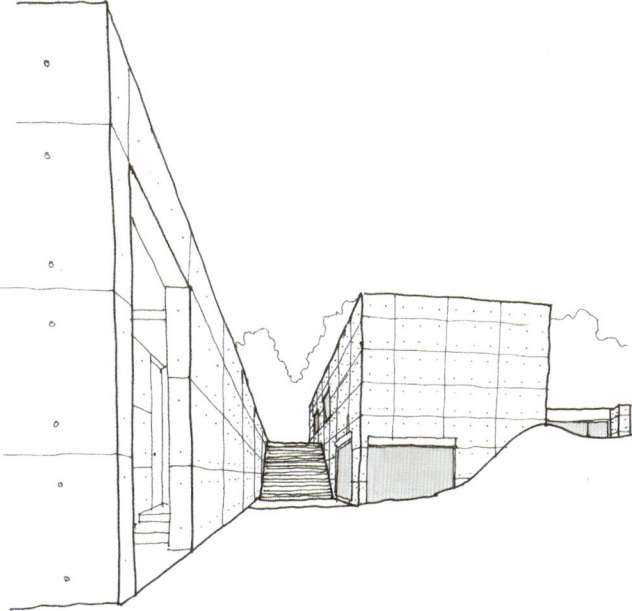

Diagram 1. Looking southwest, this view of the Koshino House highlights the exterior stairs and courtyard located between the two simple rectangular volumes. At the far right, the studio addition can be seen. Ando writes: "The courtyard is an outdoor living room, and the wide stairs receive and reflect the natural light trickling through the trees and serve as an extension of the stage for everyday life."[7]

Embedding Components

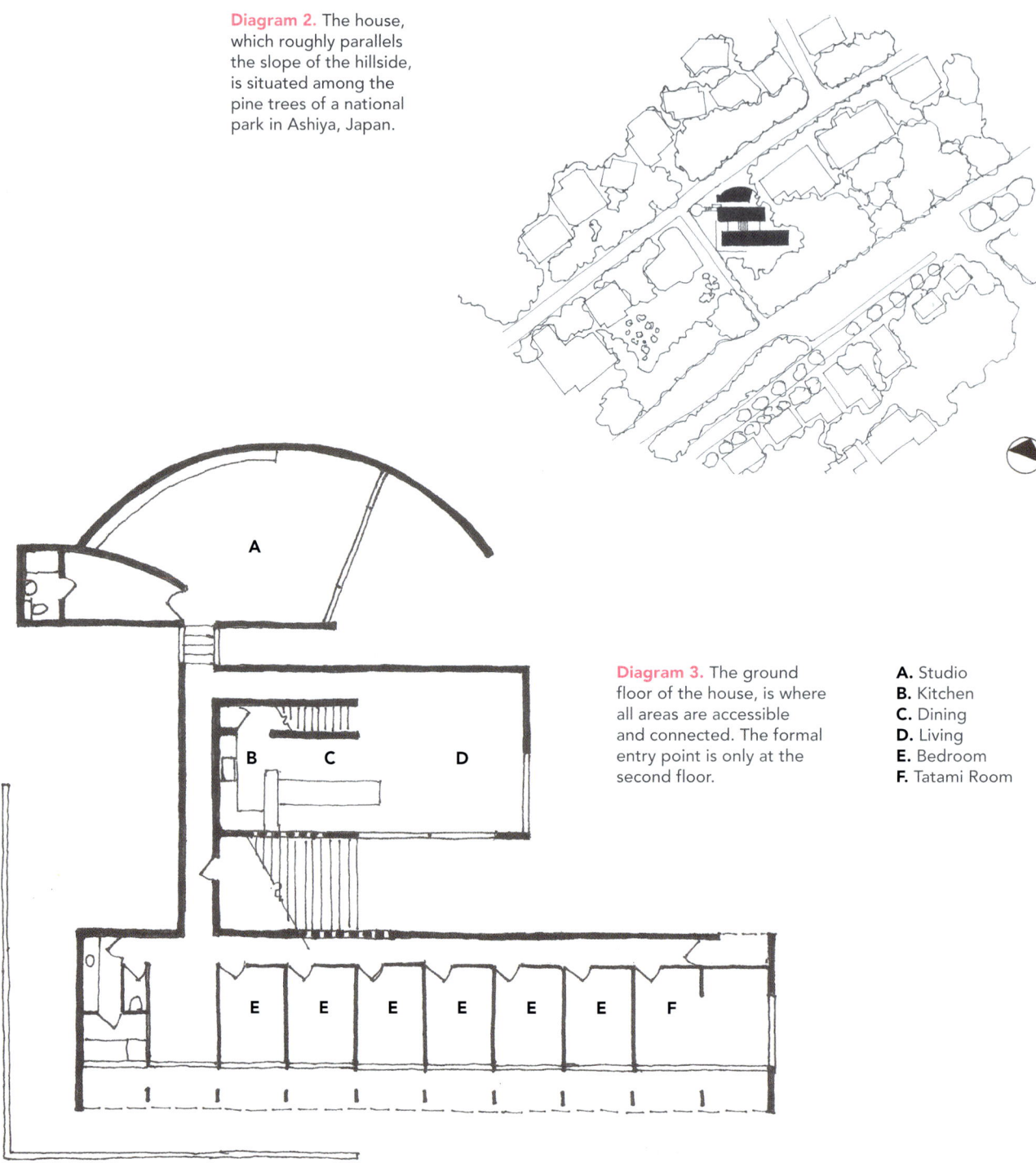

Diagram 2. The house, which roughly parallels the slope of the hillside, is situated among the pine trees of a national park in Ashiya, Japan.

Diagram 3. The ground floor of the house, is where all areas are accessible and connected. The formal entry point is only at the second floor.

A. Studio
B. Kitchen
C. Dining
D. Living
E. Bedroom
F. Tatami Room

The lower, longer rectangular volume contains six identical bedrooms, with the last space identified as a room that accommodates the width of four and a half tatami mats. Along the dimly lit corridor that joins these areas, small slats of vertical openings puncture the smooth, thick concrete walls. As light enters through them, a reflection is cast on the ceiling, wall, and floor, creating a rhythm of light and darkness.

Perhaps one of the most compelling attributes of the Koshino House—irrefutable proof of Ando's mastery of light and unparalleled use of concrete—is the gentle arc that forms part of the studio. As he describes it, this wall "is in strong contrast to the rectilinear patterns of light" as seen in the main house.[5] With the ceiling held away from this curve, light streams in from this void, washing the concrete wall with the warmth of the sun's rays. Part of a beam is visible in this gap, which casts a cool, dark shadow, its presence marking the wall like a fragment of a large sundial. Introspective and restrained, Ando's architecture brings the shadows and stillness into keen focus. It is not surprising that he holds strongly to the belief that architecture "is an act of contemplation, a search to find the best solution amid the abstract and concrete aspects unique to each project."[6]

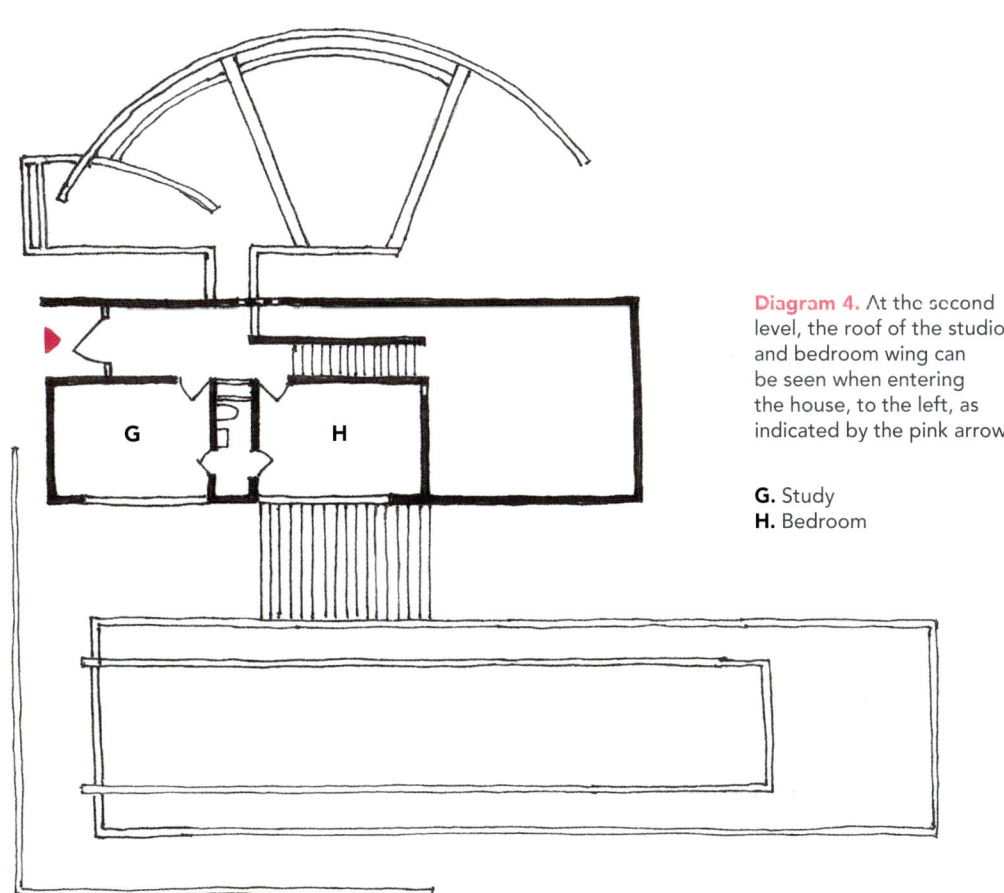

Diagram 4. At the second level, the roof of the studio and bedroom wing can be seen when entering the house, to the left, as indicated by the pink arrow.

G. Study
H. Bedroom

Embedding Components

5

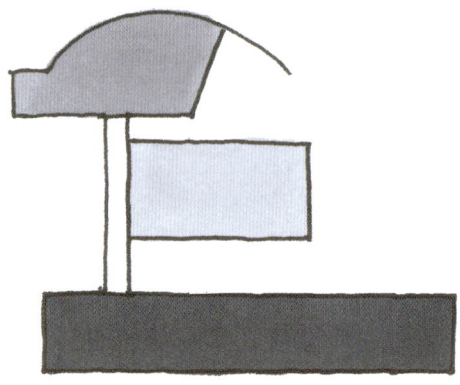

6

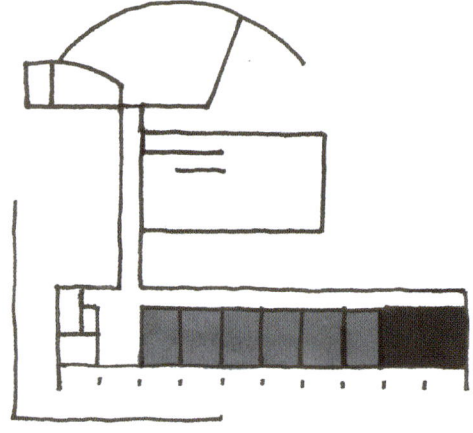

7

Diagram 5. The passageway in gray, which links the three volumes, is not revealed until one enters the house as nearly all of this connecting space is submerged.

Diagram 6. The darkest gray zone represents the most private areas of the house. In the middle, shown in light gray, a mix of public and private rooms is contained. At the top, the studio—semi-public space—is colored in medium gray.

Diagram 7. Six bedrooms available for guests, grouped in a linear organization, give this volume its length (shown in medium gray). The darkest gray area represents a space identified as a tatami room.

Koshino House

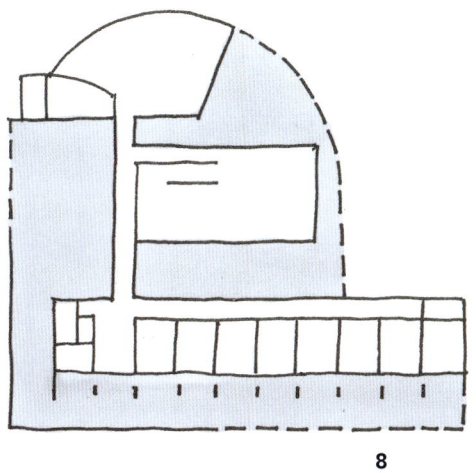

8

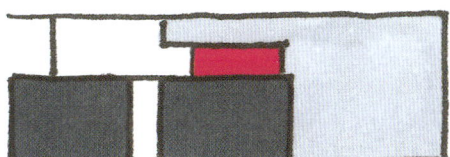

9

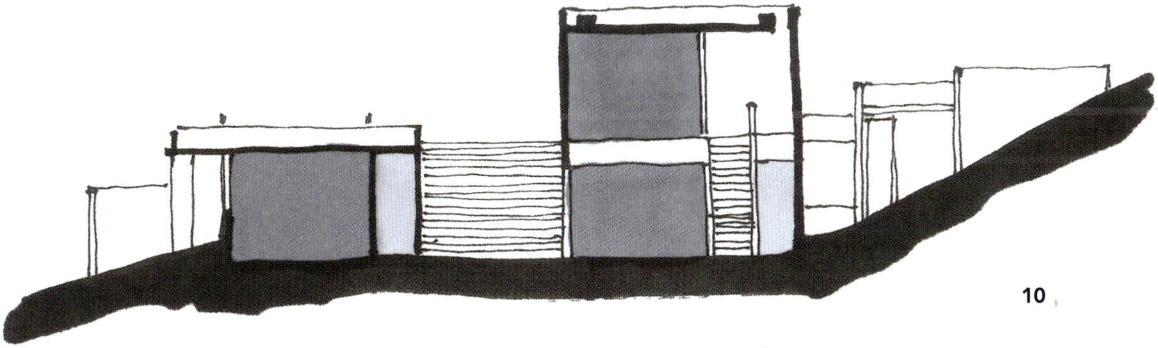

10

Diagram 8. Exterior zones (shown in light gray), above and below grade, are an essential part of the experience of the house. In fact, Ando writes that "Architecture . . . becomes a medium by which man comes into contact with nature . . . Wind and rain . . . activate space, make us aware of the season, and nurture within us a finer sensibility."[8]

Diagram 9. In this simplified plan showing the second level of the two-story volume, private rooms (a bedroom and study), are shown in dark gray. A double-height living room, in light gray, comes into view as one walks down the stairs, abstracted as a pink box.

Diagram 10. This section cuts perpendicular to the length of the rectangles, depicting the private zones in dark gray and circulation in light gray.

Embedding Components

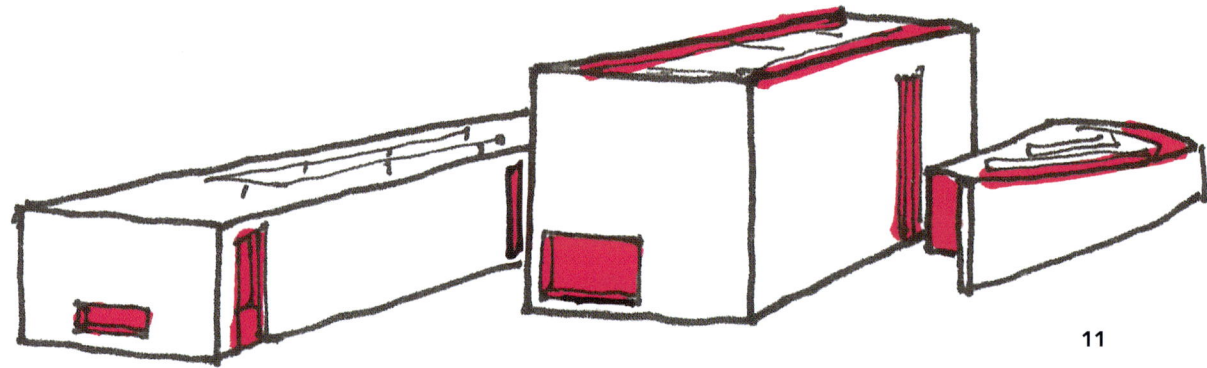

11

Diagram 11. Openings, shown in pink, permit views to nature and give shape to the quality of daylight that enliven the interiors.

Diagram 12 (opposite). This south view captures the thin, concrete columns shown in pink. This colonnade mimics the vertical lines of light that pierce the wall within this single-story volume of bedrooms.

Koshino House

12

20 CLUSTERING OBJECTS
Winton Guest House

Sculptural shapes, clustered like objects in a still-life painting, create an uncommon architectural composition; each space is its own unique structure and sensation.

Winton Guest House

In Wayzata, Minnesota, the Winton Guest House once stood like a piece of sculpture on a site that has the distinction of having another house—the primary residence—designed by Philip Johnson. After Mike and Penny Winton purchased this property from Richard S. Davis, the previous owner, the couple approached the renowned architect to design an additional structure for their bourgeoning family of children and grandchildren to stay when visiting. Their inquiry never elicited a response from Johnson. The Wintons, keen to find an architect, contacted Frank Gehry in 1982 after reading an article featuring his work in the *New York Times Magazine*.

As a cluster of multi-colored and textured forms, the guest house stands in sharp contrast to the minimal and restrained Modernist design by Johnson. Gehry's treatment of the existing structure is nearly deferential; he "didn't want to mess around with Uncle Philip's baby,"[1] as he would later recall. Rather than feeling encumbered by the presence of such a notable work of architecture already on the site, Gehry's response is, in large part, a study in contrast. Greatly influenced by urban planning, he is compelled to design contextually responsive buildings. As he has stated, "Compositionally I do not exclude the building across the road; I explore[d] that composition."[2]

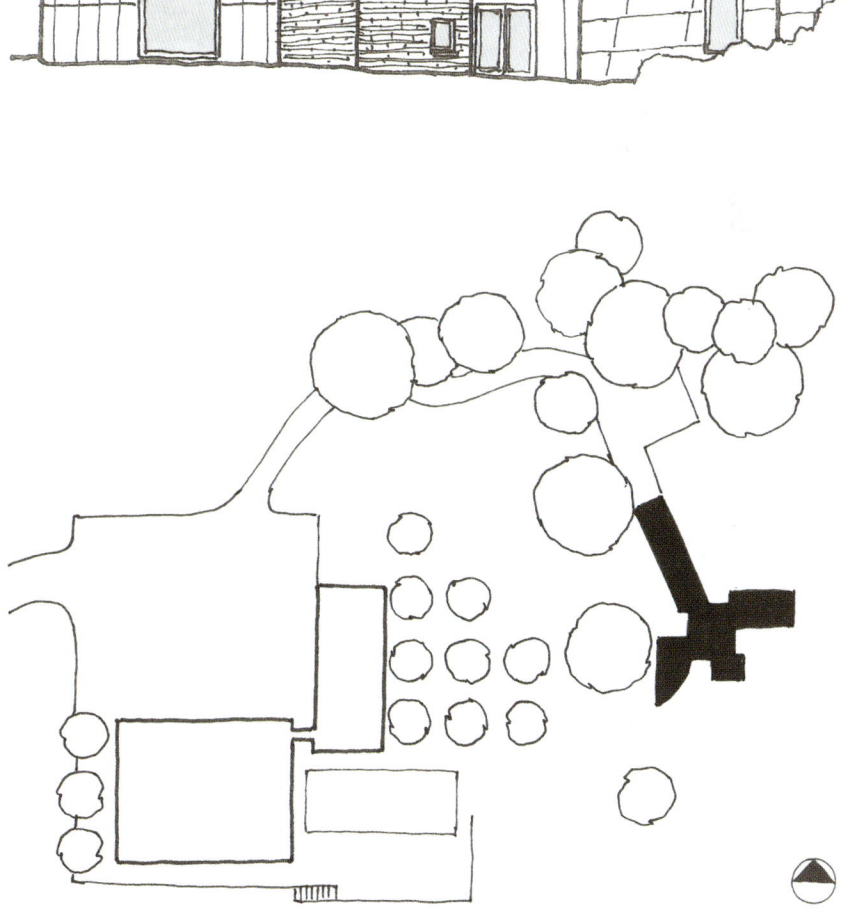

Diagram 1 (above). A view of the house, looking northwest.
Diagram 2 (right). The Winton Guest House can be seen with its relationship to the main house, designed by Philip Johnson, to the left.

Clustering Objects

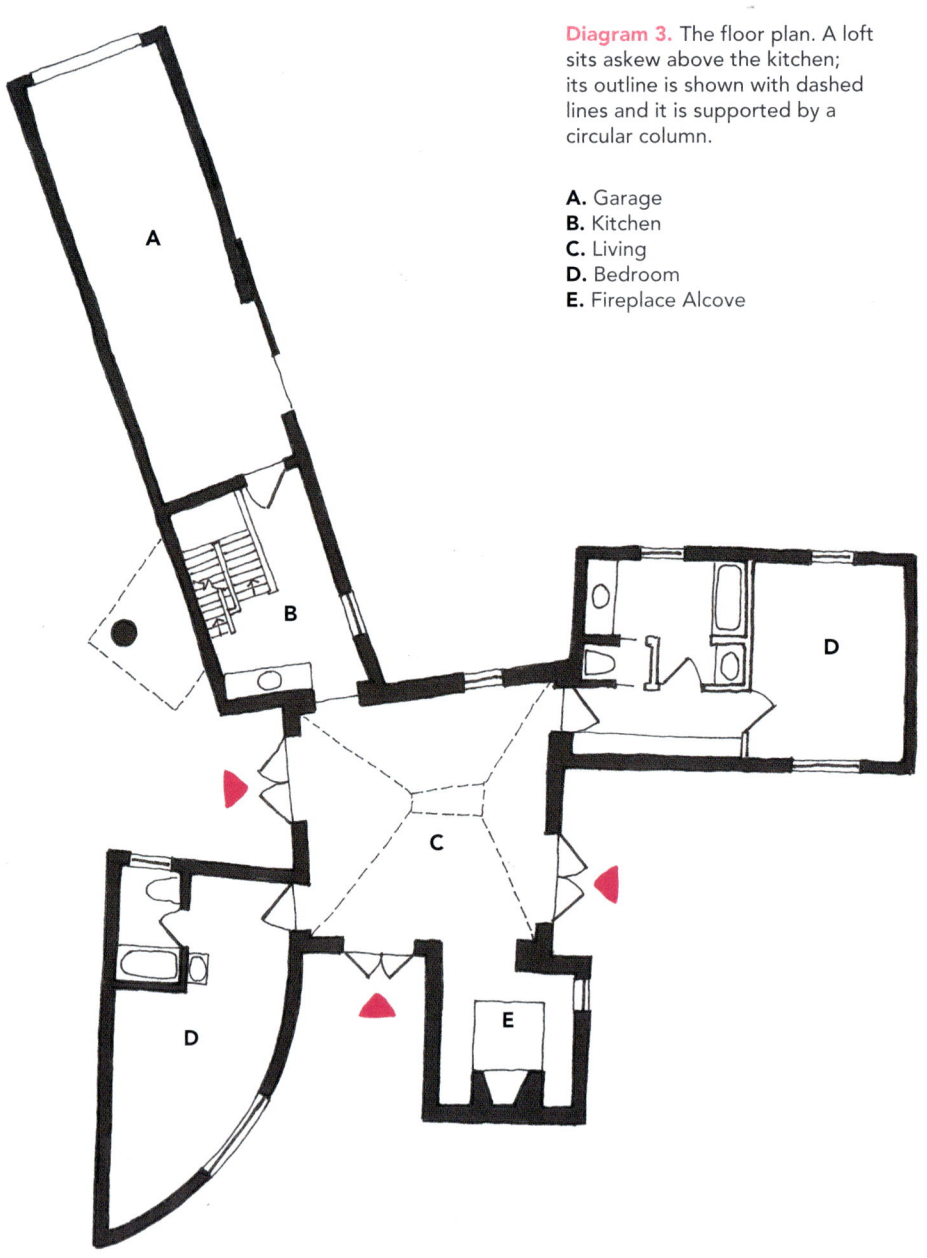

Diagram 3. The floor plan. A loft sits askew above the kitchen; its outline is shown with dashed lines and it is supported by a circular column.

A. Garage
B. Kitchen
C. Living
D. Bedroom
E. Fireplace Alcove

Winton Guest House

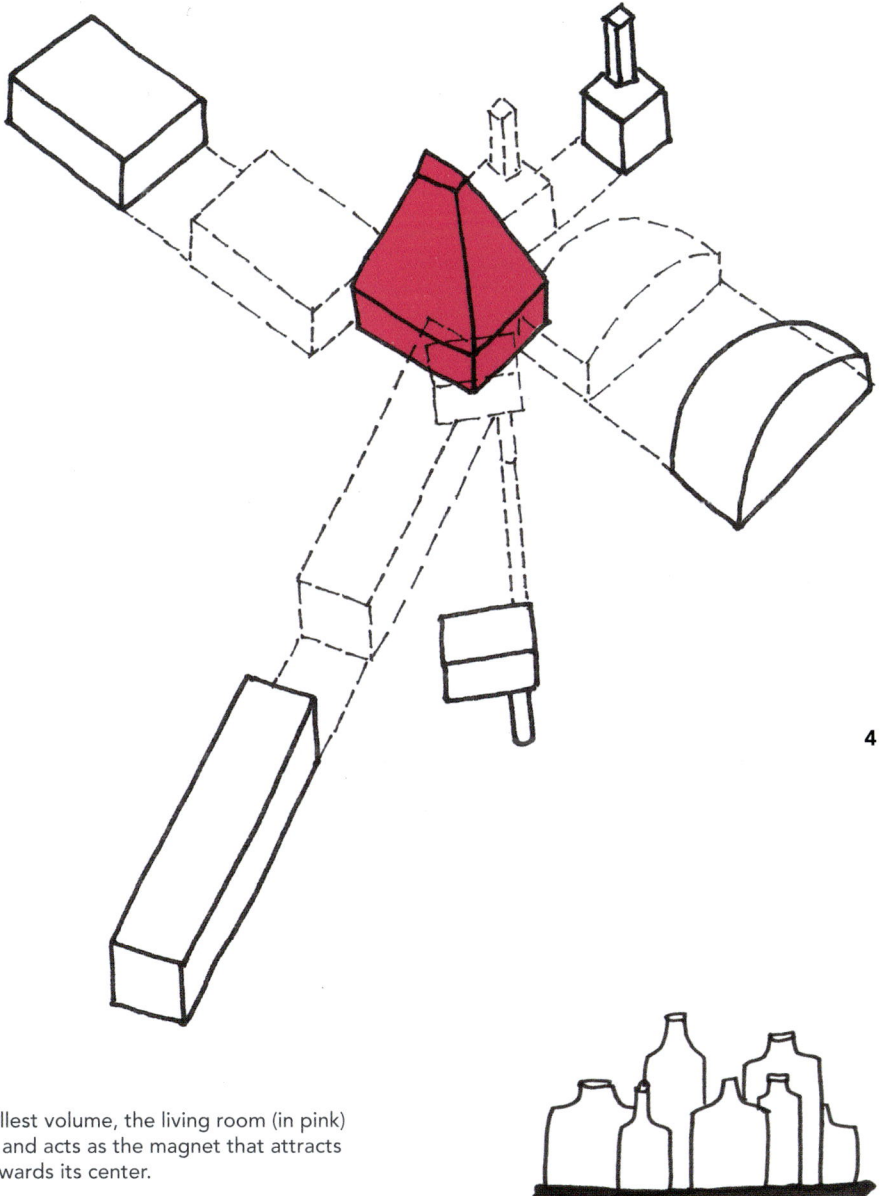

Diagram 4. As the tallest volume, the living room (in pink) establishes hierarchy and acts as the magnet that attracts the other volumes towards its center.

Diagram 5. Clustered bottles, painted frequently by Italian artist Giorgio Morandi, have often been cited as the source of inspiration for the design of the house.

Clustering Objects

The forms are also an acknowledgement of the influences that weigh heavily in Gehry's work—artists such as Clas Oldenburg, Coosje van Bruggen, and Richard Serra—which underscores his penchant for regarding his "architecture as a painting."[3] Most notably, myriad images of jars and bottles by the painter Giorgio Morandi are the actuators for the Winton Guest House's configuration that resembles **clustered objects**.

Six discrete volumes join together to include bedrooms, living areas, kitchen, and garage. One of the shapes—a small brick cube, replete with an oversized chimney—contains a fireplace with low, built-in seats to avert the cold Minnesota winters. The living room tower is the pyramidal shape at the center, sheathed in black metal, from where nearly all the rooms are accessed and the main point of entry is located. The loft area is a rectangular box obliquely perched atop the plywood-clad kitchen; it is the only space detached from the living room. Buff-colored limestone covers one of the bedrooms; its curved lines, visible in plan and elevation, break the rigidity of its neighboring forms.

Because the volumes are composed in a loose cluster and they are articulated uniquely through a diversity of materials and shapes, the view of the house varies from every perspective, both inside and out. Commonly, a house is designed as a container, with its spaces inside divided to form rooms and areas; with the Winton Guest House, Gehry creates "each room [as] a different thing",[4] essentially fragmenting the container and reassembling the pieces into a grouping. This ensemble sits as a sculpture, an assemblage of simple yet carefully detailed pieces, as expressed by the joinery or seams of the exterior materials. It is too easy to dismiss the composition as random; Gehry establishes a harmonious relationship between the hierarchy of a central,

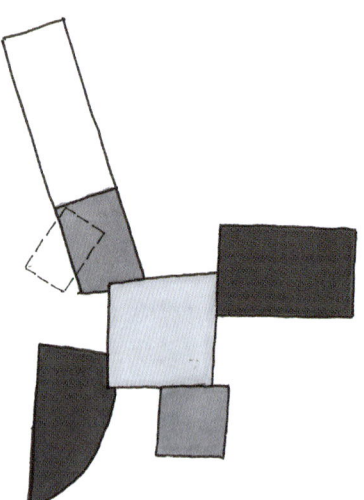

Diagram 6. Access into the house is gained through the living room, the most public area, rendered in the lightest gray. The medium gray represents semi-public spaces: kitchen and alcove with a fireplace. Lastly, the two bedrooms are shown in the darkest gray.

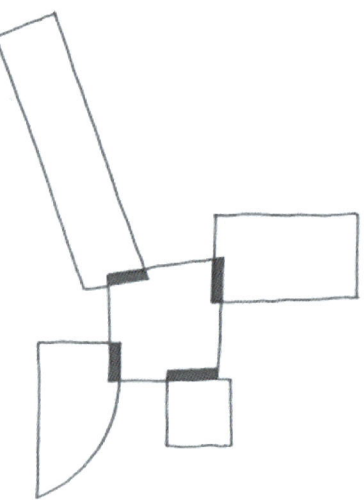

Diagram 7. With the exception of the loft, all volumes connect with the central space. In order to maintain purity of each form, the points of contact are subtle.

35-foot tall living room tower with the other, laterally oriented, volumes. Ada Louise Huxtable, the acclaimed architectural critic, wrote an essay as a Pritzker Architecture Prize Juror when Gehry won the award. Of the house, she noted that, "What may look like arbitrary . . . abstract geometry outside reveals itself inside as a series of unusual and inviting relationships achieved through a thoughtful analysis of the program in terms of a multidimensional concept of sensuously orchestrated space."[5]

Mediating between the primary core of the tower and the horizontality are "minor" vertical elements such as the chimney and loft above the garage and kitchen spaces. When considered from nearly any position, the overall composition is quite balanced and harmonious but very dynamic. The informality of the clustered organization also evokes a sense of whimsy and playfulness, "a place that our grandchildren would love to come to," as the Wintons noted.[6]

Along with other accolades, the Los Angeles Chapter of the American Institute of America presented Gehry with its Award of Honor after the completion of the house in 1987. As a fitting coda, Philip Johnson wrote to the Wintons: "I can't get the guest house out of my mind. An architectural masterpiece. The house of the 80's."[7]

Diagram 8. An imaginary boundary inscribing the building highlights the irregular shape of the void.

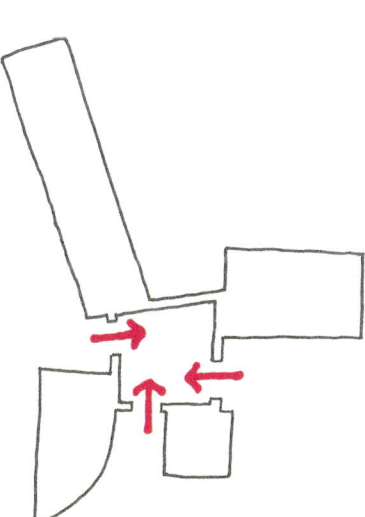

Diagram 9. The pockets of space between the volumes create intuitive points of entry. As a piece of sculpture to be experienced from many perspectives, there is no "true" front of the house but rather, multiple entrances that underscore the freedom to approach the building from nearly any side.

Diagram 10. The mirrored footprint of each form creates an alternative perspective of the uniquely shaped floor plan.

Clustering Objects

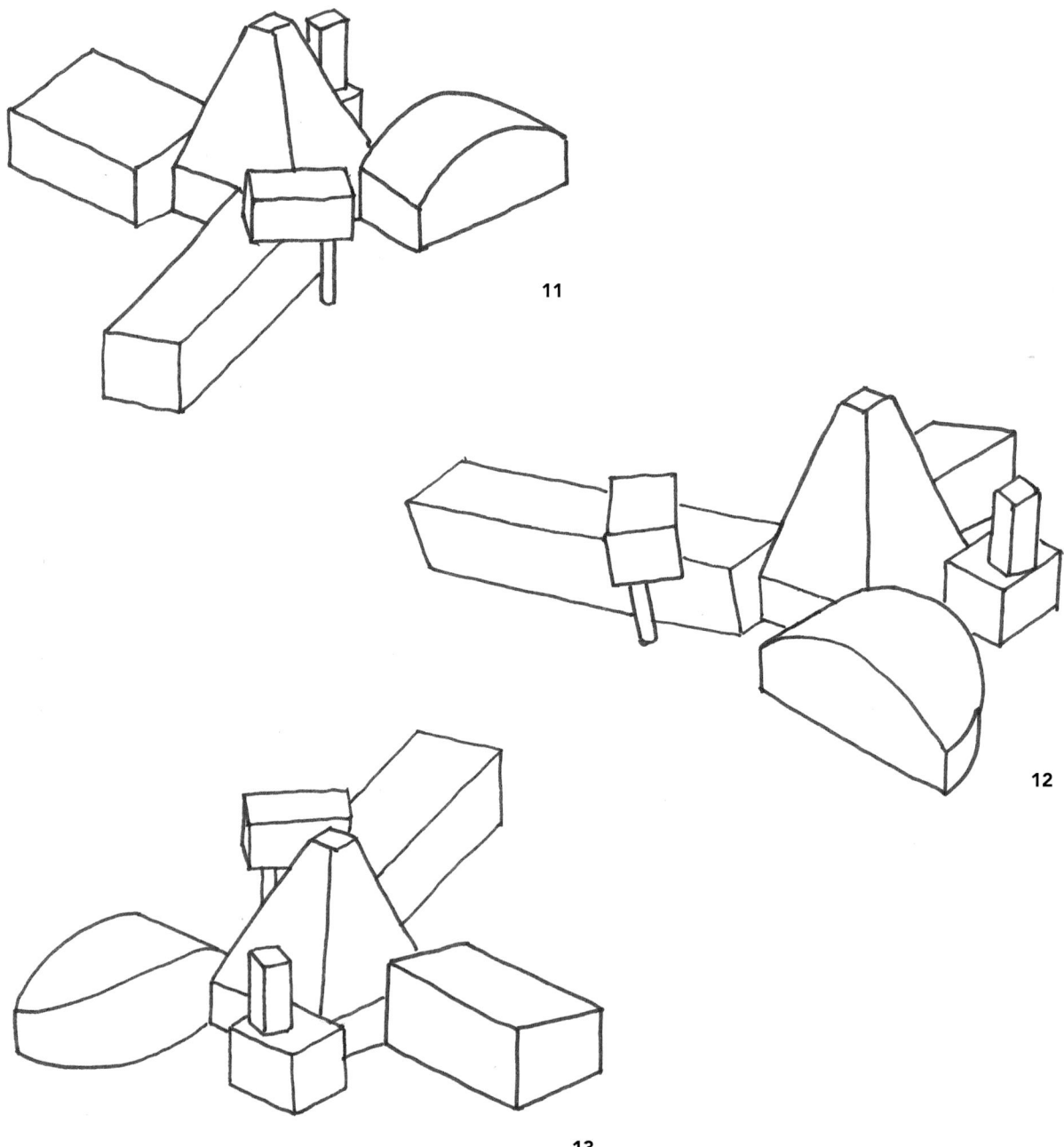

11

12

13

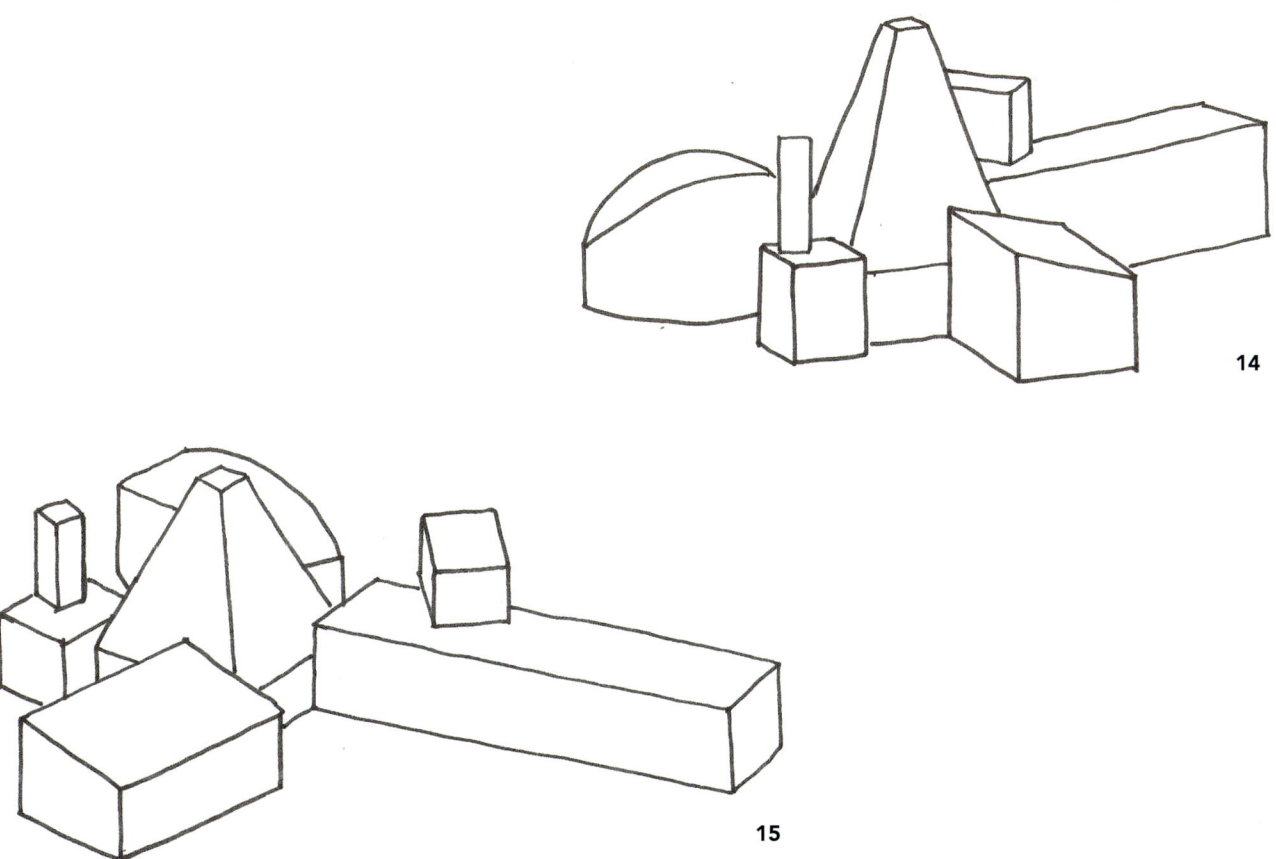

Diagrams 11, 12, 13, 14, 15. The house, studied as a collection of shapes, recalls Gehry's childhood experience playing with wood blocks alongside his grandmother, who purchased burlap bags filled with scrap pieces of irregular shapes from the local woodshop. He would fondly recall the happy times as "the most fun I ever had in my life" while creating buildings and small-scaled cities.[8] Seeing the artfully composed volumes of the Winton Guest House from any angle, it is easy to draw parallels between this early influence and his architecture. Diagram 11 is looking southeast; Diagram 12 is looking northeast; Diagram 13 is looking northwest; Diagram 14 is looking west; Diagram 15 is looking southwest.

21 ENGAGING PROCESSION
Church on the Water

A thoughtfully choreographed procession to any structure will always be memorable and engaging.

Church on the Water

Built in 1988 as a wedding chapel for a nearby resort hotel in Hokkaido, Japan, the Church on the Water is a serene and beautiful structure because of its restraint and simplicity. The architect, Tadao Ando, who did not receive a formal architectural education, intuitively understood that "travel was [his] single most important teacher."[1] Crafting his own curriculum by visiting particular sites throughout Europe, such as the Pantheon, he intuitively grasped that "to truly understand architecture, you must experience spaces with your own five senses."[2] For over forty years, he has designed deeply emotive spaces that evoke a vast sense of stillness. Nowhere can this be felt more profoundly than at the Church on the Water.

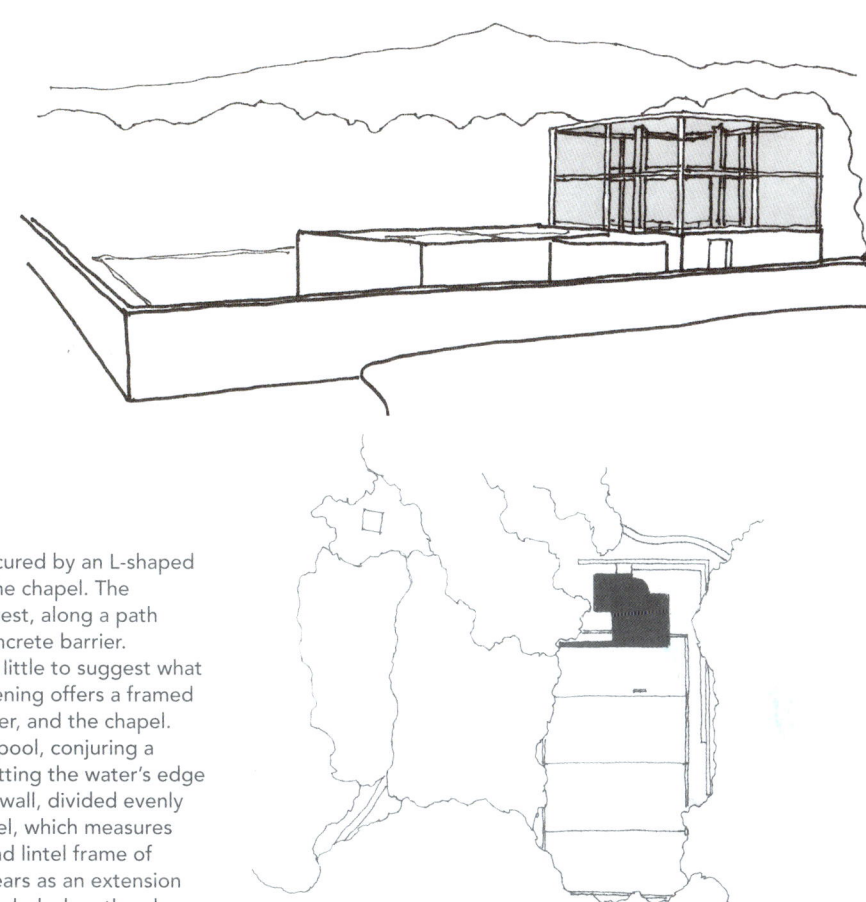

A substantial portion of the structure is obscured by an L-shaped wall, defining the south and east edges of the chapel. The procession begins by walking towards the west, along a path that follows this seemingly impenetrable concrete barrier. Anticipation builds as the promenade offers little to suggest what is on the other side; eventually, a simple opening offers a framed view of the sky, surrounding mountains, water, and the chapel. An unadorned, solitary cross sits in a tiered pool, conjuring a sense of tranquility and contemplation. Abutting the water's edge is a long, concrete box with a massive glass wall, divided evenly into four panes. This space houses the chapel, which measures nearly 49'3" squared. Next to this, a post and lintel frame of concrete of the same width and height appears as an extension of the adjacent structure. Its purpose is revealed when the glass, separating the interior of the chapel from the pool, slides open to rest within this concrete frame. Ando observes that "wind and rain through their action on the human body give colour to life. Architecture is a medium that enables man to sense the presence of nature."[3] Lastly, perched atop a portion of the chapel, four crosses stand like quiet observers with outstretched arms that nearly touch. Forming a perfect box, they nest inside a glass cube that measures nearly 32'0" squared, open to the elements above.

Diagram 1 (above). Looking west, the view of the church is partially blocked by a wall in the foreground. Walking along the south wall provides access to the entrance.

Diagram 2 (below). The site is surrounded by mountains and trees, creating a beautiful and serene backdrop for the simple and pristine church. Ando gave much thought to how the architecture would be placed within the landscape without harming the trees. Integral to the experience of this architecture is a pool of water, shown as a large rectangle, divided into four gently stepped tiers.

Although the initial view of the chapel does not indicate a discernible entry point, there is a prescribed path continuing along the long southern wall, permitting time and space for the visitor to absorb the stillness while controlling the cadence of this **engaging procession**. Ando denies visitors direct and immediate access but forces them to walk along the edges of the property.

Engaging Procession

As one follows the eastern portion of the site, an unadorned opening invites the visitor inside. Above this concrete base sits a four-sided glass structure framed by dark steel. One slowly emerges from the darkness as the path traverses two short flights of stairs ascending the sides of the concrete box. Open to the sky above and yet enclosed by glass and the four crosses, "meant as sculpture," as Ando notes,[4] the visitor is rewarded with a bird's eye view of the landscape. The beauty of nature surrounding the church is the focal point of contemplation and stillness. Ando recognizes that "Human life is not intended to oppose nature and endeavor to control it, but rather to draw nature into an intimate association in order to find union with it."[5]

Two more sets of stairs descend and lead through a semi-circular form to reveal the chapel. The dark slate floor and the concrete ceiling and walls, rather than casting a pall over the interior, focus the visitor's attention towards the light. As the eyes adjust to the cool darkness, they are drawn to a very large opening, entirely covered by very large panes of glass, evenly separated horizontally and vertically by the familiar steel cross. Beyond the glass, a sweeping view of nature is the backdrop to the tranquil pool and the cross within the water, a gesture that Ando felt would "express the idea of God as existing in one's heart and mind, rather than something that is merely presented to you by someone else."[6] The essence of spirituality and nature are sublimated in the blurred boundary of interior and exterior; Ando sees "no clear demarcation between outside and inside but rather their mutual permeation."[7]

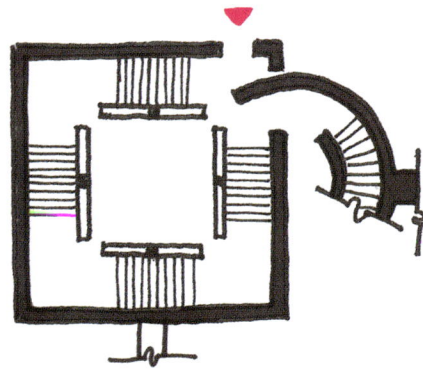

Diagram 3. At the entry, a prescribed journey begins: the visitor walks up two, short flights of stairs to a commanding view of the site, overlooking the water and landscape. Moments to pause occur at the corners of this staircase; the descent begins at the staircase opposite the entrance and continues through the semi-circular stair.

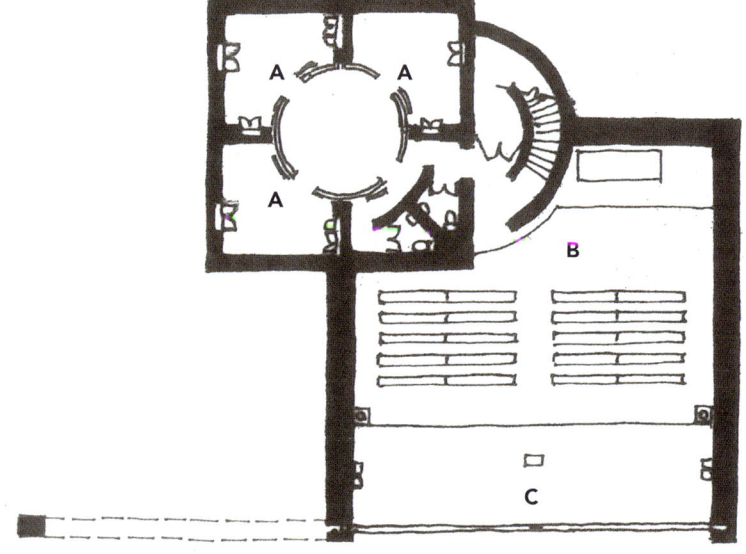

Diagram 4. After descending the stairs of the dimly lit, half-circle form on the level above, the visitor enters the ground level, a light-flooded sanctuary with a spectacular view of the water and cross.

A. Waiting Room
B. Chapel
C. Pulpit

Church on the Water

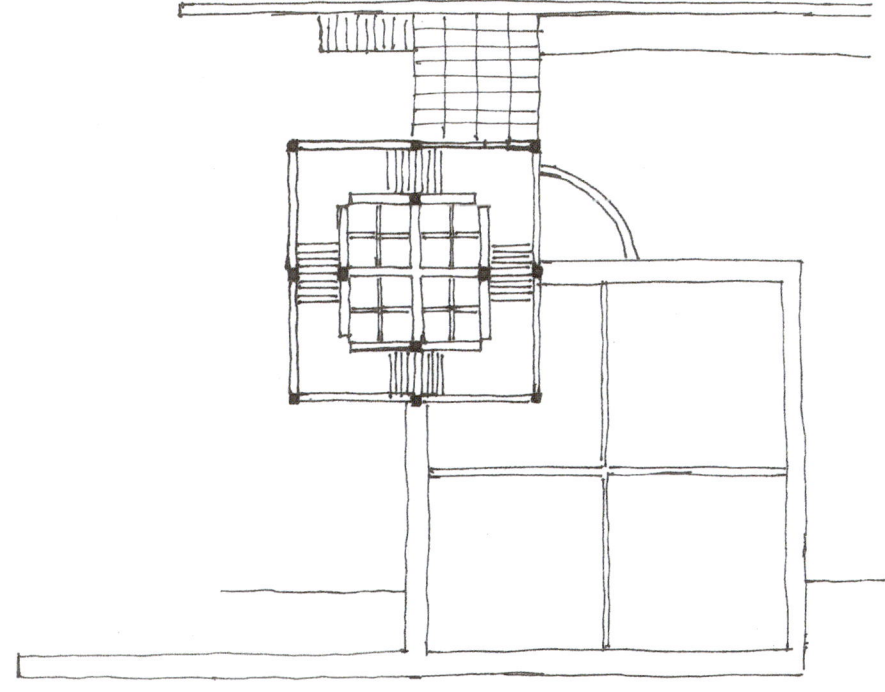

Diagram 5. The roof plan of the building shows the intricate replication of the cross, maintaining precise and proportional subdivisions of the square.

Engaging Procession

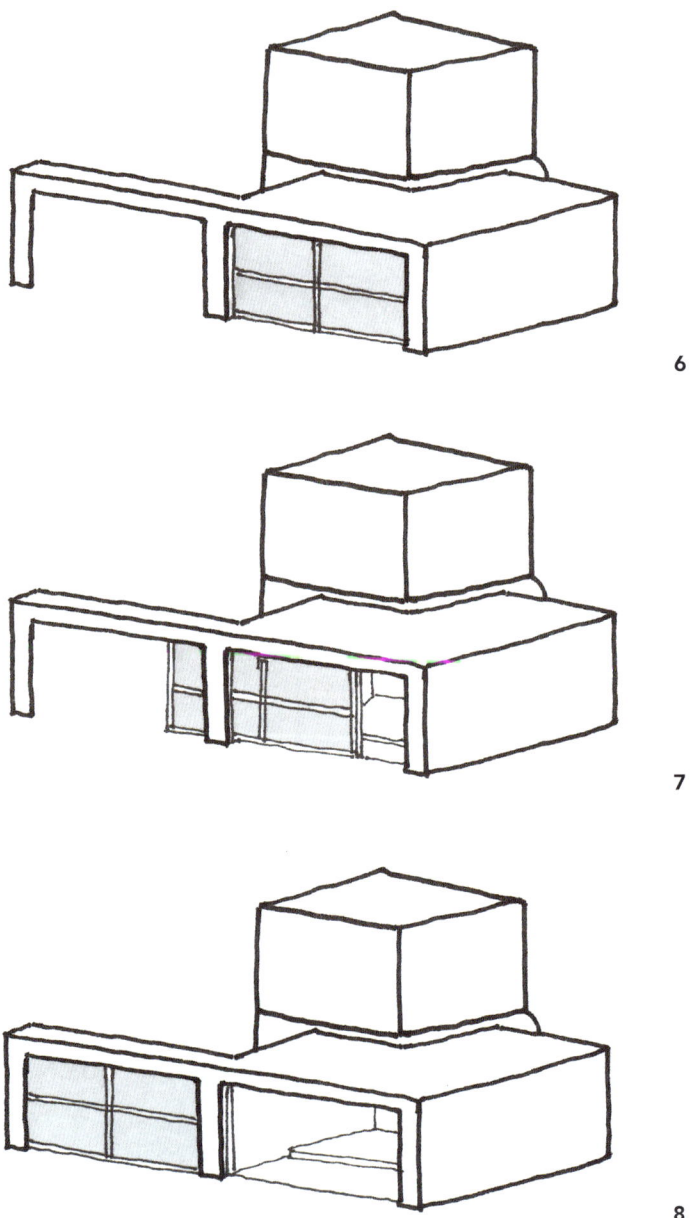

6

7

8

Diagrams 6, 7, 8. Ando's deep respect for nature is always present in his architecture; he states, "I want to give nature's power a presence in contemporary society and provide thereby the kind of stimulating places that speak directly to man's every sense as a living, corporeal being."[8] In Diagram 6, the massive glass wall (shown in gray) that separates the chapel from the elements is movable; when shifted (Diagram 7), the interior space is completely open (Diagram 8), and the outdoors is welcomed into the sanctuary. He writes, "Rustling leaves, the sound of water, and the song of birds can be heard. These natural sounds emphasize the general silence. Becoming integrated with nature, one confronts oneself. The framed landscape changes in appearance from moment to moment."[9]

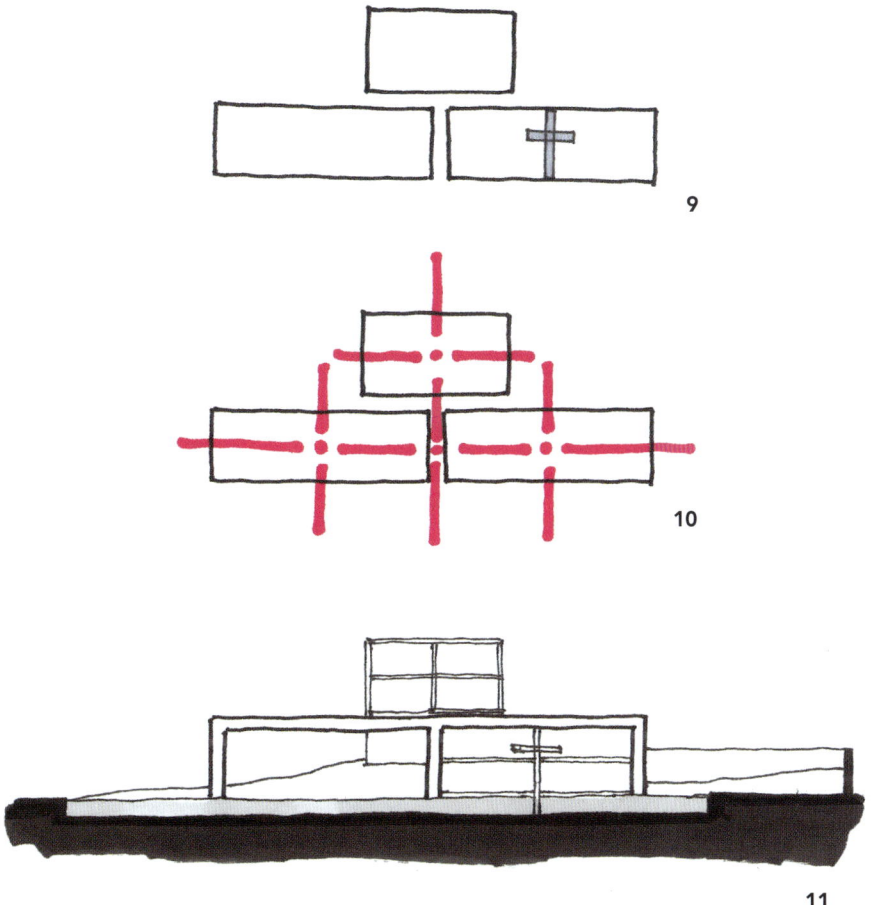

Diagram 9. In this diagram of the elevation, the balance and harmony of symmetry is evident. However, when studied three-dimensionally, the entire structure is asymmetrical as the rectangle to the left is simply a frame and not a volume. The cross in the water becomes integrated with the ever-changing scenery of nature, and acts as the background of the altar.

Diagram 10. The centerlines of each rectangle (in pink) naturally subdivide them; this is a repeated motif seen throughout other elevations of the chapel.

Diagram 11. The elevation shows the façade's most basic components.

22 LIFTING ELEMENTS
Maison à Bordeaux

Lifting elements provide an escape from the conventional, earthbound view, offering different vistas while literally and figuratively transporting you to another realm.

Maison à Bordeaux

The impetus for the design of Maison à Bordeaux in 1998, was a cataclysmic car accident: the owner, who nearly perished and was left paralyzed, had to reconsider his life confined to a wheelchair. He had considered other architects but likely found Rem Koolhaas and his Office for Metropolitan Architecture to be most receptive when he told the Dutch architect: "Contrary to what you would expect, I do not want a simple house. I want a complex house, because the house will define my world."[1] Koolhaas sensitively responds to the quotidian and aspirational desires of the family by meeting the client's severe mobility limitations and needs while creating a dwelling, finished in 1998, that his able-bodied wife and three children would find most agreeable.

As one approaches the house atop a hill, the view is dominated by a long, concrete box, impossibly floating above very large panes of glass. The random, circular perforations dotting the northeast and southwest elevations do nothing to lighten the weight of this massive box but add a touch of whimsy. Vehicular entry requires following the road that slips below the wall of a courtyard, which acts as an enormous lintel. This ascending driveway terminates in the shape of a curl at the center of the courtyard. Here, the three levels of the main house to the southwest are revealed; a maid's apartment and guest room define the opposite or northeast portion of the courtyard. Beyond the banal façade of the ground floor, composed mostly of opaque and clear glass, there are three different staircases, a TV room, wine cellar, and kitchen. Koolhaas identifies this floor as "a series of caverns carved out from the hill for the most intimate life of the family."[2]

For this house, Koolhaas writes, "a machine is its heart."[3] He is describing a platform measuring 10'0" by 10'9", which moves vertically—a **lifting element**—that enables access to all levels and anywhere in between. Identified as the client's office, this area is not delineated by walls; instead, a bookcase serving as a vertical datum line that stretches all three floors becomes the boundary at the southeast edge of the elevator platform. Because of extensive discussions Koolhaas conducted prior to designing, he was keenly aware of the client's proclivity for books; the architect notes that the house "arises from a generous reading of the client's requirements and an extreme engagement with context and program."[4]

Another notable aspect of the house is the question of how a concrete box of such considerable weight could appear to be lifted and cantilevering above the second floor that is partially encased in massive glass panels. The other half of this level is a generous terrace, completely open to the elements; only the overhead of the third floor covers this area. The impression is that nothing of great substance is supporting this mass, which threatens to collapse under its own weight. However, a single, deep, black beam stretches southwest to northeast and is supported by two columns. Positioned nearly in the center of the terrace, a highly polished cylinder—containing the circular stairs that lead to the children's bedrooms within—provides structural support. Intuitively, these do not seem adequate, but they are

Diagram 1 (above). This east view of the house emphasizes the looming, concrete box that appears to be lifted and floating—with very little structural support—over the lower levels. It is perched atop a hill, further exaggerating the presence of this heavy mass.

Diagram 2 (right). Situated in Floriac, southwest France, the residence is nestled among the trees. A private driveway terminates within an intimate courtyard, the pavement creating a near perfect donut-like shape on the manicured lawn.

175

Lifting Elements

Diagram 3. Organic and rectilinear "fingers" of the ground level burrow into the hillside at the southwest, their forms unseen from the exterior. The client's office is a movable platform, defined by a bookshelf on the southeast side. A guest bedroom and maid's suite are separated by a courtyard.

Diagram 4. The second level appears nearly devoid of solid walls. Large glass panels that slide away surround the entire living area. A rectangular column sits on the lawn, appearing somewhat detached from the structural systems. However, it is connected to a beam (shown as a double dashed line) that is supported by an interior vertical member.

Diagram 5. The bedrooms for the parents and children are on this third floor. A literal break between the two areas is connected by a small bridge.

A. Office/Movable Platform
B. Kitchen
C. TV Room
D. Courtyard
E. Guest Bedroom
F. Maid's Apartment
G. Study
H. Living
I. Outdoor Living
J. Master Bedroom
K. Bedroom

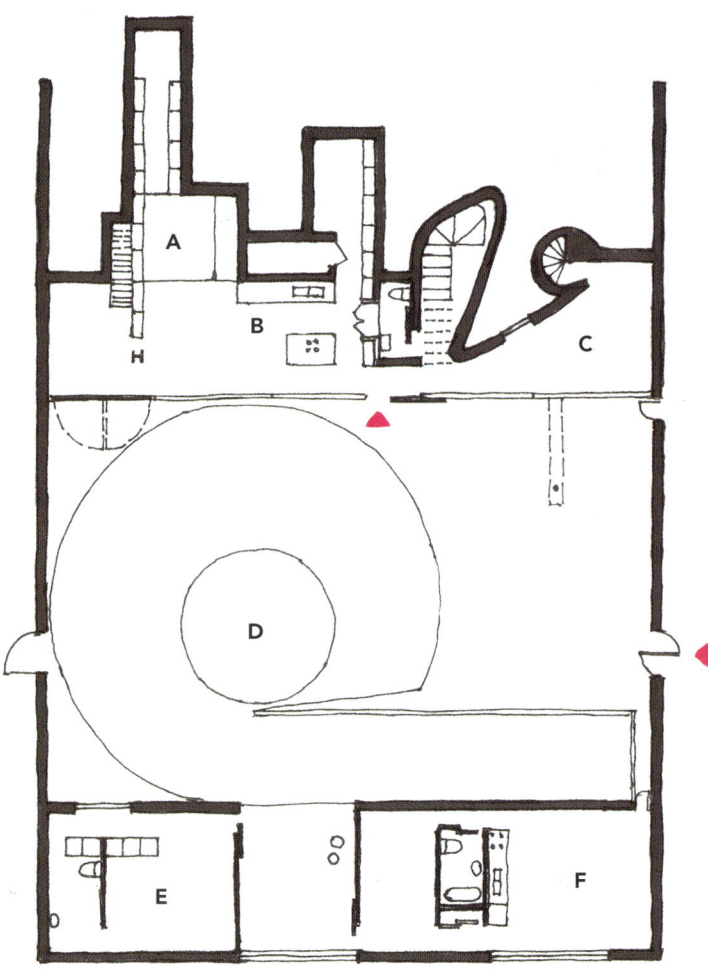

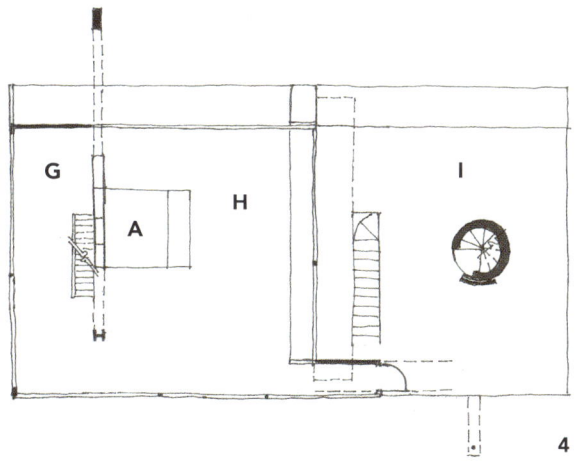
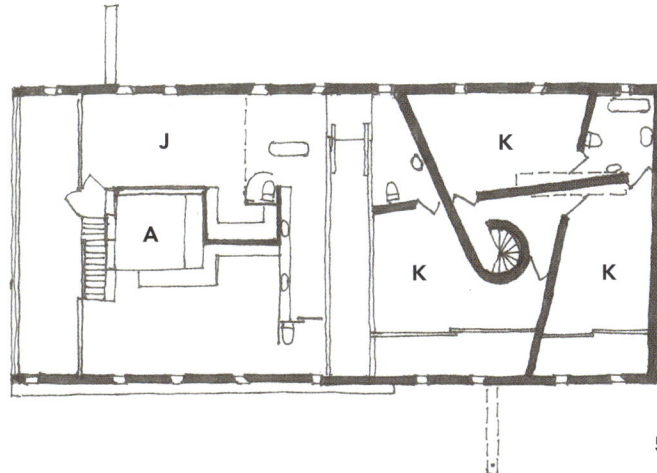

Diagram 6. Koolhaas himself describes the house as "three houses on top of each other."[8] The top, shown in dark gray, is the most private; the living room in the middle, colored the lightest gray, is literally and visually the most open; at ground level, the color is medium gray, due to the semi-public and private spaces located here.

Lifting Elements

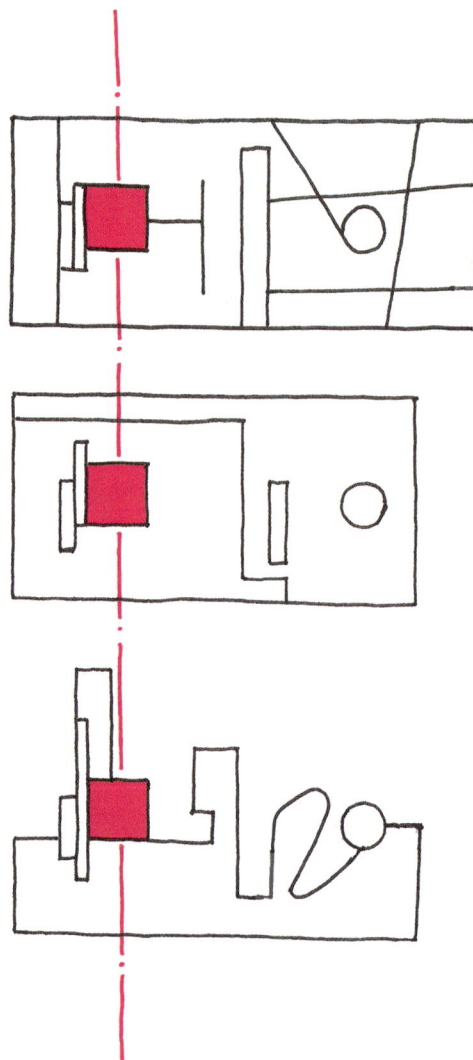

Diagram 7. A pink box highlights the office/movable platform that the client, bound to a wheelchair, employs to access all levels of his home.

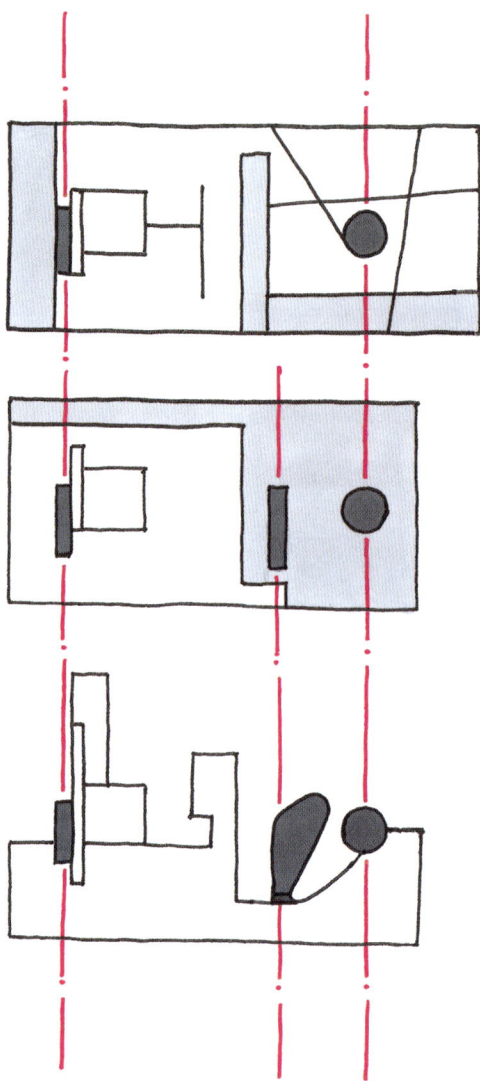

Diagram 8. The forms, shown in dark gray, are the various stairs that Koolhaas designed for vertical access to the upper levels. At the far left, a stair that leads to the client's study as well as the master bedroom is mostly used by the client's wife. Guests use the amoeba-shaped stair in the middle that only rises to the second level. The circular stairs, on the right, take the children to their bedrooms as well as the outdoor living area. Light gray zones depict balconies or areas open to the outdoors.

a part of a formidable structural system, balancing all the forces of compression and tension to provide homeostasis. Koolhaas intentionally seeks to "define the living space by the implied pressure of the floor below and the concrete form above." Paradoxically, the sensation of weightlessness is attained by the mass of the concrete. He continues, explaining that, "To achieve intimacy with and orientation to the space beyond the house, it is essential that the concrete top story appears to float. This is achieved by evacuating or exiling the support structure from the space itself."[5]

If the second level, with all its transparencies, can be characterized as extroverted, the third floor is certainly the most introverted and reclusive, despite the small porthole windows dotting the northeast and southwest concrete walls. The master bedroom, situated at the southeast end of the house, surrounds the elevator platform rising at the center. Its near-square shape is divided by only a few orthogonal walls; appropriately, this economy of partitions is most pragmatic for a person confined to a wheelchair. To the northwest, the walls are in disarray: none of the children's bedrooms and bathrooms divide neatly into rectangles. Further emphasizing this differentiation of soberness and playfulness in the bedrooms of the parents and children is a literal break between the two sides; however, a narrow bridge connects the opposing worlds. What unifies this private realm is the intimate, quiet retreat that Koolhaas creates with a balance of enclosed spaces and open expanses of glass. His strategy, to design a house full of complexity with distinct layers, or "three houses on top of each other,"[6] stems from his unique mindset about his client's physical immobility. He explains in an interview: "It was not a case of 'now we're going to do our best for an invalid'. The starting point is rather a denial of invalidity."[7]

Diagram 9. In section, the motorized platform is shown penetrating the heart of the house at the southeast.

Lifting Elements

Diagram 10. The box above, in dark gray, is nearly solid except for the portals perforating the southwest and northeast elevations. Light gray areas show glazing, and the medium gray represents places on the façade composed of opaque materials.

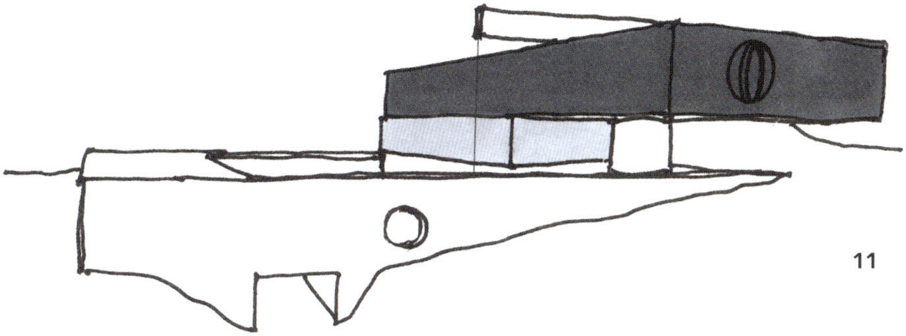

Maison à Bordeaux

11

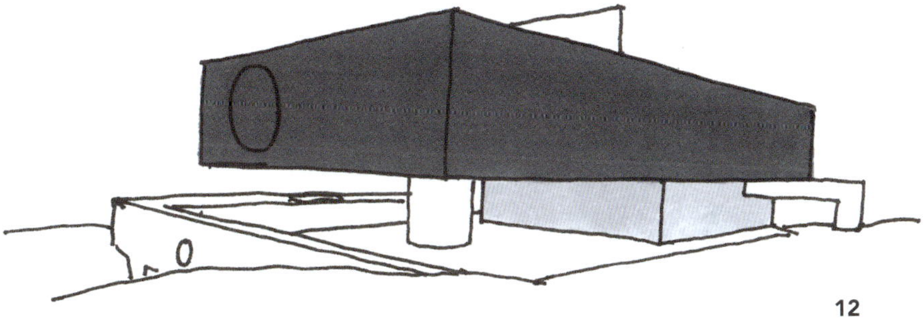

12

13

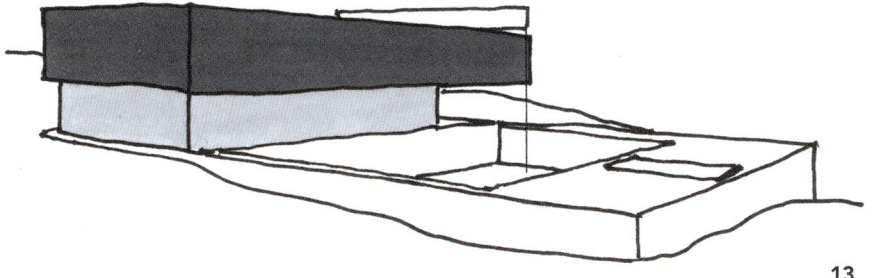

Diagrams 11, 12, 13.
No matter the view, the positioning of the massive concrete box, in dark gray, on top of the glass, in light gray, is completely counterintuitive. Rather than trying to create a sense of uneasiness, Koolhaas relies on the weight above to give presence to the airy, ethereal living space below. Diagram 11 is looking to the southeast; Diagram 12 is looking east; Diagram 13 is looking west.

23 BRANCHING MASSES
Y House

Branching masses appear like independent arms, pulling in slightly divergent directions but tethered together, firmly affixed to their location.

Y House

Completed in 1999, this weekend retreat house is nestled in the Catskill Mountains of New York for a couple and their grown children. The site is a clearing on top of a hill, which commands a view of the surrounding mountains and trees; Steven Holl recalls that he "visited the site and got excited about how one turns up and up to a hilltop, then turns and looks back at the [Catskill Mountains]."[1] As with all his projects, the design process begins with sketching and the use of watercolors. He favors these analogue methods because "I think that you must, in a way, bring the mind and the hand together to begin a project, this seed that starts the project is something you're emotionally feeling as well as intellectually feeling. The concept sketch, via watercolor, is a perfect way to begin."[2]

In plan, the house forms a "Y" and is "[l]ike a found forked stick . . . [it] makes a primitive mark on a vast site."[3] The two masses branch towards the west and crescendo from a one-story entrance at the east into two, double-story volumes; the façades composed mainly of various sized openings accessing the scenic mountain views. Balconies, with their pencil-thin steel columns, are located on the west-facing elevations; their deep roofs minimize the glare from the sun but immerse the interiors with natural light. Holl describes the point where the house cleaves as where a "slice of sky" can be seen above and light is brought "into the heart of the house."[4] The entire structure is painted in an iron-oxide red, reminiscent of the vernacular architecture of the barns and stables in upstate New York.

As simple and as straightforward as the exterior appears, this contrasts with the experiential richness of the interiors. For Holl, "the measure of excellence in architecture comes from the internal experiences rather than the exterior . . . In Le Corbusier's buildings, the interiors—their feeling of movement and light— are so intense . . . The interior experience of architecture is incredibly important."[5] Stairs connecting to the upper level are visible immediately upon entry; they bisect a dynamic and spacious hallway, forcing circulation to either side. Space that diverges to the left of the stairs houses the kitchen and dining room below and the master bedroom above. To the right of the stairs, the children's bedrooms are on the ground floor and the living room is on the second floor, inverting the order of public and private spaces, or, as Holl describes them, as "day/night" zones.[6] In section, rather than stacking programmatically similar areas or placing them side by side, there is "a sectional flip of public/private or day/night zones to animate the spaces and their activities"[7] as noted by the architect, which creates an inner complexity of circulation and the mental map of the interior is no longer perceived as layered spaces.

Inside, the architecture brings an awareness of light at the ends of each arm, due to the abundance of glazing facing the west portion of the house. Because the **masses branch** or fork, light surrounds three sides of nearly every space; the light "from early morning to sunset is to be a primary experience in the house," as Holl explains.[8] In addition to framing the movement of the

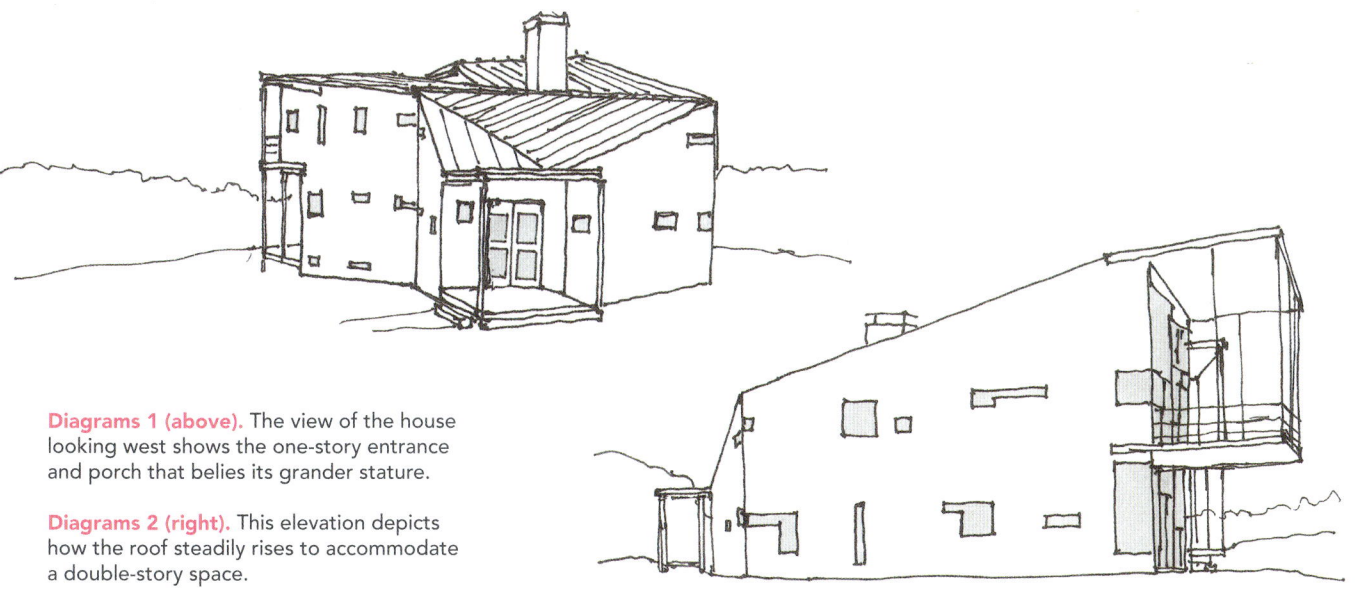

Diagrams 1 (above). The view of the house looking west shows the one-story entrance and porch that belies its grander stature.

Diagrams 2 (right). This elevation depicts how the roof steadily rises to accommodate a double-story space.

Branching Masses

sun, the ground level inside undulates gently: passage from one wing to the other requires the use of stairs or ramps. The grade changes of the floor are subtle while the articulation of the ceiling is much more visible and dynamic. Wooden slats above are not arranged in neat, linear rows that follow each rectangular arm of the "y" but rather, they change orientation at various points, giving the ceiling a faceted, animated appearance. Holl desires to create these sensory-rich experiences in his architecture:

> When we move through space with a twist and turn of the head, mysteries of gradually unfolding fields of overlapping perspectives are charged with a range of light—from the steep shadows of bright sun to the translucence of dusk. A range of smell, sound, and material—from hard stone and steel to the free billowing of silk— returns us to *primordial* experiences framing and penetrating our everyday lives.[9]

When experiencing space, its beauty is only apparent through a body in motion, and, as he writes, "personal perception. There is no more important measure of the force and potential of architecture."[10]

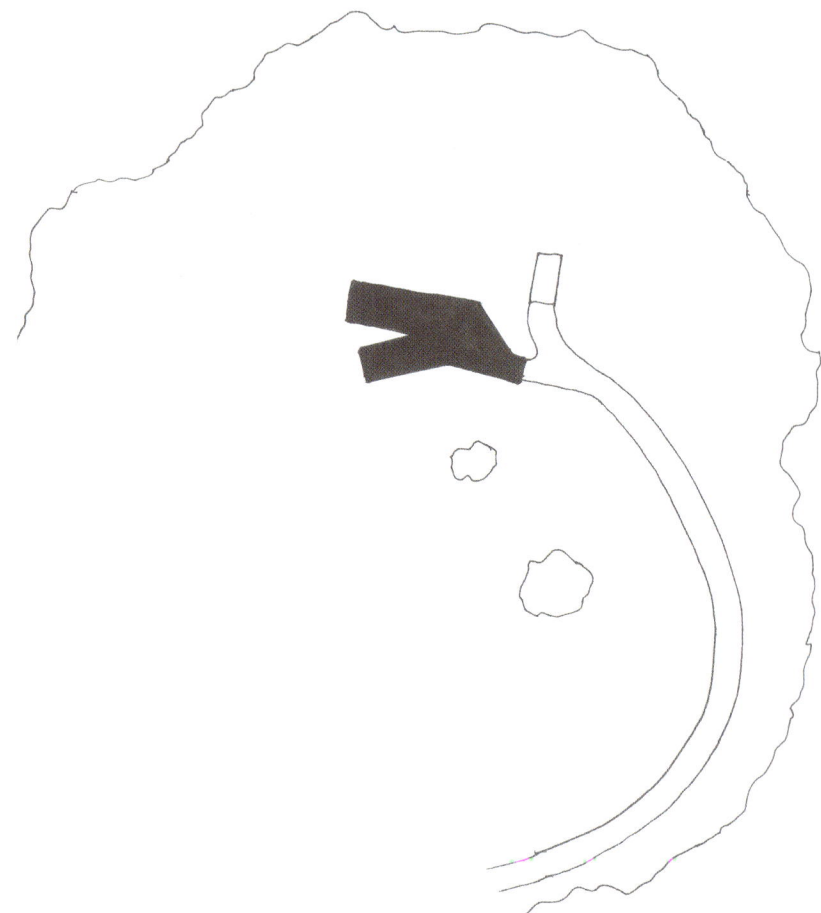

Diagram 3. A clearing on top of a hill is the site of this weekend retreat residence. Holl recalls the occasion he went to the location in the Catskill Mountains: "It's actually one of those projects that seldom happens for me: I made the basic sketch the day that I went to the site, November 16, 1997, and didn't deviate from it."[11]

Diagram 4. The roof plan does not follow any convention; rather, its standing-seam metal looks to be unfolding, giving it a faceted appearance. There is, however, a rationale for the various slopes as they tilt to funnel rainwater into a cistern.

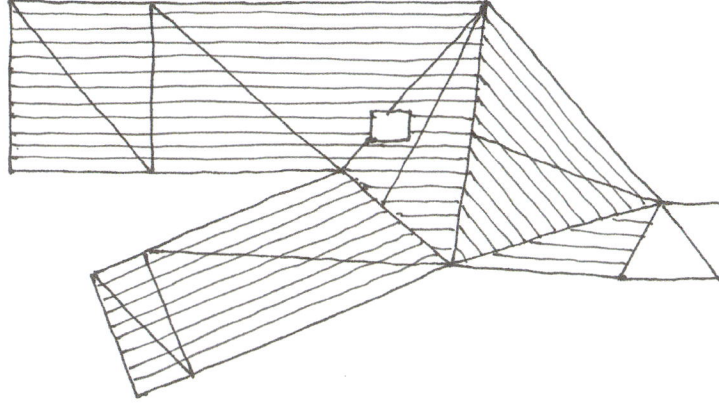

Diagram 5. On the second floor plan, the balconies extend into the landscape and elongate the two arms.

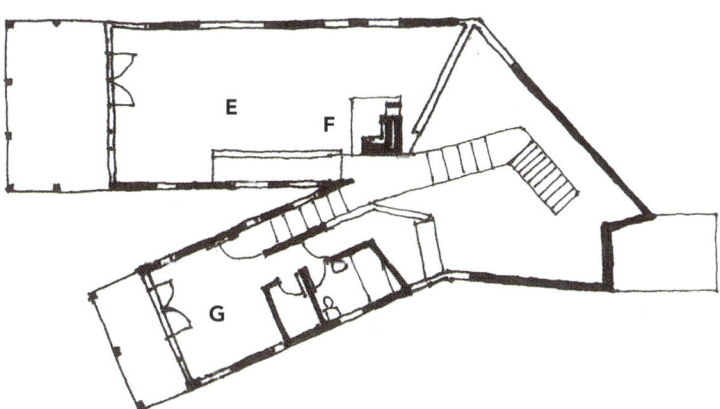

Diagram 6. The ground plan of the house is shown with its distinctive Y-shaped configuration.

A. Pool
B. Bedroom
C. Dining
D. Kitchen
E. Living
F. Fireplace
G. Master Bedroom

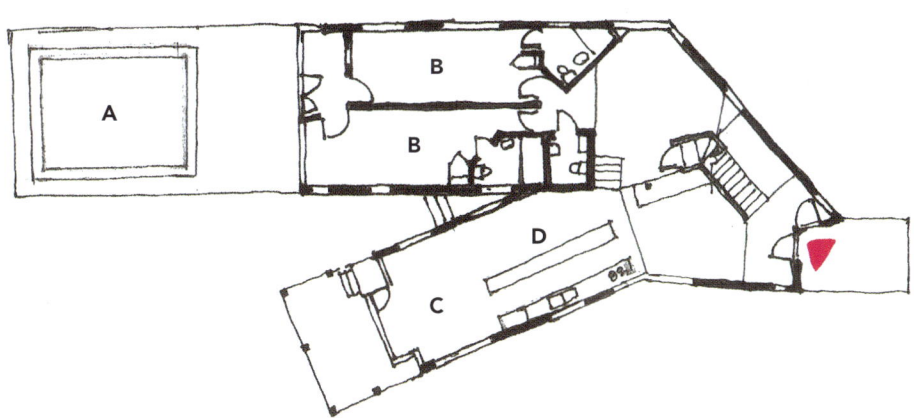

Branching Masses

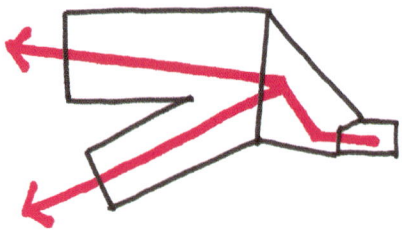

Diagram 7. The circulation leads predominately towards the beautiful views of the Catskill Mountains to the west.

Diagram 8. A staircase leading to the second level and the connection between the two branching arms can be seen in pink, forming a "Y."

a
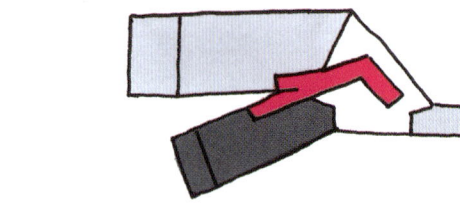

b
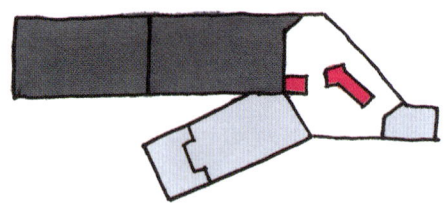

Diagram 9. On the ground level (b), the public areas—shown in light gray—are the entry, kitchen, and dining rooms. The dark gray represents the children's bedrooms. The second floor (a) with the private master bedroom in dark gray and the living room in a lighter gray. Both plans show the hallway in white with the stairs in pink.

a
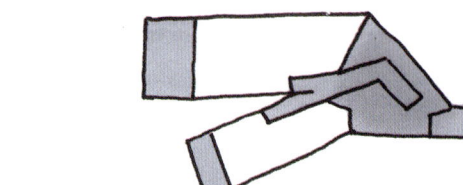

b
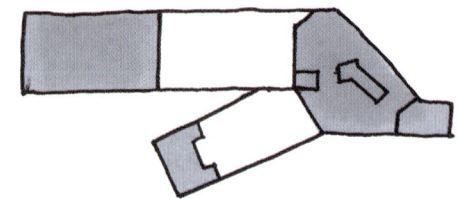

Diagram 10. The light gray represents two kinds of transitional spaces in the house: movement from inside to outside (or vice versa) and travel between the wings of the "Y."

Y House

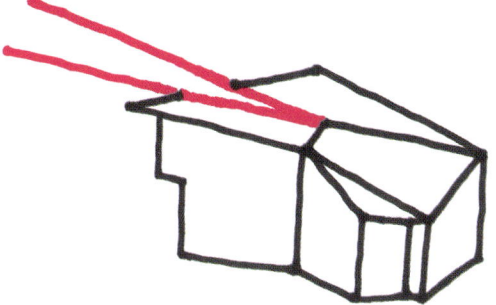

Diagram 11. Splitting the building creates more surface area for openings, allowing sunlight to enter deep inside the home.

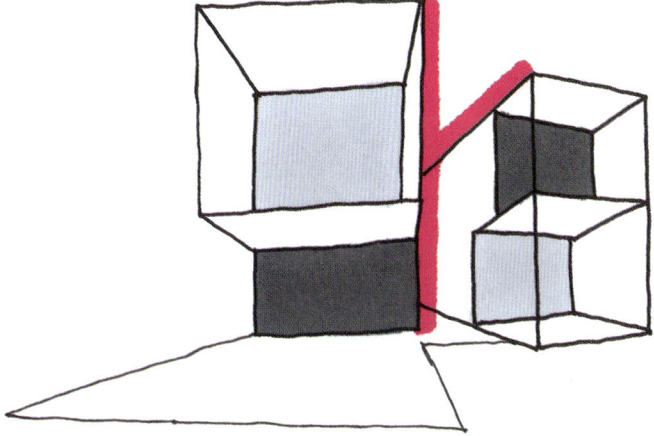

Diagram 13. In this perspective, the key elements of the house are shown: the switching of the public/private zones in each branch and the distinctive "Y" shape that makes the house so memorable.

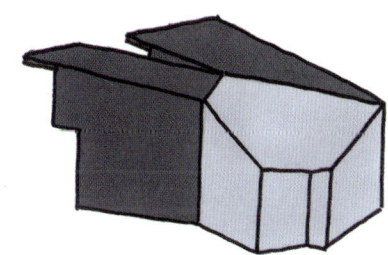

Diagram 12. Public areas (in light gray) naturally stop or break before the continuation of the private spaces, shown in dark gray.

24 NESTING RECTANGLES
House N

The spaces between nested rectangles can be as provocative as the concealed nucleus which is oftentimes a reserved space that only a few may access.

House N

At a cursory glance, it is immediately apparent that this is no conventional house; it does not share any characteristics of the dwellings that surround it, such as shingle-covered pitched roofs, doors, or windows. The cool, crisp white box perforated with large rectangular cut-outs, stands in sharp contrast with its unassuming neighbors in this residential district of Oita, Japan. Designed by Sou Fujimoto in 2008 for a retired couple, these **nested rectangles**, or as the architect describes them, "a box within a box with a box,"[1] investigate the gradation of public and private spaces. He states that "I have always had doubts about streets and houses being separated by a single wall, and wondered that a gradation of rich domain accompanied by various senses of distance between streets and houses might be a possibility, such as: a place inside the house that is fairly near the street; a place that is a bit far from the street; and a place far off the street, in secure privacy."[2]

The wall establishes a binary relationship; you are either on this side or that side, inside or outside. Fujimoto challenges this dichotomy and examines an alternative: "What is between inside and outside? . . . [I]f you say between inside and outside . . . not inside, not outside, but something between, then we have to think about something new, some new definition or some new space . . . that is the power of thinking about something between."[3] It is clear that he is most intrigued by "architecture as a sort of background,"[4] as he notes, whereby the dwelling occurs in the spaces *between* the layers.

The largest box encloses the entire plot of land; its 24-foot height is in keeping with the adjacent houses. Due to the large, glass-free openings, trees grow within the courtyard of this container, reminding one of nature's constant presence. Rather than acting as a barrier between the residence and the street, it is a highly porous envelope that simultaneously provides engagement with the road and the house. Fujimoto has taken the *engawa*, or porch, of a Japanese traditional house and reinterpreted it in a refreshing and unconventional way. This in-between space allows for exchanges with neighbors and views of the sky that are framed by the large openings; the outermost shell is not perceived as a rigid barrier but, rather, as a permeable screen. The architect describes the sensation of inhabiting this space as "you are almost half inside of something but definitely, you are outside, half-covered."[5]

Diagram 1. The façade's unique appearance, looking north, captures the cut-outs of the flat roof as well as the sides of the house. Trees are in an open courtyard, obscuring the line between what is "inside" and "outside."

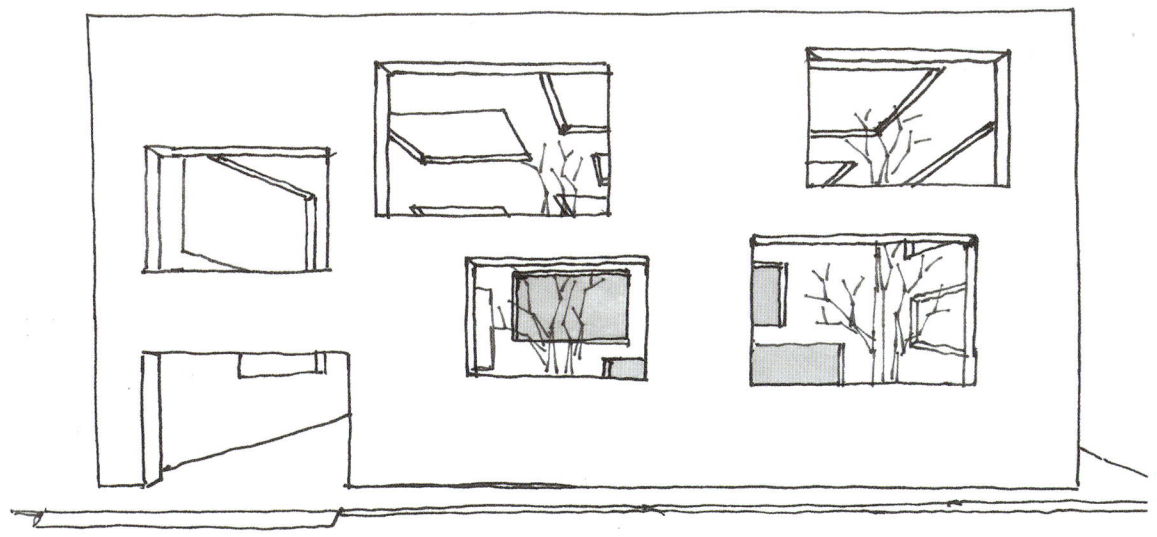

Nesting Rectangles

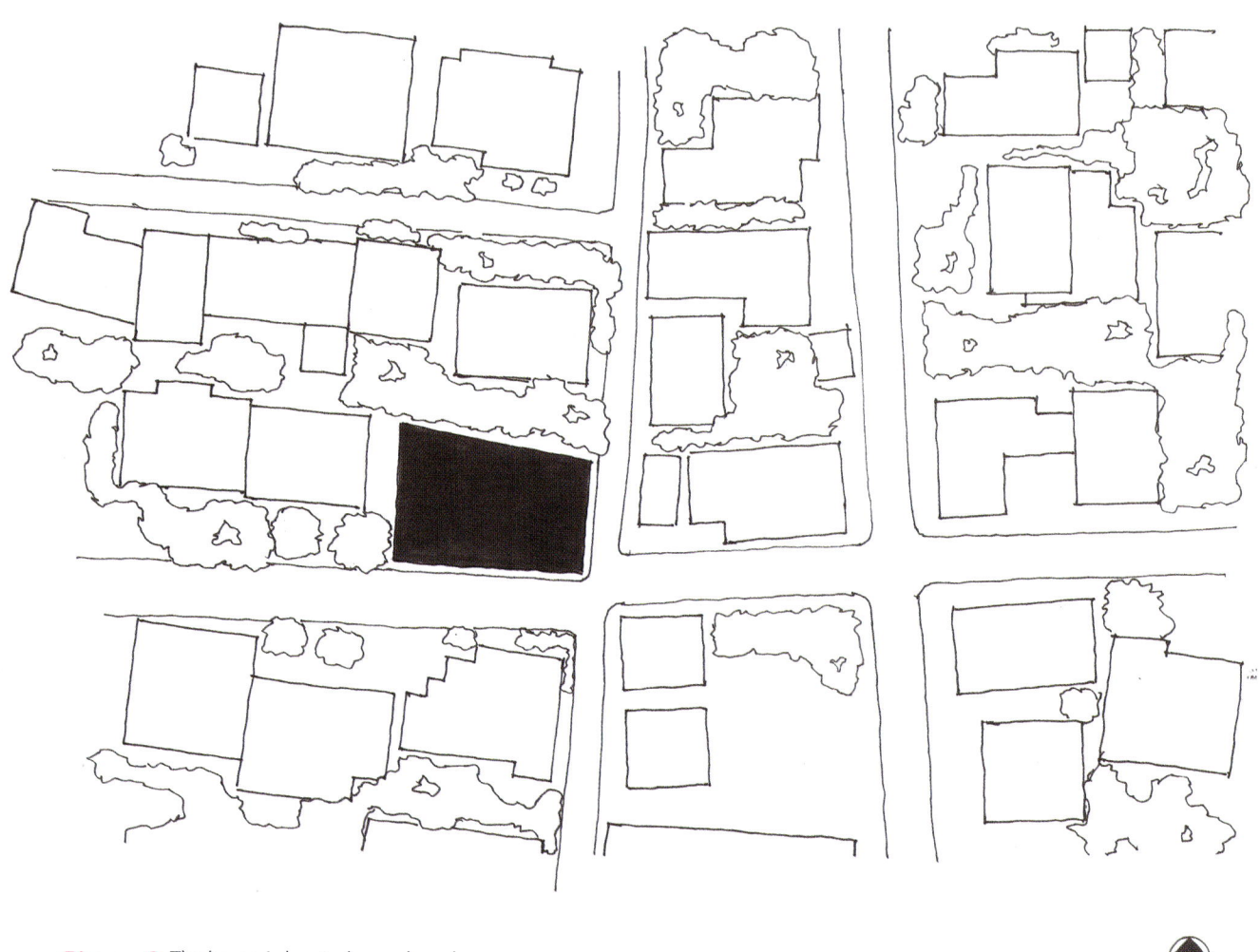

Diagram 2. The house is located on a densely populated but quiet residential neighborhood in Oita, Japan. In this view, Fujimoto's architecture seems to mimic the form of the other houses, but this is where the similarity ends.

House N

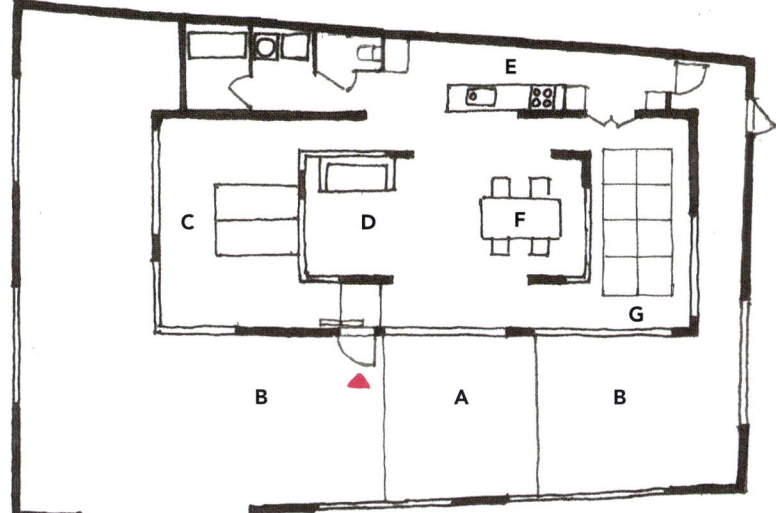

Diagram 3. Sparsely furnished, the home elegantly suits the needs of the retired owners.

A. Porch
B. Garden
C. Bedroom
D. Living
E. Kitchen
F. Dining
G. Tatami Room

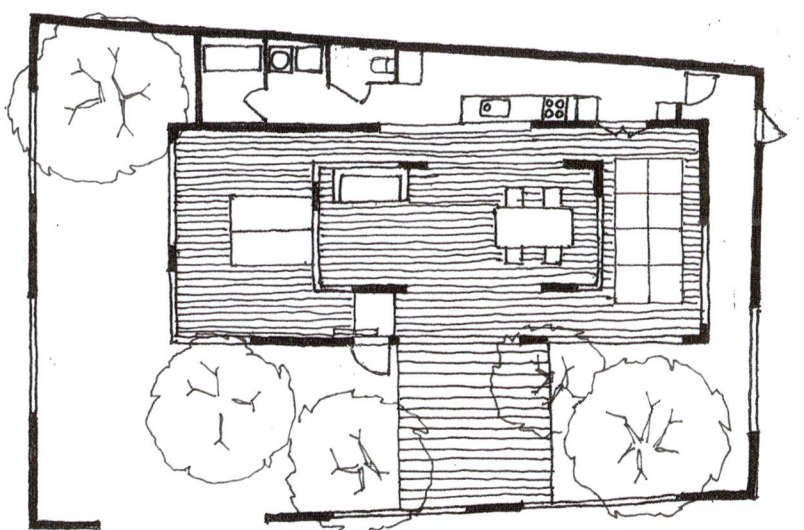

Diagram 4. This plan emphasizes the wood flooring that is brought through the house. The architect envisioned "things get[ing] placed in between the layers."⁹

Nesting Rectangles

Diagram 5. Instead of dividing a large box into a series of rooms, Fujimoto's approach is quite singular—he nests boxes, which generate their own levels of privacy and function.

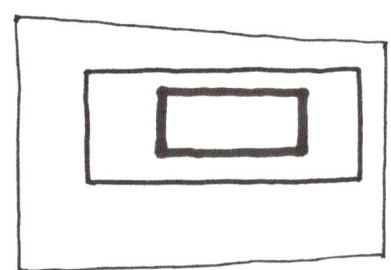

Diagram 6. The private bedroom and tatami room are not located in the heart of the house; they are shown in the darkest gray. Fujimoto designated the smallest area for living and dining, shown in medium gray. The most public area is the zone between the street and the house (in lightest gray).

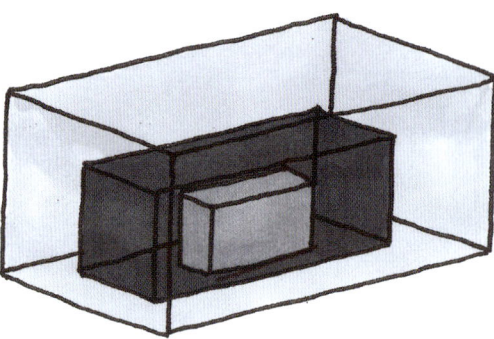

Diagram 7. Surprisingly, from the center or heart of the structure (in pink), there is still a sense of openness; the large rectangular cut-outs at the walls and ceilings allow one to view the layers and through them, provide a connection to the immediate surroundings and the streetscape beyond.

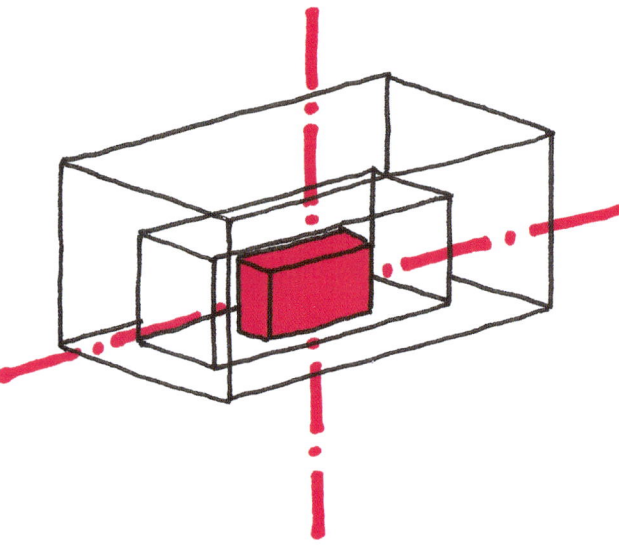

House N

The 14-foot-tall second shell, fully enclosed with operable windows, an entrance door, and fixed glazing, contains a bedroom and a tatami room. Its northern wall abuts a bathroom and kitchen, located furthest away from the entrance. Nested within this second shell is the smallest and most intimate box—at 9 feet tall—that holds the living and dining areas. Because the spaces are not fully enclosed or strictly delineated by four walls and a door, the definition of the rooms is ambiguous; Fujimoto has described living in this house as, "resembles to living among the clouds. A distinct boundary is nowhere to be found, except for a gradual change in the domain."[6] The experience within House N is dynamic and fluid. One's position in the house restricts or reveals how much is seen through the openings, and, despite all the layers, from inside the smallest box, a sense of openness pervades.

While the forms—seemingly so simple, placed inside one another like *matryoshka* nesting dolls—create rich and complex spaces for living, Fujimoto's macro interpretation of House N extends beyond dwelling. He writes that, "This is a presentation of an ultimate house in which everything from the origins of the world to a specific house is conceived together under a single method."[7] Examples of this "method" include: Beijing's Forbidden City, which is a replica of the cosmos, constructed as a series of complex walled areas and encircled by a moat; the human heart, while protected by the ribcage, is composed of many layers to ensure its vitality; and Earth's location nested within numerous zones—Inner Solar System, Heliosphere, Milky Way Galaxy, and the Virgo Supercluster, to name a few. A house that models the universe while thoughtfully designing "architecture that is not about space nor about form, but simply about expressing the riches of what are 'between'"[8] with such simplicity is indeed worthy of high praise and thorough analysis.

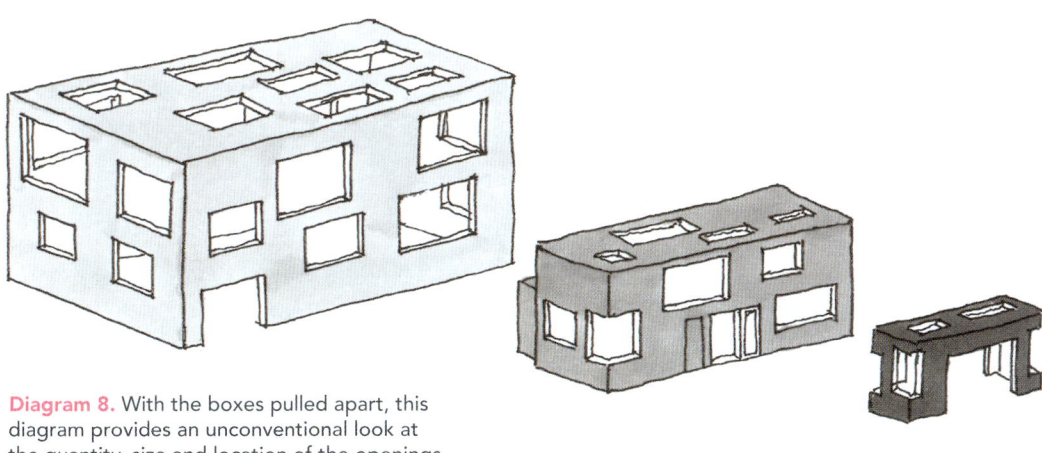

Diagram 8. With the boxes pulled apart, this diagram provides an unconventional look at the quantity, size and location of the openings scattered over the façades of the three boxes.

25 STACKING SHAPES
Tokyo Apartment

Highly unconventional, stacked shapes express their individual forms, to create a singular architectural expression.

Tokyo Apartment

The city of Tokyo, teeming with over nine million people and encompassing everything that defines a mega-metropolis, is the context for Sou Fujimoto's aptly named project, Tokyo Apartments. He writes, "This collective housing is a miniature of Tokyo . . . My intention was to make an infinitely rich place that is crowded and disorderly."[1] Despite his deep affinity to nature (he was always surrounded by the serenity of the outdoors in Hokkaido, where he was born), he came to embrace the chaos, density, and the various scales that he observed while studying and living in Japan's largest city: "For all its maze of concrete, metal, glass and wood, I walk around the city as if it were a forest."[2]

From Fujimoto's perspective, both environments are similar; facilely, he is able to harmonize these dichotomous worlds. He states: "I thought there is a strange similarity between nature and artificial things, even in such a contrast."[3] This helped him to "think about architecture as equal [to] nature."[4] Perhaps this view of architecture and Fujimoto's uncommon vision attracted the client, Shunzo Ueda, to hire the architect. Mr. Ueda, who was caring for his ill wife, was unable to work; to alleviate his financial predicament he considered building rental units on the existing plot of land he owned to generate income. The result, finished in 2010, is a four-unit structure, including one for the admiring owner, that displays the disarray of the city but keeps the chaos at bay by, as Fujimoto writes, "resisting being totally dissolved into that disorder."[5]

Piled impossibly and precariously on top of each other, these **stacked shapes** or pitch-roofed "houses" with gleaming white standing-seam metal sheeting belie their varied organization. Each unit is not an individual dwelling but, instead, consists of either two or three rooms that are adjacent, above, and/or below one another. The volumes sit slightly askew, providing the inhabitants with a unique view of the city while their configuration reveals cavities of the most irregular shapes in plan and elevation. Entries into individual rental spaces are interspersed at various points on the site, requiring the use of exterior stairs that interlace the building. The act of climbing to a dwelling requires one to be aware of the sights, sound, and smells of the environment or, as Fujimoto notes, "the whole city is experienced as part of your house"; he has even described the act of scaling or ascending into a house as "climbing a high mountain."[6]

The structural complexity is masked but only to a point. In plain view, vertical elements and other bracing members prop the volumes that appear to be balancing precariously along the ridges of the pitched roofs. Inside, columns pierce through the volumes and diagonal supports cut across windows, mimicking the crisscrossing electrical lines and other cables that construct the layered landscape.

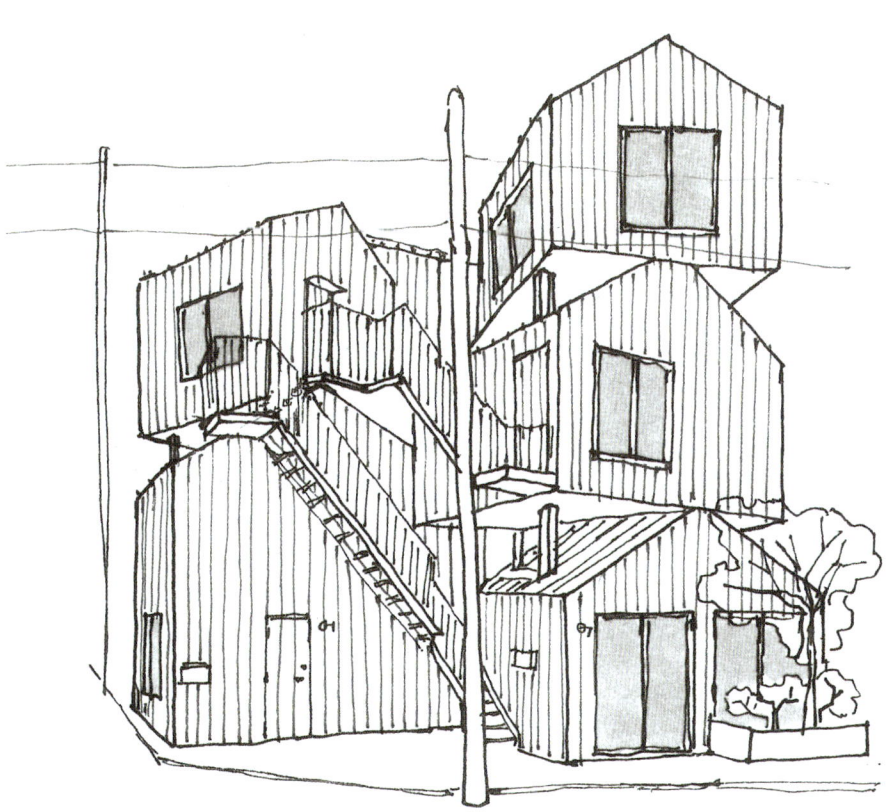

Diagram 1. A view of the apartments, looking at the northeast corner of the site. Although the overall height of the structure is very similar to the surrounding houses, the composition of the stacked "houses" is unexpected.

Stacking Shapes

Diagram 2. The site is fairly small, but undeterred, Fujimoto is able to design four unique units on this corner lot. The two façades facing the street are the most expressive, while the southwest corner of the building conforms to the orthogonal houses on either side.

Tokyo Apartment

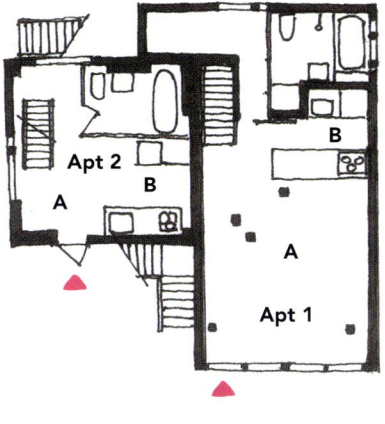

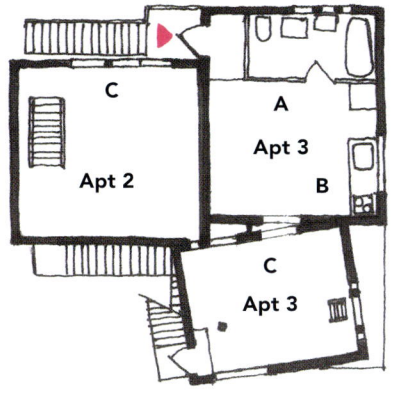

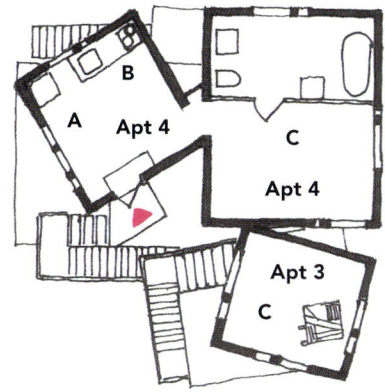

3

4

5

Diagrams 3, 4, 5. Floor plans of the ground level (Diagram 3), second floor (Diagram 4), and third floor (Diagram 5) are shown. Unlike a traditional or typical plan, each level does not comprise of one apartment. Each rental is a combination of rooms that are either above, below, or adjacent to each other.

A. Living / Dining
B. Kitchen
C. Bedroom

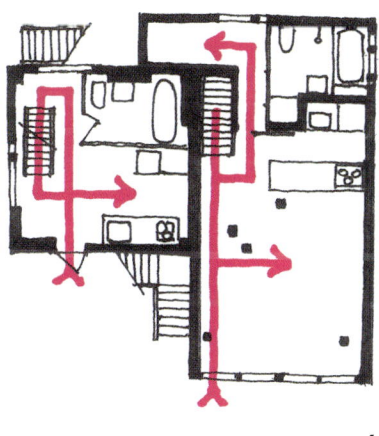

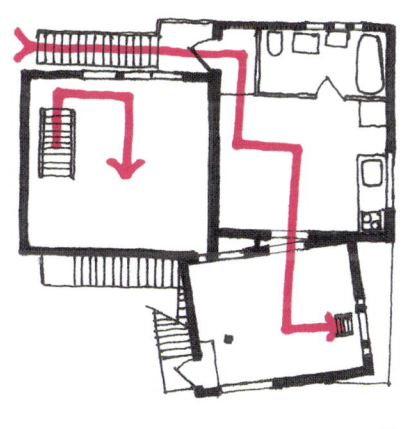

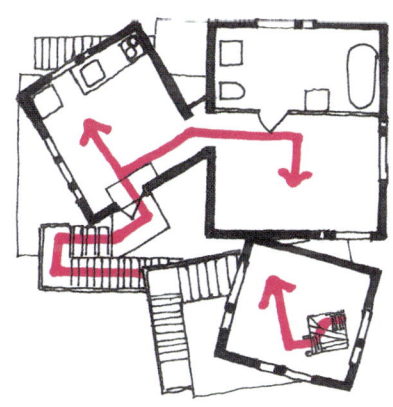

6

7

8

Diagrams 6, 7, 8. The entry points and circulation routes to adjoining volumes is shown in these diagrams. In some units, ladders are employed to traverse the levels. Diagram 6 is the ground floor; 7 is the second floor; and 8 is the third floor.

Stacking Shapes

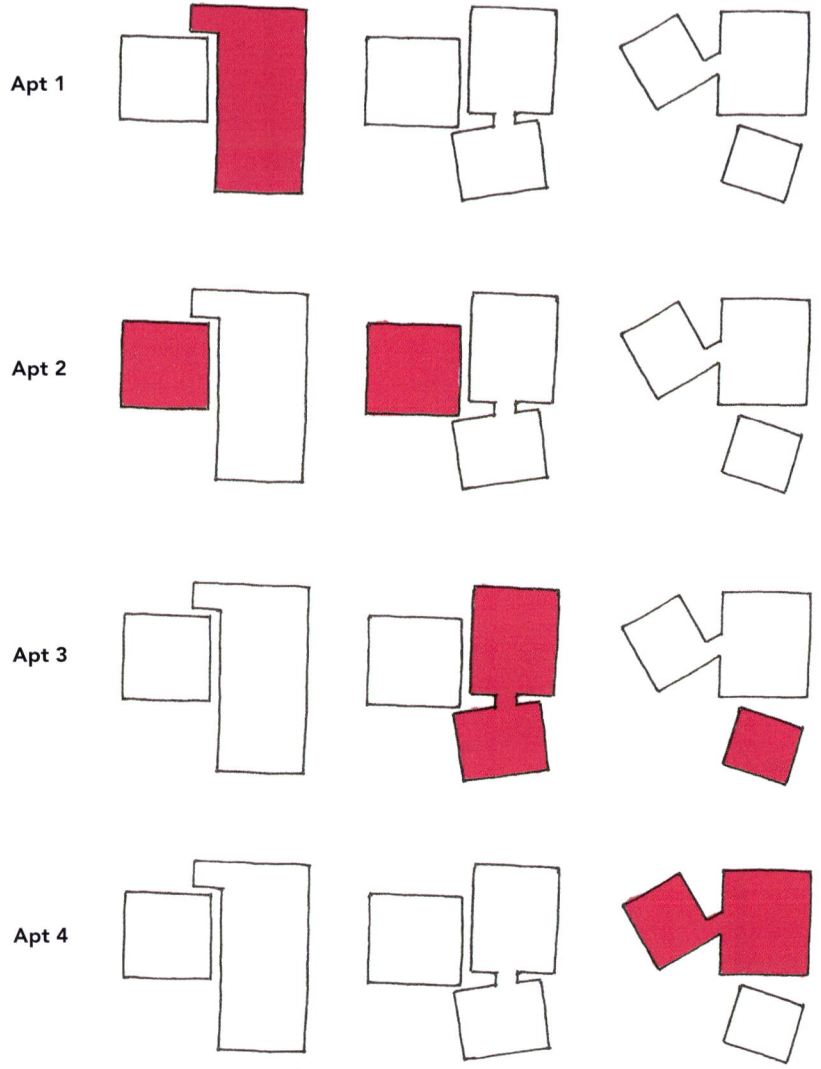

Diagram 9. These diagrams explain how each apartment is organized; each row from left to right is a simplified floor plan from the ground floor to the third. Apt 1 is a single, generously sized room (with a basement space that is not shown). Apt 2 is stacked on the ground and second floors. Apt 3 is three rooms - two are adjoined on the second floor, and the third room is above. Lastly, Apt 4 is two rooms, both on the third floor.

Tokyo Apartment

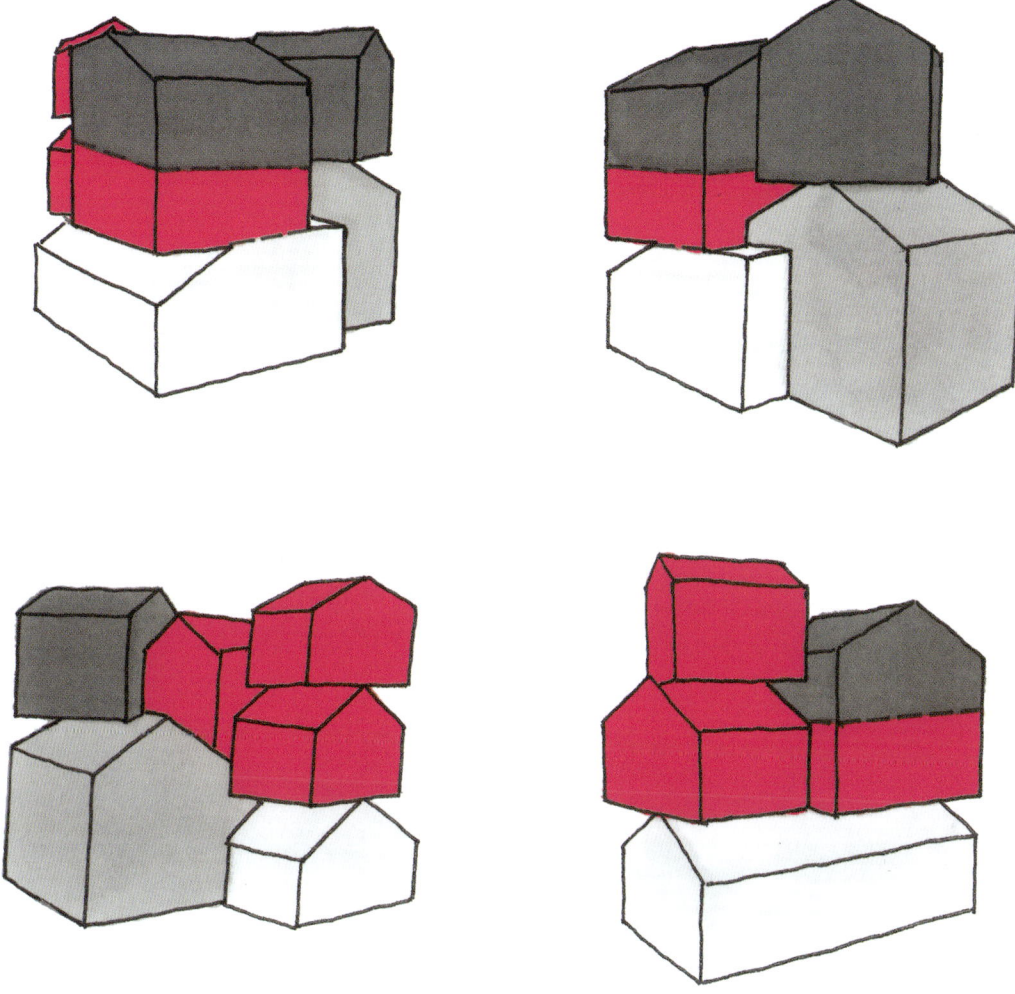

Diagram 10. Fujimoto creates different sized "houses": two-storied, small, and long. Most of them sit precariously on the ridges of the pitched roofs, while a couple of units appear to be merged – but not completely. The result is a pile of homes that seems to defy logic and resembles chaos but invites the viewer to study and look intently at the architecture with curiosity and humor. Similar to Diagram 7, this series of diagrams provide another analysis of how the apartments are organized in a three-dimensional way from various perspectives. Apt 1 is light gray; Apt 2 is medium gray; Apt 3 is pink; and Apt 4 is dark gray.

Stacking Shapes

Due to the austerity of the interiors, sunlit spaces with white walls and ceilings amplify the sense of serenity within the intimate scale of the apartments. Generously-sized windows are strategically placed to allow views of the city while providing privacy within this community of residences. Openings are cut through the sloped ceilings to accommodate ladders, permitting vertical connections within some of the units. Fujimoto's use of these ladders saves precious floor space and perhaps also mimics the joys of emerging into a child's treehouse. His love of trees is well-known, and he speaks with wonder about them:

"Trees need individual comfort zones but don't want to be isolated from each other. Their branches, leaves and shrubbery help create the balance. My architecture works in similar ways. Instead of separation, I create fragmentation which blurs boundaries and forges connections."[7] Perhaps, due to the world of artifice and chaos of Tokyo, nature is a vital part of the dwelling experience for Fujimoto. His architecture visually embodies the noise of the big city, but, paradoxically, it is also able to recreate a retreat within, enabling the presence of the solitude and calm that a forest can provide.

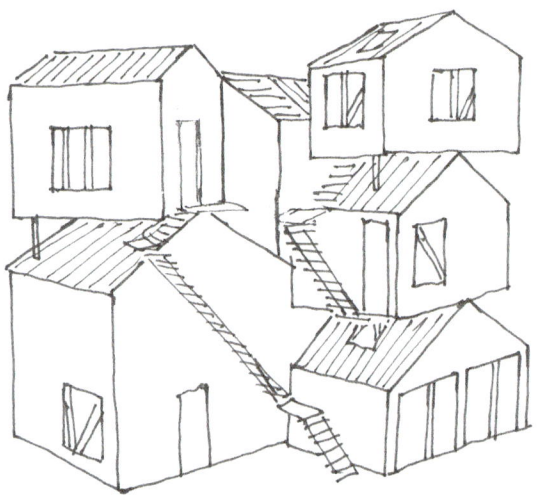

11

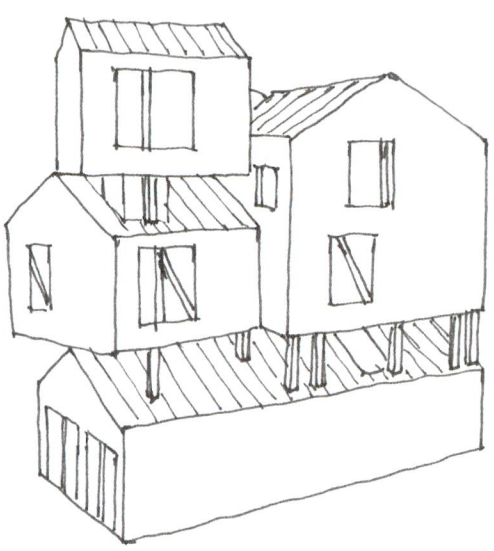

12

Tokyo Apartment

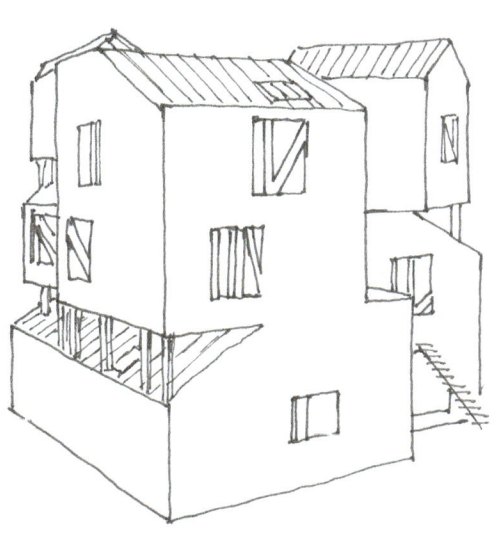

13

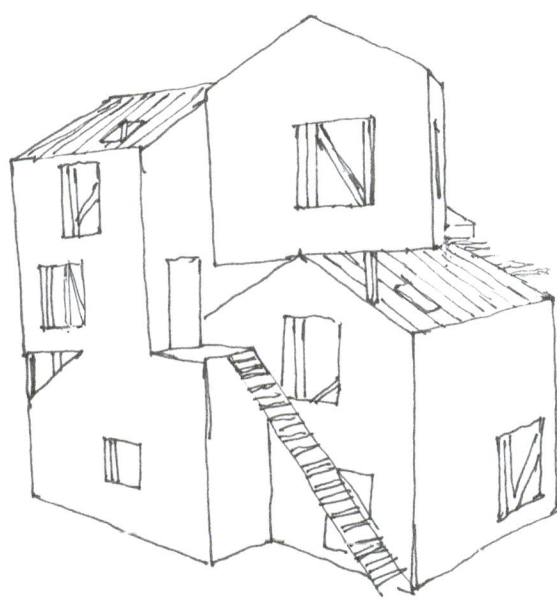

14

Diagrams 11, 12, 13, 14. Multiple views are necessary to appreciate the complexity of the form; Fujimoto created many physical models to study how the stacked units would appear.

NOTES

Introduction
1. Mik, E. "Interview: Steven Holl." *ArchIdea*, edition 42, 2010, https://view.publitas.com/forboflooring-com/archidea-42/page/1, pp. 7–8.
2. Masheck, Joseph, and Steven Holl. "Steven Holl." *BOMB*, vol. 79, 2002, *https://bombmagazine.org/articles/steven-holl/*, np.

1 Rotating L-Shapes
1. Smith, Kathryn. *Schindler House*. Harry N. Adams, 2001, p. 11.
2. Darling, Michael, et.al. *The Architecture of R. M. Schindler*. The Museum of Contemporary Art, Harry N. Abrams, 2001, p. 47.
3. Smith, Kathryn. *Schindler House*. Harry N. Adams, 2001, p. 81.
4. Park, Jin-Ho. "Rudolph M. Schindler—Proportion, Scale and the 'Row.'" *Nexus Network Journal*, vol. 5, no. 2, 2003, doi:10.1007//s00004-003-0017-9, p. 60.

2 Manipulating Volumes
1. Gropius, Walter, et al. "'The Bauhaus' and 'How Do We Build Decent, Beautiful, and Inexpensive Housing?'" *West 86th: A Journal of Decorative Arts, Design History, and Material Culture*, vol. 23, no. 1, 2016, pp. 102–124., doi:10.1086/688202, p. 122.
2. Gropius, Walter, et al. "'The Bauhaus' and 'How Do We Build Decent, Beautiful, and Inexpensive Housing?'" *West 86th: A Journal of Decorative Arts, Design History, and Material Culture*, vol. 23, no. 1, 2016, pp. 102–124., doi:10.1086/688202, p. 117.
3. Gropius, Walter, et al. "'The Bauhaus' and 'How Do We Build Decent, Beautiful, and Inexpensive Housing?'" *West 86th: A Journal of Decorative Arts, Design History, and Material Culture*, vol. 23, no. 1, 2016, pp. 102–124., doi:10.1086/688202, p. 119.
4. Gropius, Walter, et al. "'The Bauhaus' and 'How Do We Build Decent, Beautiful, and Inexpensive Housing?'" *West 86th: A Journal of Decorative Arts, Design History, and Material Culture*, vol. 23, no. 1, 2016, pp. 102–124., doi:10.1086/688202, p. 117.

3 Shifting Space
1. Sarnitz, August E. "Proportion and Beauty—The Lovell Beach House by Rudolph Michael Schindler, Newport Beach, 1922–1926." *Journal of the Society of Architectural Historians*, vol. 45, no. 4, Dec. 1986, pp. 374–388, p. 374.
2. Vallen, Michael Earl. *Housing . . . the Hillside, Los Angeles*. 1998, Virginia Polytechnic Institute, M Arch Thesis, vtechworks.lib.vt.edu/bitstream/handle/10919/36539/schindle.pdf?sequence=8&isAllowed=y, p. 29.
3. Gebhard, David. *Schindler*. William Stout Publishers, 1997, p. 147.
4. Vallen, Michael Earl. *Housing . . . the Hillside, Los Angeles*. 1998, Virginia Polytechnic Institute, M Arch Thesis, vtechworks.lib.vt.edu/bitstream/handle/10919/36539/schindle.pdf?sequence=8&isAllowed=y, p. 28.
5. Greenhalgh, Paul, editor. *Modernism in Design*. Reaktion Books, 1990, p. 116.
6. Vallen, Michael Earl. *Housing . . . the Hillside, Los Angeles*. 1998, Virginia Polytechnic Institute, M Arch Thesis, vtechworks.lib.vt.edu/bitstream/handle/10919/36539/schindle.pdf?sequence=8&isAllowed=y, p. 27.
7. Gebhard, David. *Schindler*. William Stout Publishers, 1997, p. 149.

4 Sliding Planes
1. Hosey, Lance. "The Ship of Theseus: Identity and the Barcelona Pavilion(s)." *Journal of Architectural Education (1984)*, vol. 72, no. 2, 2018, pp. 230–247, doi:10.1080/10464883.2018.1496731, p. 240.
2. Blake, Peter. *The Master Builders*. W. W. Norton & Company, 1960, p. 208.
3. Mertins, Detlef. *Mies*. Phaidon Press Limited, 2014, p. 138.
4. Kim, Ransoo. "The Tectonically Defining Space of Mies Van Der Rohe." *Architectural Research Quarterly*, vol. 13, no. 3–4, 2009, pp. 251–260, doi:10.1017/s1359135510000102, p. 252.
5. Kim, Ransoo. "The Tectonically Defining Space of Mies Van Der Rohe." *Architectural Research Quarterly*, vol. 13, no. 3–4, 2009, pp. 251–260, doi:10.1017/s1359135510000102, p. 252.
6. Unwin, Simon. *Twenty Buildings Every Architect Should Understand*. Routledge, 2010, p. 33.

5 Moving Perspectives
1. Le Corbusier (Charles-Edouard Jeanneret). *Vers Une Architecture* (*Towards a New Architecture*). Dover Publications, 2013(1923), p. 95.
2. Baltanas, Jose. *Walking Through Le Corbusier: A Tour of His Masterworks*. Thames & Hudson, 2005, p. 55.
3. Benton, Tim. *The Villas of Le Corbusier and Pierre Jeanneret, 1920–1930*. Birkhauser Architecture, 2007, p. 20.
4. Baltanas, Jose. *Walking Through Le Corbusier: A Tour of His Masterworks*. Thames & Hudson, 2005, p. 63.
5. Samuel, Flora, and Peter Blundell Jones. "The Making of Architectural Promenade: Villa Savoye and Schminke House." *Architectural Research Quarterly*, vol. 16, no. 2, 2012, pp. 108–124, doi:10.1017/S1359135512000437, p. 111.
6. Baltanas, Jose. *Walking Through Le Corbusier: A Tour of His Masterworks*. Thames & Hudson, 2005, p. 63.
7. Blake, Peter. *The Master Builders*. W. W. Norton & Company, 1960, p. 61.

8   Moulis, Antony. "Forms and Techniques: Le Corbusier, the Spiral Plan and Diagram Architecture." *Architectural Research Quarterly*, vol. 14, no. 4, 2010, pp. 317–326, doi:10.1017/S135913551100011X, p. 324.

6 Compressing Horizontals
1   Wright, Frank Lloyd. *An Autobiography*. Faber & Faber Limited, 1977, p. 424.
2   Wright, Frank Lloyd. *An Autobiography*. Faber & Faber Limited, 1977, pp. 427, 429.
3   Wright, Frank Lloyd. *An Autobiography*. Faber & Faber Limited, 1977, p. 139.
4   Wright, Frank Lloyd. *An Autobiography*. Faber & Faber Limited, 1977, p. 427.
5   Jacobs, Herbert, and Katherine Jacobs. *Building with Frank Lloyd Wright: An Illustrated Memoir*. Southern Illinois University Press, 1996, p. 53.
6   Jacobs, Herbert, and Katherine Jacobs. *Building with Frank Lloyd Wright: An Illustrated Memoir*. Southern Illinois University Press, 1996, pp. 16, 57, 50.
7   Jacobs, Herbert, and Katherine Jacobs. *Building with Frank Lloyd Wright: An Illustrated Memoir*. Southern Illinois University Press, 1996, p. 53.

7 Expanding Volumes
1   Hoffmann, Donald. *Frank Lloyd Wright's Fallingwater: The House and Its History*. Dover Publications, 1978, p. 74.
2   Hoffmann, Donald. *Frank Lloyd Wright's Fallingwater: The House and Its History*. Dover Publications, 1978, pp. 13, 17.
3   McCarter, Robert. *Fallingwater: Frank Lloyd Wright*. Phaidon Press, 2002, p. 24.
4   Kauffmann, Jr., Edgar. *Fallingwater. A Frank Lloyd Wright Country House*. Cross River Press, Ltd., 1986, p. 172.
5   McCarter, Robert. *Fallingwater: Frank Lloyd Wright*. Phaidon Press, 2002, p. 17.
6   Hoffmann, Donald. *Frank Lloyd Wright's Fallingwater: The House and Its History*. Dover Publications, 1978, Introduction.
7   McCarter, Robert. *Fallingwater: Frank Lloyd Wright*. Phaidon Press, 2002, p. 15.

8 Extending Rectangles
1   Dodds, George. (2002). "Richard Neutra's Venetian lecture." *Architectural Research Quarterly*, vol. 6, pp. 257–267, doi:10.1017/S1359135503001751, pp. 264, 265.
2   Dodds, George. (2002). "Richard Neutra's Venetian lecture." *Architectural Research Quarterly*, vol. 6, pp. 257–267, doi:10.1017/S1359135503001751, p. 267.
3   Tippey, Brett. "Richard Neutra's Search for the Southland: California, Latin America and Spain." *Architectural History*, vol. 59, 2016, pp. 311–352, doi:10.1017/arh.2016.10, p. 340.

4   Dodds, George. (2002). "Richard Neutra's Venetian lecture." *Architectural Research Quarterly*, vol. 6, pp. 257–267, doi:10.1017/S1359135503001751, p. 264.
5   Neutra, Dion. "The View from Inside: An Overview of the Neutra Practice." *Richard and Dion Neutra Architecture*, vol. 1, Oct. 2000, neutra.org/the-view-from-inside-an-overview-of-the-neutra-practice/, np.
6   Niedenthal, Simon. "'Glamourized Houses': Neutra, Photography, and the Kaufmann House." *Journal of Architectural Education (1984–)*, vol. 47, no. 2, 1993, pp. 101–112, doi:10.2307/1425171, p. 108.
7   Dodds, George. (2002). "Richard Neutra's Venetian lecture." *Architectural Research Quarterly*, vol. 6, pp. 257–267, doi:10.1017/S1359135503001751, p. 264.

9 Splitting Zones
1   McAvoy, Christy, et al. "Eames House." National Historic Landmark Nomination Form. Washington, DC: U.S. Department of the Interior, National Park Service, May 2005, p. 12.
2   McAvoy, Christy, et al. "Eames House." National Historic Landmark Nomination Form. Washington, DC: U.S. Department of the Interior, National Park Service, May 2005, p. 19.

10 Offsetting Interior/Exterior
1   Harris, Randy. "Here's Looking Through You, Kid." *The New York Times*, 12 December 2013, www.nytimes.com/slideshow/2013/12/12/garden/20131212-GLASSHOUSE/s/20131212-GLASSHOUSE-slide-8YCA.html, np.
2   Mason, Christopher. "Behind the Glass Wall." *The New York Times*, 7 June 2007, www.nytimes.com/2007/06/07/garden/07glass.html?ref=philip_johnson, np.
3   Clouette, Bruce, and Hoang Tinh. "Philip Johnson's Glass House." National Historic Landmark Nomination Form. Washington, DC: U.S. Department of the Interior, National Park Service, 1996, p. 11.

11 Layering Planes
1   Wong, Yoke-Sum. "Edith Doesn't Live Here Anymore: A Story of Farnsworth House." In D. Gafijczuk and D. Sayer (eds.), *The Inhabited Ruins of Central Europe*. Palgrave Macmillan, 2013, doi:10.1057/9781137305862_7, p. 34.
2   Kim, Ransoo. "The Tectonically Defining Space of Mies Van Der Rohe." *Architectural Research Quarterly*, vol. 13, no. 3–4, 2009, pp. 251–260, doi:10.1017/s1359135510000102, p. 257.
3   Kim, Ransoo. "The Tectonically Defining Space of Mies Van Der Rohe." *Architectural Research Quarterly*, vol. 13, no. 3–4, 2009, pp. 251–260, doi:10.1017/s1359135510000102, p. 259.

Notes

4 Wong, Yoke-Sum. "Edith Doesn't Live Here Anymore: A Story of Farnsworth House." In D. Gafijczuk and D. Sayer (eds.), *The Inhabited Ruins of Central Europe*. Palgrave Macmillan, 2013, doi:10.1057/9781137305862_7, p. 32.
5 Kim, Ransoo. "The Tectonically Defining Space of Mies Van Der Rohe." *Architectural Research Quarterly*, vol. 13, no. 3–4, 2009, pp. 251–260, doi:10.1017/s1359135510000102, p. 252.
6 Kim, Ransoo. *The Art of Building (Baukunst) of Mies Van Der Rohe*. PhD dissertation, Georgia Institute of Technology, August 2006, hdl.handle.net/1853/11465, p. 127.

12 Undulating Forms
1 Niemeyer, Oscar. *The Curves of Time: The Memoirs of Oscar Niemeyer*. Phaidon Press, 2000, p. 3.
2 Niemeyer, Oscar. *The Curves of Time: The Memoirs of Oscar Niemeyer*. Phaidon Press, 2000, p. 171.
3 Philippou, Styliane. "The Dancing Curves of Oscar Niemeyer's House at Canoa." *Revue - Articles - Textes Originale - Werk, Bauen + Wohnen*, www.wbw.ch/fr/revue/articles/textes-originalw/2013-3-the-dancing-curves-of-oscar-niemeyers-house-at-canoa.html, np.
4 Segawa, Hugo. "Oscar Niemeyer: A Misbehaved Pupil of Rationalism." *The Journal of Architecture*, vol. 2, no. 4, 1997, pp. 291–312, doi:10.1080/136023697374333, p. 293.
5 Niemeyer, Oscar. *The Curves of Time: The Memoirs of Oscar Niemeyer*. Phaidon Press, 2000, p. 168.
6 Underwood, David Kendrick. *Oscar Niemeyer and Brazilian Free-form Modernism*. George Braziller Inc., 1994, p. 22.

13 Manipulating Light
1 Le Corbusier (Charles-Edouard Jeanneret). *Vers Une Architecture* (*Towards a New Architecture*). Dover Publications, 2013(1923), p. 29.
2 Watson, Caitlin Turski. "Flesh and Form: Light and the Sacred at Notre-Dame-Du-Haus." *Faith & Form*, https://faithandform.com/feature/flesh-and-form/, np.

14 Interlocking Cubes
1 Solomon, Susan. *Louis I. Kahn's Trenton Jewish Community Center*. Princeton Architectural Press, 2000, p. 137.
2 McCarter, Robert. *Louis I. Khan*. Phaidon Press, 2005, p. 91.
3 Solomon, Susan. *Louis I. Kahn's Trenton Jewish Community Center*. Princeton Architectural Press, 2000, p. 85.
4 Solomon, Susan. *Louis I. Kahn's Trenton Jewish Community Center*. Princeton Architectural Press, 2000, p. 137.
5 McCarter, Robert. *Louis I. Khan*. Phaidon Press, 2005, p. 222.
6 Scully, Vincent, cast member, as himself. *My Architect: A Son's Journey*. Directed by Nathaniel Kahn, New Yorker Films, 2003, np (quote from film).

15 Connecting Forms
1 Schwarb, Amy Wimmer. "Modern Family: The Miller Home." *Indianapolis Monthly*, 1 May 2011, www.indianapolismonthly.com/arts-and-culture/modern-family-the-miller-home, np.
2 Roman, Antonio. *Eero Saarinen: An Architecture of Multiplicity*. Princeton Architectural Press, 2006, p. 205.
3 Keller, Hadley. "AD Remembers the Extraordinary Word of Eliel and Eero Saarinen." *Architectural Digest*, 31 July 2014, www.architecturaldigest.com/story/saarinen-father-and-son, np.

16 Lengthening Views
1 Steele, James, and David Jenkins. *Pierre Koenig*. Phaidon Press, 1998, p. 15.
2 Bussel, Amy. "Perspectives: An Architect for Better Living." *Progressive Architecture*, May 1993, p. 113.
3 Steele, James, and David Jenkins. *Pierre Koenig*. Phaidon Press, 1998, p. 15.
4 Steele, James, and David Jenkins. *Pierre Koenig*. Phaidon Press, 1998, p. 15.
5 Steele, James, and David Jenkins. *Pierre Koenig*. Phaidon Press, 1998, p. 15.

17 Overlapping Circles
1 Carder, James N. "Critical Appraisal of the Philip Johnson Pavilion." *Dumbarton Oaks*, www.doaks.org/resources/philip-johnson/critical-appraisal-of-the-philip-johnson-pavilion, np.
2 Carder, James N. "Last Concerns: Installation of the Collection, Landscaping, and 'the Acoustical Problem.'" *Dumbarton Oaks*, www.doaks.org/resources/philip-johnson/last-concerns-installation-of-the-collection-landscaping-and-201cthe-acoustical-problem201d, np.
3 Tamulevich, Susan. *Dumbarton Oaks: Garden Into Art*. Montacelli Press, 2001, p. 18.
4 Carder, James N. "Critical Appraisal of the Philip Johnson Pavilion." *Dumbarton Oaks*, www.doaks.org/resources/philip-johnson/critical-appraisal-of-the-philip-johnson-pavilion, np.
5 "Maestro of Modernism: Interview with Philip C. Johnson." *Academy of Achievement*, 1992, achievement.org/achiever/philip-johnson/#interview, np.
6 Carder, James N. "Last Concerns: Installation of the Collection, Landscaping, and 'the Acoustical Problem.'" *Dumbarton Oaks*, www.doaks.org/resources/philip-johnson/last-concerns-installation-of-the-collection-landscaping-and-201cthe-acoustical-problem201d, np.

18 Rotating Blocks
1 Marcus, George H., and William Whitaker. *The Houses of Louis Kahn*. Yale University Press, 2013, p. 196.

2. Booher, Pierson William, "Louis I. Kahn's Fisher House: A Case Study on the Architectural Detail and Design Intent." Theses (Historic Preservation), 132, 2009, repository.upenn.edu/hp_theses/132/, p. 20.
3. Booher, Pierson William, "Louis I. Kahn's Fisher House: A Case Study on the Architectural Detail and Design Intent." Theses (Historic Preservation), 132, 2009, repository.upenn.edu/hp_theses/132/, p. 32.
4. Booher, Pierson William, "Louis I. Kahn's Fisher House: A Case Study on the Architectural Detail and Design Intent." Theses (Historic Preservation), 132, 2009, repository.upenn.edu/hp_theses/132/, p. 60.
5. Booher, Pierson William, "Louis I. Kahn's Fisher House: A Case Study on the Architectural Detail and Design Intent." Theses (Historic Preservation), 132, 2009, repository.upenn.edu/hp_theses/132/, p. 65.
6. Booher, Pierson William, "Louis I. Kahn's Fisher House: A Case Study on the Architectural Detail and Design Intent." Theses (Historic Preservation), 132, 2009, repository.upenn.edu/hp_theses/132/, p. 64.
7. Booher, Pierson William, "Louis I. Kahn's Fisher House: A Case Study on the Architectural Detail and Design Intent." Theses (Historic Preservation), 132, 2009, repository.upenn.edu/hp_theses/132/, p. 68.
8. Booher, Pierson William, "Louis I. Kahn's Fisher House: A Case Study on the Architectural Detail and Design Intent." Theses (Historic Preservation), 132, 2009, repository.upenn.edu/hp_theses/132/, p. 57.
9. Romero, Melissa. "What Lou Taught Me: Growing Up in Kahn's Fisher House." *Curbed Philadelphia*, updated 15 April 2019, philly.curbed.com/2018/2/20/16886274/louis-kahn-fisher-house-first-person-essay, np.
10. Marcus, George H., and William Whitaker. *The Houses of Louis Kahn*. Yale University Press, 2013, p. 204.
11. Booher, Pierson William, "Louis I. Kahn's Fisher House: A Case Study on the Architectural Detail and Design Intent." Theses (Historic Preservation), 132, 2009, repository.upenn.edu/hp_theses/132/, p. 49.
12. McCarter, Robert. *Louis I. Khan*. Phaidon Press, 2005, p. 468.
13. Marcus, George H., and William Whitaker. *The Houses of Louis Kahn*. Yale University Press, 2013, p. 198.
14. Romero, Melissa. "What Lou Taught Me: Growing Up in Kahn's Fisher House." *Curbed Philadelphia*, updated 15 April 2019, philly.curbed.com/2018/2/20/16886274/louis-kahn-fisher-house-first-person-essay, np.

19 Embedding Components
1. Jodidio, Philip. *Tadao Ando: Houses*. Rizzoli, 2013, p. 12.
2. Jodidio, Philip. *Tadao Ando: Houses*. Rizzoli, 2013, p. 12.
3. Jodidio, Philip. *Tadao Ando: Houses*. Rizzoli, 2013, p. 11.
4. Jodidio, Philip. *Tadao Ando: Houses*. Rizzoli, 2013, p. 11.
5. Ando, Tadao. *Tadao Ando: 1983–1993*. Madrid: El Croquis Editorial, 1994, p. 47.
6. Jodidio, Philip. *Tadao Ando: Houses*. Rizzoli, 2013, p. 11.
7. Ando, Tadao. *Tadao Ando: 1983–1993*. Madrid: El Croquis Editorial, 1994, p. 47.
8. Dal, Co Francesco, and Tadao Ando. *Tadao Ando: Complete Works*. Phaidon Press, 2000, p. 449.

20 Clustering Objects
1. Young, Victoria. "The Art of Architecture Frank Gehry's Winton Guest House." *Wright Design Masterworks Auction Catalogue*, 19 May 2015, www.wright20.com/auctions/2015/05/design-masterworks/frank-gehrys-winton-guest-house, np.
2. Ledgerwood, Angela, and Ross Miller. "New Again: Frank Gehry." *Interview Magazine*, 19 Sept. 2012, //www.interviewmagazine.com/art/new-again-frank-gehry, np.
3. Ledgerwood, Angela, and Ross Miller. "New Again: Frank Gehry." *Interview Magazine*, 19 Sept. 2012, //www.interviewmagazine.com/art/new-again-frank-gehry, np.
4. Young, Victoria. "The Art of Architecture Frank Gehry's Winton Guest House." *Wright Design Masterworks Auction Catalogue*, 19 May 2015, www.wright20.com/auctions/2015/05/design-masterworks/frank-gehrys-winton-guest-house, np.
5. Huxtable, Ada Louis. "Frank Gehry: 1989 Laureate Essay." The Pritzker Architecture Prize, https://www.pritzkerprize.com/sites/default/files/inline-files/1989_essay.pdf, np.
6. Viladas, Pilar. "Outdoor Sculpture." *Progressive Architecture*, 16 Dec. 1987, p. 60.
7. Young, Victoria. "The Art of Architecture Frank Gehry's Winton Guest House." *Wright Design Masterworks Auction Catalogue*, 19 May 2015, www.wright20.com/auctions/2015/05/design-masterworks/frank-gehrys-winton-guest-house, np.
8. Goldberger, Paul. "Frank Gehry's First Playground of the Imagination." *The Toronto Star*, 28 Sept. 2015, www.thestar.com/news/insight/2015/09/28/frank-gehrys-first-playground-of-the-imagination.html, np.

21 Engaging Procession
1. Ando, Tadao. *Tadao Ando: Conversations with Students*. Translated by Matthew Hunter, Princeton Architectural Press, 2013, p. 14.
2. Ando, Tadao. *Tadao Ando: Conversations with Students*. Translated by Matthew Hunter, Princeton Architectural Press, 2013, p. 14.
3. Dal, Co Francesco, and Tadao Ando. *Tadao Ando: Complete Works*. Phaidon Press, 2000, p. 451.
4. *Tadao Ando*. Directed by Michael Blackwood, Michael Blackwood Productions, 1988, np (quote from film).

Notes

5. Frampton, Kenneth, et al. *Tadao Ando*. Museum of Modern Art, 1991, p. 76.
6. *Tadao Ando*. Directed by Michael Blackwood, Michael Blackwood Productions, 1988, np (quote from film).
7. Frampton, Kenneth, et al. *Tadao Ando*. Museum of Modern Art, 1991, p. 76.
8. Drew, Philip. *Tadao Ando Church on the Water, Church of the Light: Tadao Ando*. Phaidon Press, 1996, p. 23.
9. Dal, Co Francesco, and Tadao Ando. *Tadao Ando: Complete Works*. Phaidon Press, 2000, p. 455.

22 Lifting Elements
1. "Maison à Bordeaux." *OMA*, 1994–98, https://oma.eu/projects/maison-a-bordeaux, np.
2. "Maison à Bordeaux." *OMA*, 1994–98, https://oma.eu/projects/maison-a-bordeaux, np.
3. "Maison à Bordeaux." *OMA*, 1994–98, https://oma.eu/projects/maison-a-bordeaux, np.
4. Davies, Colin. "Machine for Living." *Architectural Record*, vol. 87, Dec. 1998, p. 80.
5. Davies, Colin. "Machine for Living." *Architectural Record*, vol. 87, Dec. 1998, p. 79.
6. "Maison à Bordeaux." *OMA*, 1994–98, https://oma.eu/projects/maison-a-bordeaux, np.
7. Haan, Jasper de. "Interview with Rem Koolhaas." *www.jasperdehaanarchitecten.nl/en/jasper-de-haan-architects/writings/interview-with-rem-koolhaas.aspx*, np.
8. "Maison à Bordeaux." *OMA*, 1994–98, https://oma.eu/projects/maison-a-bordeaux, np.

23 Branching Masses
1. Masheck, Joseph, and Steven Holl. "Steven Holl." *BOMB*, vol. 79, 2002, https://bombmagazine.org/articles/steven-holl/, np.
2. McCarter, Robert. *Steven Holl*. Phaidon Press, 2015, p. 328.
3. "Y House." *Steven Holl Architects*, 1999, www.stevenholl.com/projects/y-house, np.
4. "Y House." *Steven Holl Architects*, 1999, www.stevenholl.com/projects/y-house, np.
5. Fisher, Thomas. "Conversation with Steven Holl." *Architectural Research Quarterly*, vol. 6, no. 2, 2002, pp. 121–129, doi:10.1017/s1359135502001598, p. 124.
6. Holl, Steven. *House: Black Swan Theory*. Princeton Architectural Press, 2007, p. 75.
7. Third quote ("a sectional flip. . ."): Pg140, Riley, Terence. *The Un-Private House*. Museum of Modern Art, 1999.
8. Holl, Steven. *House: Black Swan Theory*. Princeton Architectural Press, 2007, p. 75.
9. Holl, Steven. *Intertwining*. Princeton Architectural Press, 1996, p. 11.
10. Peters, Michael Brady. "Constructing the Experience of Movement." Submitted in Partial Fulfillment of the Requirements for the Degree of Master of Architecture, Dalhousie University, July 2001, p. 16.
11. Masheck, Joseph, and Steven Holl. "Steven Holl." *BOMB*, vol. 79, 2002, https://bombmagazine.org/articles/steven-holl/, np.

24 Nesting Rectangles
1. Moore, Rowan. "Interview: Sou Fujimoto and Building with Nature." *The Guardian*, 26 May 2013, www.theguardian.com/artanddesign/2013/may/25/sou-fujimoto-serpentine-pavilion-interview, np.
2. "House N / Sou Fujimoto Architects." *ArchDaily*, 14 Sept. 2011, www.archdaily.com/7484/house-n-sou-fujimoto, np.
3. Fujimoto, Sou. Lecture, "Between Nature and Architecture." The Architectural League, 15 Apr. 2014, New York, NY, www.youtube.com/watch?v=YPeZ4l1tdjs.
4. Fujimoto, Sou. Lecture, "Between Nature and Architecture." The Architectural League, 15 Apr. 2014, New York, NY, www.youtube.com/watch?v=YPeZ4l1tdjs.
5. Fujimoto, Sou. Lecture, "Between Nature and Architecture." The Architectural League, 15 Apr. 2014, New York, NY, www.youtube.com/watch?v=YPeZ4l1tdjs.
6. "House N / Sou Fujimoto Architects." *ArchDaily*, 14 Sept. 2011, www.archdaily.com/7484/house-n-sou-fujimoto, np.
7. "House N / Sou Fujimoto Architects." *ArchDaily*, 14 Sept. 2011, www.archdaily.com/7484/house-n-sou-fujimoto, np.
8. "House N / Sou Fujimoto Architects." *ArchDaily*, 14 Sept. 2011, www.archdaily.com/7484/house-n-sou-fujimoto, np.
9. "Office Talk with Sou Fujimoto." *a+u Architecture and Urbanism Magazine*, au-magazine.com/interviews/four-questions-to-sou-fujimoto/, np.

25 Stacking Shapes
1. Tokyo Apartment. *Sou Fujimoto: 2003/2010*. Madrid: El Croquis Editorial, 2012, p. 150.
2. Hagenberg, Roland. "Rethinking Urban Space." *Audi Magazine*, http://audi-magazine.otterbach.de/magazine/5/lifestyle/319-rethinking-urban-space, np.
3. Fujimoto, Sou. Lecture, "Between Nature and Architecture." The Architectural League, 15 Apr. 2014, New York, NY, www.youtube.com/watch?v=YPeZ4l1tdjs.
4. Fujimoto, Sou. Lecture, "Between Nature and Architecture." The Architectural League, 15 Apr. 2014, New York, NY, www.youtube.com/watch?v=YPeZ4l1tdjs.
5. Worrall, Julian. "Sou Fujimoto's Tokyo Apartment." *Icon Magazine*, 14 July 2010, www.iconeye.com/architecture/features/item/4476-sou-fujimoto-s-tokyo-apartment, np.
6. Tokyo Apartment. *Sou Fujimoto: 2003/2010*. Madrid: El Croquis Editorial, 2012, p. 150.
7. Hagenberg, Roland. "Rethinking Urban Space." *Audi Magazine*, http://audi-magazine.otterbach.de/magazine/5/lifestyle/319-rethinking-urban-space, np.

BIBLIOGRAPHY

Abbe, Mary. "Frank Gehry's Winton Guest House to Be Auctioned May 19 in Chicago." *Star Tribune*, 2 Mar. 2015, www.startribune.com/variety/Artcetera/.

Aguar, Charles E., and Berdeana Aguar. *Wrightscapes: Frank Lloyd Wrights Landscape Designs*. VGM Career Books, 2002.

Alford, John. "Creativity and Intelligibility in Le Corbusier's Chapel at Ronchamp." *The Journal of Aesthetics and Art Criticism*, vol. 16, no. 3, Mar. 1958, pp. 293–305.

Alter, Kevin. "Looking Forward." *The AIA Journal*, vol. 88, Oct. 1999, p. 75.

Ando, Tadao. *Tadao Ando: 1983–1993*. Madrid: El Croquis Editorial, 1994.

Ando, Tadao. *Tadao Ando: Conversations with Students*. Translated by Matthew Hunter, Princeton Architectural Press, 2013.

Andreoli, Elisabetta, and Adrian Forty. *Brazil's Modern Architecture*. Phaidon, 2004.

Arsitadulako. "Frank Gehry (Applause and Effect)." *Frank Gehry (Applause and Effect)*, 1 Jan. 1970, arsitadulako.blogspot.com/2007/05/frank-gehry-applause-and-effect.html.

Ascher, Barbara Elisabeth. "The Bauhaus: Case Study Experiments in Education." *Wiley Online Library*, John Wiley & Sons, Ltd, 9 Mar. 2015, www.onlinelibrary.wiley.com/doi/abs/10.1002/ad.1873.

Aynsley, J. "Bauhaus Houses and the Design Canon: 1923-2019." *From De Stijl to Dutch design: canonising design 2.0*, Amsterdam: Stichting Designgeschiedenis Nederland, 2017, pp. 25–33.

Baek, Jin. "Shintai and the Empty Cross." *Architectural Theory Review*, vol. 14, pp. 55–70, doi:10.1080/13264820902740781.

Baltanas, Jose. *Walking Through Le Corbusier: A Tour of His Masterworks*. Thames & Hudson, 2005.

Benton, Tim. *The Villas of Le Corbusier and Pierre Jeanneret, 1920–1930*. Birkhauser Architecture, 2007.

Bevan, Robert. "In the Pursuit of Pleasure: The Not So Fleeting Life of the Pavilion and Its Ilk." *Architectural Design*, vol. 85, no. 3, 2015, pp. 16–25, doi:10.1002/ad.1896.

Bierig, Aleksander. "Modest Monument Revived." *Architectural Record*, vol. 198, no. 9, pp. 34–34.

Blake, Peter. *The Master Builders*. W. W. Norton & Company, 1960.

Booher, Pierson William, "Louis I. Kahn's Fisher House: A Case Study on the Architectural Detail and Design Intent." Theses (Historic Preservation), 132, 2009, repository.upenn.edu/hp_theses/132/.

Brooks, Bradley C., and Maxwell Lincoln. Anderson. *Miller House and Garden*. Assouline Publishing, 2011.

Brownlee, David Bruce., and David Gilson De Long. *Louis I. Kahn*. Rizzoli, 2005.

Brunner, Matthias. "Richard Neutra's Ambiguous Relationship to Luxury." *Arts*, vol. 7, no. 75, 2008, 10.3390/arts7040075.

Bussel, Amy. "Perspectives: An Architect for Better Living." *Progressive Architecture*, May 1993.

Carder, James N. "Critical Appraisal of the Philip Johnson Pavilion." *Dumbarton Oaks*, www.doaks.org/resources/philip johnson/critical-appraisal-of-the-philip-johnson-pavilion.

Carder, James N. "Last Concerns: Installation of the Collection, Landscaping, and 'the Acoustical Problem.'" *Dumbarton Oaks*, www.doaks.org/resources/philip-johnson/last-concerns-installation-of-the-collection-landscaping-and-201cthe acoustical-problem201d.

"The City as Built Forest." *Stylepark*, www.stylepark.com/en/news/the-city-as-built-forest.

Clouette, Bruce, and Hoang Tinh. "Philip Johnson's Glass House." National Historic Landmark Nomination Form. Washington, DC: U.S. Department of the Interior, National Park Service, 1996.

Colomina, Beatriz, and Bianca Lleo. "A Machine Was Its Heart." *Assemblage, No.37*, The MIT Press, 1 Dec. 1998, www.jstor.org/stable/3171354.

Corcuff, Marie-Pascale. "Modularity and Proportions in Architecture and Their Relevance to a Generative Approach to Architectural Design." *Architecture, Systems Research and Computational Sciences*, 2012, pp. 53–73, doi:10.1007/978-3-0348-0393-9_6.

Craven, Jackie. "Maison à Bordeaux, Koolhaus in High-Tech Gear." *ThoughtCo*, 17 Mar. 2019, www.thoughtco.com/maison-a-bordeaux-rem-koolhaas-178058.

Crippa, Maria Antonietta, and Françoise Caussé. *Le Corbusier: The Chapel of Notre Dame Du Haut at Ronchamp*. Royal Academy of Arts, 2015.

Cromley, Elizabeth Collins. "Frank Lloyd Wright in the Kitchen." *Buildings & Landscapes: Journal of the Vernacular Architecture Forum*, vol. 19 no. 1, 2012, p.18–42. Project MUSE, doi:10.1353/bdl.2012.0010.

Curtis, Penelope. "The Modern Eye-Catcher: Mies Van Der Rohe and Sculpture." *Architectural Research Quarterly*, vol. 7, no. 3–4, 2003, pp. 361–370, doi:10.1017/s135913550300229x.

Dal, Co Francesco, and Tadao Ando. *Tadao Ando: Complete Works*. Phaidon Press, 2000.

Bibliography

Darling, Michael, et.al. *The Architecture of R. M. Schindler*. The Museum of Contemporary Art, Harry N. Abrams, 2001.

Davies, Colin. *Key Houses of the Twentieth Century: Plans, Sections and Elevations*. W.W. Norton & Company, 2006.

Davies, Colin. "Machine for Living." *Architectural Record*, vol. 87, Dec. 1998.

Dawes, Michael J., and Michael J. Ostwald. "Testing the 'Wright Space': Using Isovists to Analyse Prospect-Refuge Characteristics in Usonian Architecture." *The Journal of Architecture*, vol. 19, no. 5, Mar. 2014, pp. 645–666, doi:10.1080/13602365.2014.965722.

Deitz, Paula. "Louis Kahn's Trenton Bath House in New Jersey Is Fondly Remembered." *Architectural Record*, vol. 195, no. 6, June 2007, pp. 63–64.

Dodds, George. (2002). "Richard Neutra's Venetian lecture." *Architectural Research Quarterly*, vol. 6, pp. 257–267, doi:10.1017/S1359135503001751.

Drew, Philip. *Tadao Ando Church on the Water, Church of the Light: Tadao Ando*. Phaidon Press, 1996.

Drexler, Arthur, et al. *The Architecture of Richard Neutra: from International Style to California Modern*. Museum of Modern Art, 1984.

Dunham, Donald. *Utopian Studies*, 1 Apr. 2014, www.jstor.org/stable/10.5325/utopianstudies.25.1.0150.

Dynes, Wayne R. "Medievalism and Le Corbusier." *The University of Chicago Press on Behalf of the International Center of Medieval Art*, vol. 45, 2006, pp. 89–94.

Ellis, Charlotte. "Koolhaas in Bordeaux." *The Architectural Review*, May 1998, p. 22.

Fisher, Thomas. "Conversation with Steven Holl." *Architectural Research Quarterly*, vol. 6, no. 2, 2002, pp. 121–129, doi:10.1017/s1359135502001598.

Frampton, Kenneth, et al. *Tadao Ando*. Museum of Modern Art, 1991.

Freiman, Ziva. "Back to Neutra." *Progressive Architecture*, vol. 76, Nov. 1995, p. 72.

Fujimoto, Sou. Lecture, "Between Nature and Architecture." The Architectural League, 15 Apr. 2014, New York, NY, www.youtube.com/watch?v=YPeZ4l1tdjs.

Futagawa, Yukio. *Steven Holl: Stretto House, Dallas, Texas, U.S.A.,1989–92: "Y" House Catskill Mountains, New York, U.S.A., 1997–99*. Tokyo A.D.A. Edita, 2010.

Gebhard, David. *Schindler*. William Stout Publishers, 1997.

Giesecke, Annette, and Naomi Jacobs. *The Good Gardener? Nature, Humanity and the Garden*. Artifice Books on Architecture, 2015.

Goldberger, Paul. "Frank Gehry's First Playground of the Imagination." *The Toronto Star*, 28 Sept. 2015, www.thestar.com/news/insight/2015/09/28/frank-gehrys-first-playground-of-the-imagination.html.

Grabow, Stephen. "The Role of Memory in the Perception of Architecture: Reading the Trenton Bath House from Auschwitz." *Structurist*, no. 37/38, 1997, pp. 41–45.

Greenhalgh, Paul, editor. *Modernism in Design*. Reaktion Books, 1990.

Gregory, Rob. "Sou Fujimoto Architects." *The Architectural Review*, vol. 255, Apr. 2009, p. 48.

Gropius, Walter, et al. "'The Bauhaus' and 'How Do We Build Decent, Beautiful, and Inexpensive Housing?'" *West 86th: A Journal of Decorative Arts, Design History, and Material Culture*, vol. 23, no. 1, 2016, pp. 102–124, doi:10.1086/688202.

Haan, Jasper de. "Interview with Rem Koolhaas." www.jasperdehaanarchitecten.nl/en/jasper-de-haan-architects/writings/interview-with-rem-koolhaas.aspx.

Hagenberg, Roland. "Rethinking Urban Space." *Audi Magazine*, http://audi-magazine.otterbach.de/magazine/5/lifestyle/319-rethinking-urban-space.

Harris, Randy. "Here's Looking Through You, Kid." *The New York Times*, www.nytimes.com/slideshow/2013/12/12/garden/20131212-GLASSHOUSE/s/20131212-GLASSHOUSEslide-8YCA.html.

Hay, David. "A Modernist Masterpiece in the Desert Is Reborn." *Architectural Record*, vol. 187, no. 9, Sept. 1999, pp. 92–98.

Heilmeyer, Florian. "Gropius' Ghosts Bauhaus Reinterpreted Not Reconstructed in Dessau." *Uncube Magazine*, 22 May 2014, www.uncubemagazine.com/blog/13113621.

Hien, Pham Thanh. *Abstraction and Transcendence: Nature, Shintai, and Geometry in the Architecture of Tadao Ando*. Dissertation.Com, 1998.

Hildner, Claudia. *Future Living: Collective Housing in Japan*, Birkhauser, 2013.

Hill, John. "Iconic Architecture: 10 Homes You Must See." *Houzz*, 15 Dec. 2017, www.houzz.in/magazine/iconic-architecture-10-homes-you-must-see-stsetivw-vs~98361167.

Hines, Thomas S., and Richard Joseph Neutra. *Richard Neutra and the Search for Modern Architecture*. University of California Press, 1982.

Hiroshi, Watanabe. "Ando Tadao, an Architect Who Disdains Comfort." *Japan Quarterly*, vol. 40, Oct. 1993, p. 426.

Historic American Buildings Survey, Creator, et al. *Lovell Beach House, West Ocean Front, Newport Beach, Orange County, CA*. Retrieved from the Library of Congress. www.loc.gov/item/ca0448/.

Hitchcock, Henry Russell, and David Gebhard. *Schindler*. William Stout Publisher, 1997.

Hoffmann, Donald. *Frank Lloyd Wright's Fallingwater: The House and Its History*. Dover Publications, 1978.

Holl, Steven. *House: Black Swan Theory*. Princeton Architectural Press, 2007.

Holl, Steven. *Intertwining*. Princeton Architectural Press, 1996.

Hosey, Lance. "The Ship of Theseus: Identity and the Barcelona Pavilion(s)." *Journal of Architectural Education (1984)*, vol. 72, no. 2, 2018, pp. 230–247, doi:10.1080/10464883.2018.1496731.

"House N / Sou Fujimoto Architects." *ArchDaily*, 14 Sept. 2011, www.archdaily.com/7484/house-n-sou-fujimoto.

Huxtable, Ada Louis. "Frank Gehry: 1989 Laureate Essay." The Pritzker Architecture Prize, https://www.pritzkerprize.com/sites/default/files/inline-files/1989_essay.pdf.

Jacobs, Herbert, and Katherine Jacobs. *Building with Frank Lloyd Wright: An Illustrated Memoir*. Southern Illinois University Press, 1996.

James-Chakraborty, Kathleen. *Architecture Since 1400*. University of Minnesota Press, 2014.

Jetsonen, Jari, and Sirkkaliisa Jetsonen. *Saarinen Houses*. Princeton Architectural Press, 2014.

Jodidio, Philip. *Tadao Ando: Houses*. Rizzoli, 2013.

Johnson, Philip Cortelyou. *The Glass House*. Skira Rizzoli, 2012.

Johnson, Philip. *Deconstructivist Architecture*. The Museum of Modern Art, 1988.

Kahn, Louis. "The Room, the Street, and Human Agreement." *Louis Kahn: Essential Texts*, edited by Robert Twombly, W. W. Norton & Co., 2003.

Kauffmann, Jr., Edgar. *Fallingwater: A Frank Lloyd Wright Country House*. Cross River Press, Ltd., 1986.

Keller, Hadley. "AD Remembers the Extraordinary Word of Eliel and Eero Saarinen." *Architectural Digest*, 31 July 2014, www.architecturaldigest.com/story/saarinen-father-and-son.

Kim, Ransoo. *The Art of Building (Baukunst) of Mies Van Der Rohe*. PhD dissertation, Georgia Institute of Technology, August 2006, hdl.handle.net/1853/11465.

Kim, Ransoo. "The Tectonically Defining Space of Mies Van Der Rohe." *Architectural Research Quarterly*, vol. 13, no. 3–4, 2009, pp. 251–260, doi:10.1017/s1359135500000102.

Krohn, Carsten, and Mies van der Rohe. *Mies van der Rohe: The Built Work*. Birkhauser, 2014.

Kroll, Andrew. "AD Classics: Kaufmann House / Richard Neutra." *ArchDaily*, 16 Jan. 2011, www.archdaily.com/104112/adclassics-kaufmann-house-richard-neutra.

Krstić, Hristina, et al. "Interior-Exterior Connection in Architectural Design Based on the Incorporation of Spatial in between Layers. Study of Four Architectural Projects." *Spatium*, no. 36, 2016, pp. 84–91, doi:10.2298/spat1636084k.

Kucker, Patricia. "Framework: Construction and Space in the Architecture of Frank Lloyd Wright and Rudolf Schindler." *The Journal of Architecture*, vol. 7, no. 2, 2002, pp. 171–190, doi:10.1080/13602360210145097.

Le Corbusier (Charles-Edouard Jeanneret). *Vers Une Architecture (Towards a New Architecture)*. Dover Publications, 2013(1923).

Ledgerwood, Angela, and Ross Miller. "New Again: Frank Gehry." *Interview Magazine*, 19 Sept. 2012, //www.interviewmagazine.com/art/new-again-frank-gehry.

Lemonier, Aurélien, et al. *Frank Gehry*. Prestel, 2015.

Levrat, Frédéric. *ANY: Architecture New York*, Anyone Corporation, 1 May 1994, www.jstor.org/stable/41845656.

Lovine, Julie V. "The Miller House, Reborn." *The Wall Street Journal*, Dow Jones & Company, 28 May 2011, www.wsj.com/articles/SB10001424052702304520804576345351194866790.

MacCormac, Richard. "'A Sense of the Marvelous—Frank Lloyd Wright's Fallingwater." *RSA Journal*, vol. 143, Oct. 1995, pp. 40–51.

Maddex, Diane. *Wright-Sized Houses: Frank Lloyd Wright's Solutions for Making Small Houses Feel Big*. Harry N. Abrams, 2003.

"Maestro of Modernism: Interview with Philip C. Johnson." *Academy of Achievement*, 1992, achievement.org/achiever/philip-johnson/#interview.

"Maison à Bordeaux." *OMA*, 1994–98, https://oma.eu/projects/maison-a-bordeaux.

Marcus, George H., and William Whitaker. *The Houses of Louis Kahn*. Yale University Press, 2013.

Masheck, Joseph, and Steven Holl. "Steven Holl." *BOMB*, vol. 79, 2002, https://bombmagazine.org/articles/steven-holl/.

Mason, Christopher. "Behind the Glass Wall." *The New York Times*, 7 June 2007, www.nytimes.com/2007/06/07/garden/07glass.html?ref=philip_johnson.

"Masters' Houses by Walter Gropius (1925–26)." *Bauhaus | Dessau*, www.bauhaus-dessau.de/en/architecture/bauhaus-buildings-in-dessau/masters-houses.html.

McAvoy, Christy, et al. "Eames House." National Historic Landmark Nomination Form. Washington, DC: U.S. Department of the Interior, National Park Service, May 2005.

McCarter, Robert, and Juhani Pallasmaa. *Understanding Architecture*. Phaidon Press, 2012.

McCarter, Robert. *Fallingwater: Frank Lloyd Wright*. Phaidon Press, 2002.

McCarter, Robert. *Louis I. Khan*. Phaidon Press, 2005.

McCarter, Robert. *Steven Holl*. Phaidon Press, 2015.

McCoy, Esther. *Five California Architects*. Hennessey + Ingalls, 2004.

McGrew, Patrick. "The Hidden History of the Kaufmann House." *KCET*, 31 Aug. 2017, www.kcet.org/shows/artbound/the-hidden-history-of-the-kaufmann-house.

Melendo, Jose Manuel Almodovar, et al. "Similarities Between R.M. Schindler House and Descriptions of Traditional Japanese Architecture." *Journal of Asian Architecture and Building Engineering*, vol. 13, no. 1, 2014, pp. 41–48, doi:10.3130/jaabe.13.41.

Melhuish, Clare. *Modern House 2*. Phaidon Press, 2008.

Mertins, Detlef. *Mies*. Phaidon Press Limited, 2014.

Bibliography

"Mies Van Der Rohe's 'Barcelona Pavilion' to Be Reconstructed." *Museum of Modern Art*, vol. 27, 1983, pp. 2–4.

Migayrou, Frederic, and Aurelien Lemonier. *Frank Gehry*. Prestel Verlag, 2015.

Mik, E. "Interview: Steven Holl." *ArchIdea*, edition 42, 2010, pp. 4–11, https://view.publitas.com/forboflooring-com/archidea-42/page/1.

"Miller Garden." *The Landscape Architecture Legacy of Dan Kiley | The Cultural Landscape Foundation*, tclf.org/sites/default/files/microsites/kiley-legacy/MillerGarden.html.

Miller, Irwin. "Modern Medicis." *Architectural Record*, vol. 199, no. 8, 16 Aug. 2011.

Moore, Rowan. "Interview: Sou Fujimoto and Building with Nature." *The Guardian*, 26 May 2013, www.theguardian.com/artanddesign/2013/may/25/sou-fujimoto-serpentine-pavilion-interview.

Moulis, Antony. "Forms and Techniques: Le Corbusier, the Spiral Plan and Diagram Architecture." *Architectural Research Quarterly*, vol. 14, no. 4, 2010, pp. 317–326, doi:10.1017/S135913551100011X.

Nancrede, Sally Falk. "After 1st Year of Tours, Miller House Gets Inside-Outside Improvements." *Indianapolis Star*, 27 Oct. 2012.

The National Trust for Historic Preservation. *The Glass House: Visitors Guide*, 2011.

"New Again: Frank Gehry." *Interview Magazine*, 19 Sept. 2012, www.interviewmagazine.com/art/new-again-frank-gehry.

Neutra, Dion. "The View from Inside: An Overview of the Neutra Practice." *Richard and Dion Neutra Architecture*, vol. 1, Oct. 2000, neutra.org/the-view-from-inside-an-overview-of-the-neutra-practice/.

Newman, Morris. "Revisiting the Kaufmann House – The delicate art of marketing Palm Springs' most famous house." *Palm Springs Life*, 29 Apr. 2009, www.palmspringslife.com/Revisiting-the-Kaufmann-House/.

Niedenthal, Simon. "'Glamourized Houses': Neutra, Photography, and the Kaufmann House." *Journal of Architectural Education (1984–)*, vol. 47, no. 2, 1993, pp. 101–112, doi:10.2307/1425171.

Niemeyer, Oscar. *The Curves of Time: The Memoirs of Oscar Niemeyer*. Phaidon Press, 2000.

Ochsner, Jeffrey Karl. "The Experience of Prospect and Refuge: Frank Lloyd Wright's Houses as Holding Environments." *American Imago*, Johns Hopkins University Press, 25 July 2018, doi.org/10.1353/aim.2018.0010.

"Office Talk with Sou Fujimoto." *a+u Architecture and Urbanism Magazine*, au-magazine.com/interviews/four-questions-to-sou-fujimoto/.

Oldham, Todd, et al. *Alexander Girard*. AMMO, 2015.

O'Neil, Dan. "'To Schindler, the Act of Dwelling Is One of the Most Basic and Continuing Human Activities'." *Architectural Review*, 7 July, 2016, www.architectural-review.com/essays/to-schindler-the-act-of-dwelling-is-one-of-the-most-basic-and-continuing-human-activities/10008410.article.

Padua, Otilia Portillo. "Domestic Bliss." *The Architects' Journal*, vol. 228, 16 Oct. 2008, p. 41.

Park, Jin-Ho. "Rudolph M. Schindler—Proportion, Scale and the 'Row.'" *Nexus Network Journal*, vol. 5, no. 2, 2003, pp. 60–72, doi:10.1007/s00004-003-0017-9.

Peponis, John, and Tahar Bellal. "Fallingwater: The Interplay between Space and Shape." *Environment and Planning B: Planning and Design*, vol. 37, no. 6, 2010, pp. 982–1001, doi:10.1068/b36052.

Pérez-Gómez A, Anne Cormier, and Annie Pedret. "Change Over Time: The J. Irwin Miller House in the Photography of Balthazar Korab." *Where Do You Stand: 99th Acsa Annual Meeting, March 3–6, 2011, Montre?al, Canada*. Washington, DC: ACSA Press, 2011.

Peters, Michael Brady. "Constructing the Experience of Movement." Submitted in Partial Fulfillment of the Requirements for the Degree of Master of Architecture, Dalhousie University, July 2001.

Philippou, Styliane. "The Dancing Curves of Oscar Niemeyer's House at Canoa." *Revue - Articles - Textes Originale - Werk, Bauen + Wohnen*, www.wbw.ch/fr/revue/articles/textesoriginalw/2013-3-the-dancing-curves-of-oscar-niemeyershouse-at-canoa.html.

Pool, Bob. "Modernist Stahl Home Caps Historic Preservation Tour." *Los Angeles Times*, 5 Nov. 2000.

Purves, Alexander. "This Goodly Frame, the Earth." *Perspecta*, vol. 25, 1989, p. 178, doi:10.2307/1567143.

Ramos, Ana Lopes. "Walter Gropius in Dessau. Part II, The Masters' Houses." John Desmond Ltd., 3 Aug. 2017, www.johndesmond.com/blog/design/Walter-Gropius-dessau-partii-the-masters-houses/.

Rauterberg, Hanno. *Talking Architecture: Interviews with Architects*. Prestel, 2012.

Riley, Terence, and Peter Reed. *Frank Lloyd Wright, Architect: The Museum of Modern Art, New York*. The Museum of Modern Art, 1994.

Riley, Terence. *The Un-Private House*. Museum of Modern Art, 1999.

Roman, Antonio. *Eero Saarinen: An Architecture of Multiplicity*. Princeton Architectural Press, 2006.

Romero, Melissa. "What Lou Taught Me: Growing Up in Kahn's Fisher House." *Curbed Philadelphia*, updated 15 April 2019, philly.curbed.com/2018/2/20/16886274/louis-kahn-fisher-house-first-person-essay.

Bibliography

Rykwert, Joseph, and Roberto Schezen. *Louis Kahn.* Harry N. Abrams, 2001.

Saieh, Nico. "House N / Sou Fujimoto Architects." *ArchDaily,* ArchDaily, 14 Sept. 2011, www.archdaily.com/7484/house-n-sou-fujimoto.

Samuel, F. The Representation of Mary in the Architecture of Le Corbusier's Chapel at Ronchamp, *Church History,* 68(2), 1999, pp. 398-416. doi: 10.2307/3170863.

Samuel, Flora, and Peter Blundell Jones. "The Making of Architectural Promenade: Villa Savoye and Schminke House." *Architectural Research Quarterly,* vol. 16, no. 2, 2012, pp. 108–124, doi:10.1017/S1359135512000437.

Sarnitz, August E. "Proportion and Beauty—The Lovell Beach House by Rudolph Michael Schindler, Newport Beach, 1922–1926." *Journal of the Society of Architectural Historians,* vol. 45, no. 4, Dec. 1986, pp. 374–388.

Schwarb, Amy Wimmer. "Modern Family: The Miller Home." *Indianapolis Monthly,* 1 May 2011, www.indianapolismonthly.com/arts-and-culture/modern-family-the-miller-home.

Scully, Vincent, cast member, as himself. *My Architect: A Son's Journey.* Directed by Nathaniel Kahn, New Yorker Films, 2003.

Segawa, Hugo. "Oscar Niemeyer: A Misbehaved Pupil of Rationalism." *The Journal of Architecture,* vol. 2, no. 4, 1997, pp. 291–312, doi:10.1080/136023697374333.

Sergeant, John. "Frank Lloyd Wright's Usonian Houses." *Frank Lloyd Wright's Usonian Houses,* Billboard, pp. 16–19.

Siebenbrodt, Michael, and Klaus Weber. *Bauhaus: A Conceptual Model.* Hatje Cantz, 2009.

Sharr, Adam, editor. "Sculpture." *Architectural Research Quarterly,* vol. 7, 2003.

Smith, Kathryn. *Schindler House.* Harry N. Adams, 2001.

Solomon, Susan. *Louis I. Kahn's Trenton Jewish Community Center.* Princeton Architectural Press, 2000.

"Sou Fujimoto Architects: Tokyo Apartment." *DOMUS,* www.domusweb.it/en/architecture/2010/10/12/sou-fujimoto-architects-tokyo-apartment.html.

"Sou Fujimoto Interview." *Designboom,* 16 Apr. 2014, www.designboom.com/architecture/designboom-interview-soufujimoto/.

Speaks, Michael. "Rem Koolhaas and OMA Lead the Dutch onto New Turf." *Architectural Record,* vol. 188, no. 7, July 2000, pp. 92–99.

Spikol, Liz. "What Lou Taught Me: Growing Up in Kahn's Fisher House." *Curbed Philly,* 17 July 2012, philly.curbed.com/2012/7/17/10351070/what-lou-taught-me-growing-up-in-kahns-fisher-house.

Steele, James, and David Jenkins. *Pierre Koenig.* Phaidon Press, 1998.

Tadao Ando. Directed by Michael Blackwood, Michael Blackwood Productions, 1988.

Takeyama, Kiyoshi. "Tadao Ando: Heir to a Tradition." *Perspecta,* 1 Jan. 1983, www.jstor.org/stable/1567072.

Tamulevich, Susan. *Dumbarton Oaks: Garden Into Art.* Montacelli Press, 2001.

Thöner Wolfgang. *The Bauhaus Life: Life and Work in the Masters' Houses Estate in Dessau.* Seemann, 2006.

Thornburg, Barbara. "CASE STUDY HOUSE NO. 22; AN L.A. DREAM; To the Stahl family, it was just home." *Los Angeles Times,* 27 June 2009.

Tippey, Brett. "Richard Neutra's Search for the Southland: California, Latin America and Spain." *Architectural History,* vol. 59, 2016, pp. 311–352, doi:10.1017/arh.2016.10.

Tokyo Apartments. Sou Fujimoto: 2003/2010. Madrid: El Croquis Editorial, 2012.

Treib, Marc. "Simplicity and Belief." *Architectural Research Quarterly,* vol. 11, no. 3–4, 2007, pp. 223–236, doi:10.1017/s1359135500000725.

Underwood, David Kendrick. *Oscar Niemeyer and Brazilian Free-form Modernism.* George Braziller Inc., 1994.

Unwin, Simon. *Twenty Buildings Every Architect Should Understand.* Routledge, 2010.

Vallen, Michael Earl. *Housing . . . the Hillside, Los Angeles.* 1998, Virginia Polytechnic Institute, M Arch Thesis, https://vtechworks.lib.vt.edu/handle/10919/36539.

Vandenberg, Maritz. *Farnsworth House: Ludwig Mies Van Der Rohe.* Phaidon Press, 2010.

Vanstiphout, Wouter. "Rockbottom: Villa by OMA." *Harvard Design Magazine,* www.harvarddesignmagazine.org/issues/5/rockbottom-villa-by-oma.

Viladas, Pilar. "Outdoor Sculpture." *Progressive Architecture,* 16 Dec. 1987.

Vlasopoulos, Michail. "Pre-Stressed Body." *Abitare,* 14 Feb. 2012, www.abitare.it/en/research/2012/02/14/pre-stressed-body-revisiting-maison-a-bordeaux/?refresh_ce-cp.

Walker, David. "Plasticity at Ronchamp: The Interrelationship of Form and Light and Its Plastic Manifestation." *Architectural Research Quarterly,* vol. 16, no. 4, 2012, pp. 349–361, doi:10.1017/s1359135513000237.

"Walker Art Center." *Winton Guest House,* walkerart.org/minnesotabydesign/objects/winton-guest-house.

Watson, Caitlin Turski. "Flesh and Form: Light and the Sacred at Notre-Dame-Du-Haus." *Faith & Form,* https://faithandform.com/feature/flesh-and-form/.

Weber, Anne E. "Authenticity and an Original Designer at Louis Kahn's Trenton Bath House." *Australia ICOMOS,* www.aicomos.com/wp content/uploads/2009_UnlovedModern_Weber_Anne_Louis-Kahns-Trenton-Bath-House_Paper.pdf.

Bibliography

Weber, Nicholas Fox. "HISTORIC ARCHITECTURE: THE BAUHAUS - Revisiting Walter Gropius's Seminal Buildings in Dessau, Germany: Architectural Digest: DECEMBER 1991." *Architectural Digest: The Complete Archive*, Architectural Digest, 1 Dec. 1991, archive.architecturaldigest.com/article/1991/12/historic-architecture-the-bauhaus—-revisiting-walter-gropiuss-seminal-buildings-in-dessau-germany.

Weisberg, Robert W. "Frank Lloyd Wright's Fallingwater: A Case Study in Inside-the-Box Creativity." *Creativity Research Journal*, vol. 23, no. 4, 2011, pp. 296–312, doi:10.1080/10400419.2011.621814.

Weston, Richard, and Richard Weston. *Key Buildings of the 20th Century: Plans, Sections and Elevations*. W.W. Norton & Co., 2010.

Willette, Jeanne. "Walter Gropius: The Masters' Houses of the Bauhaus." *Art History Unstuffed*, 31 Mar. 2017, arthistoryunstuffed.com/walter-gropius-masters-houses-bauhaus/.

"Winton Guest House." *SAH ARCHIPEDIA*, 17 June 2019, sah-archipedia.org/buildings/MN-01-147-0001.

Wong, Yoke-Sum. "Edith Doesn't Live Here Anymore: A Story of Farnsworth House." In D. Gafijczuk and D. Sayer (eds.), *The Inhabited Ruins of Central Europe*. Palgrave Macmillan, 2013, doi:10.1057/9781137305862_7.

Worrall, Julian. "Sou Fujimoto's Tokyo Apartment." *Icon Magazine*, 14 July 2010, www.iconeye.com/architecture/features/item/4476-sou-fujimoto-s-tokyo-apartment.

Wright, Frank Lloyd. *An Autobiography*. Faber & Faber Limited, 1977.

Wright, Frank Lloyd. "Usonian House: An Autobiography." *PBS*, Public Broadcasting Service, www.pbs.org/flw/buildings/usonia/usonia_interior.html.

Wyatt, Edward. "A Landmark Modernist House Heads to Auction." *The New York Times*, The New York Times, 31 Oct. 2007, www.nytimes.com/2007/10/31/arts/design/31hous.html.

"Y House." *Steven Holl Architects*, 1999, www.stevenholl.com/projects/y-house.

Young, Victoria M. "Frank Gehry: From Architect to Icon." *St. Thomas Newsroom*, 11 July 2014, news.stthomas.edu/frankgehry-from-architect-to-icon/.

Young, Victoria. "The Art of Architecture Frank Gehry's Winton Guest House." *Wright Design Masterworks Auction Catalogue*, 19 May 2015, www.wright20.com/auctions/2015/05/design-masterworks-frank-gehrys-winton-guest-house.

Zalewski, Daniel. "Intelligent Design." *The New Yorker*, 5 Mar. 2005, www.newyorker.com/magazine/2005/03/14/intelligentdesign.

INDEX

Acropolis, 37
Alba (Kolbe), 35
American Institute of Architects, 165
American Modernism, 73
Ando, Tadao
    Church on the Water, 169–70, 172
    Koshino House, 153, 155, 157
Arts & Architecture (magazine), 73, 131

Barcelona International Exposition (1929), 31
Barcelona Pavilion, 30–5
    composition, 35
    floor plans, 31, 32
    Mies van der Rohe, Ludwig, 31
    partitions and walls, 33, 34
    photograph, 30
    site plan, 32
    sliding planes, 35
    travertine floor, 34
Bath House. *See* Trenton Bath House
Bauhaus school
    Gropius, Walter, 19
    Mies van der Rohe, Ludwig, at, 89
    philosophy of, 19
Beijing's Forbidden City, 193
Bill, Max, 97
Bliss, Mildred, 137
Bliss, Robert, 137
branching masses, Y House, 182, 183
Burial of Phocion (Poussin painting), 81, 84

Casa das Canoas, 96–105
    curves and lines of floor plan, 101
    floor plan, 99
    Niemeyer, Oscar, 97, 99, 100
    photograph, 96
    pool, 97, 98, 99, 100
    public and private areas, 102
    side views, 104–5
    undulating forms, 97
    views and access to nature, 103

Case Study House Program, 73, 131
    Case Study House No. 8 (Eames House), 73
    Case Study House No. 9, 73
    Case Study House No. 22 (Stahl House), 131
Catskill Mountains, Y House, 183, 184, 186
Ceschiatti, Alfredo, 100
Chapel of Notre-Dame du Haut at Ronchamp, 106–13
    chapels, 113
    floor plan, 109, 110
    forms and lines defining spaces, 111, 112
    Le Corbusier, 107, 108, 110–13
    light manipulation, 107, 113
    photograph, 106
    side view, 107
    site plan, 108
    Virgin Mary statue, 107, 113
Chace, Clyde, 13, 15, 16
Chace, Marian, 13, 15, 16
Christ the Redeemer statue, 100
Church on the Water, 168–73
    Ando, Tadao, 169–70, 172
    elevation, 173
    engaging procession, 169
    floor plan, 170
    photograph, 168
    pool, 168, 169
    respect for nature, 172
    roof plan, 171
    side view, 169
    staircases, 170
    symmetry, 173
clustered objects, Winton Guest House, 164
color, Chapel of Notre-Dame du Haut at Ronchamp, 107
compressed horizontals, Jacobs House, 50
concept, generating, 11

connecting forms, Miller House, 122–9
Cummins Engine Company, 123
The Curves of Time (Niemeyer), 97

Davis, Richard S., 161
DeStijl paintings, 35
diagrams, hand-drawn, 11
Dumbarton Oaks Museum, 137, 139

Eames, Charles, 73
Eames, Ray, 73, 76
Eames House, 72–9
    Case Study House No. 8, 73
    exterior view, 73, 78
    floor plans, 75
    photograph, 72
    public and private spaces, 74–7, 79
    site plan, 74
    splitting zones, 76
embedding components, Koshino House, 153
Entenza, John, 73, 131
expanding volumes, Fallingwater, 60
extending rectangles, Kaufmann House, 65

Fallingwater, 54–63
    cantilevering terraces, 61
    cascading levels, 60
    expanding volumes, 60
    floor plans, 57–9, 62–3
    photograph, 54
    site plan, 56
    terraces, 62–3
    Wright, Frank Lloyd, 55–7, 60–1, 65
Farnsworth, Edith, 89, 90, 95
Farnsworth House, 88–95
    floor plan, 91
    geometry, 89, 95
    layered planes, 89, 92–4
    Mies van der Rohe, Ludwig, 83, 89–90, 92, 95, 134
    photograph, 88

Index

privacy, 95
river and house, 90, 92
side view, 89
Feininger, Lyonel, 19, 21
Fisher, Dr. and Mrs., 145–6, 150
Fisher, Nina, 146, 150
Fisher House, 144–51
    floor plan, 147
    Kahn, Louis, 145–6, 147, 148, 150
    light and spaces, 149, 150
    living and sleeping spaces, 148
    photograph, 144
    rotating blocks, 145, 151
    side view, 145
    site plan, 146
Fujimoto, Sou
    House N, 189, 190, 192, 193
    Tokyo Apartment, 195, 196, 199, 200, 201

Gehry, Frank, 83
    Winton Guest House, 161, 164–5, 167
German National Pavilion, 31
Ghost House, 83
Girard, Alexander, 123, 124
Glass House, 80–7
    floor plan, 82
    furniture in, 86
    Johnson, Philip, 81, 83, 84
    offsetting, 81, 83
    photograph, 80
    private and public spaces, 85
    side view, 81, 87
    site plan, 81, 83, 86
Gran Plaza de la Fuente Magica, 32
Great Depression, 47
Gropius, Walter
    Bauhaus founder and director, 19
    Masters' Houses, 19, 21

Harvard University, 137
Hesse, Fritz, 19
Holl, Steven, 11, 183, 184
Hollyhock House for Aline Barnsdall, 13
House N, 188–93
    floor plan, 191
    Fujimoto, Sou, 189, 190, 192, 193
    nested rectangles, 189, 192, 193
    photograph, 188
    side view, 189
    site plan, 190

House of Canoas. *See* Casa das Canoas
Huxtable, Ada Louise, 137, 138, 165

Illinois Institute of Technology, 89
Indian Institute of Management, 145
interlocking cubes, Trenton Bath House, 115, 119
International Style, Kaufmann House, 67

Jacobs, Herbert, 47, 50, 52
Jacobs, Katherine, 47, 50
Jacobs House, 46–53
    clerestory windows, 52
    compressed horizontals, 50
    floor plan, 48
    garden in, 53
    horizon and horizontal lines, 49
    photograph, 46
    Wright, Frank Lloyd, 47–53
Johnson, Philip
    Glass House, 81, 83, 84
    Pre-Columbian Pavilion, 137, 138
    Winton Guest House, 161, 165
Judd, Donald, 81

Kahn, Louis
    Fisher House, 145–6, 147, 148, 150
    Trenton Bath House, 115, 117, 119–20
Kandinsky, Wassily, 19
Kaufmann, Edgar, Jr., 60
Kaufmann, Edgar J., 55, 65
Kaufmann, Liliane, 60
Kaufmann House, 64–71
    extending rectangles, 65
    exterior spaces, 71
    floor plans, 66, 67, 71
    Neutra, Richard, 65–7, 71
    perspectives from, 68, 69
    photograph, 64
    private spaces, 70
    site plan, 65, 67
    terrain of, 65
Kiley, Dan, 124
Klee, Paul, 19
Klee-Kandinsky House, 21
Koenig, Pierre, Stahl House, 131, 132, 134, 135
Kolbe, Georg, 35
Koolhaas, Rem, Maison à Bordeaux, 175, 177, 178, 179, 181
Koshino, Junko, 153

Koshino House, 152–9
    Ando, Tadao, 153, 155, 157
    embedding components, 153
    floor plan, 154
    photograph, 152
    public and private zones, 156, 157
    side views, 153, 158, 159
    site plan, 154
    studio and bedroom wing, 155

layered planes, Farnsworth House, 89, 92, 93, 94
Le Corbusier, 183
    Chapel of Notre-Dame du Haut at Ronchamp, 107, 108, 110–13
    Niemeyer, Oscar, and, 97, 100
    Villa Savoye, 37–8, 41–2
lifting elements, Maison à Bordeaux, 174, 175
light manipulation, Chapel of Notre-Dame du Haut at Ronchamp, 107, 113
Los Angeles Times (newspaper), 25
Lovell, Phillip, 25, 28
Lovell Beach House, 24–9
    basic structural rhythm, 28
    floor plans, 26, 29
    photograph, 24
    Schindler, Rudolph, 25–6, 28–9
    shifting space, 25, 27

Maison à Bordeaux, 174–81
    concrete forms, 175, 179, 181
    floor plans, 176, 177
    Koolhaas, Rem, 175, 177, 178, 179, 181
    lifting elements, 174, 175
    photograph, 174
    side view, 175, 180, 181
    site plan, 175
    stairs, 178
manipulating light, Chapel of Notre-Dame du Haut at Ronchamp, 107, 113
Masters' Houses, 18–23
    asymmetric and box-like volumes of, 19
    floor plans, 20, 22
    Gropius, Walter, 19, 21
    manipulating volumes, 21
    photograph, 18
    three dimensional views, 23

matryoshka nesting dolls, 193
Meisterhauser, 19
Mies van der Rohe, Ludwig
    Barcelona Pavilion, 31–5, 81
    Farnsworth House, 83, 89–90, 92, 95, 134
    furniture, 81
Miller, J. Irwin, 123
Miller House, 122–9
    connecting forms, 123
    floor plan, 125
    grid, 128, 129
    landscape plan, 124
    photograph, 122
    private and public spaces, 127
    rectangular forms, 126
    Saarinen, Eero, 123–4, 128
    side view, 123
Modernism, 76
Moholy-Nagy, Laszlo, 19
Morandi, Giorgio, 163, 164
Mosher, Bob, 55
Muche, Georg, 19
Museum of Modern Art, 83

Nadelman, Elie, 84
National Trust for Historic Preservation, 83
nested rectangles, House N, 189, 192, 193
Neutra, Dion, 67
Neutra, Richard, Kaufmann House, 65–7, 71
New York Times Magazine, 161
Niemeyer, Oscar, Casa das Canoas, 97, 99, 100

Oeuvre Complete (Le Corbusier), 38
Office of Metropolitan Architecture, Rem Koolhaas and, 175
offsetting, Glass House, 81, 83
Oldenburg, Clas, 164

Pantheon, 169
papillon, 31
Parthenon, 37
perspectives move, Villa Savoye, 38
pilotis, 37
planes, sliding, 30, 35
Poussin, Nicolas, 84
Pre-Columbian Gallery, 136–43
    columns and arcs of glass, 137, 141, 143

Dumbarton Oaks, 137
    floor plan, 139, 142
    Johnson, 137, 138
    overlapping circles, 137, 140
    photograph, 136
    site plan, 138

Ronchamp (Le Corbusier), 113
rotating blocks, Fisher House, 145, 151
rotating L-shaped, Schindler Chace House, 14, 16

Saarinen, Eero, Miller House, 123–4, 128
Saarinen, Eliel, 124
Salk Institute for Biological Studies, 145
Savoye, Pierre, 37, 39
Schindler, Pauline, studio of, 13, 15, 16
Schindler, Rudolph M., 13, 14
    Lovell Beach House, 25–6, 28–9
    studio of, 13, 15, 16
Schindler Chace House, 12–17
    floor plan, 15
    landscape, 14
    outdoor spaces, 17
    photograph, 12
    rotating L-shaped arrangement, 14, 16
    Schindler, Rudolph, 13–17
    side view, 13
    site plan, 14
Schlemmer, Oskar, 19
Scully, Vincent, 117
Serra, Richard, 11, 164
shifting space, Lovell Beach House, 25
Shulman, Julius, 131
sliding planes, Barcelona Pavilion, 30, 35
stacked shapes, Tokyo Apartment, 195, 199
Stahl, Buck, 131
Stahl, Carlotta, 131
Stahl House, 130–5
    floor plan, 133, 135
    Koenig, Pierre, 131, 132, 134, 135
    lengthened view, 134
    photograph, 130
    private and public spaces, 135
    Shulman, Julius, 131
    site plan, 132, 134
Stella, Frank, 83

terra firma, 60, 131
Tokyo Apartment, 194–201

circulation routes, 197
floor plans, 197
Fujimoto, Sou, 195, 196, 199, 200, 201
organization of, 198, 199
photograph, 194
side views of, 200, 201
site plan, 196
stacked shapes, 195, 199
Towards a New Architecture (Le Corbusier), 37, 107
Trenton Bath House, 114–21
    floor plan, 116, 117
    grid, 119, 120
    interlocking cubes, 115, 119
    Kahn, Louis, 115, 117, 119–20
    layout of central plan, 115
    photograph, 114
    private and public space, 119
    roofs, 117, 118
    side view, 121
    site plan, 116
Trenton Jewish Community Center, 115
Two Circus Women (Nadelman sculpture), 81, 84

Ueda, Shunzo, 195
undulating forms, Casa das Canoas, 97
Usonia, etymology of, 47
Usonian Houses, 47, 48, 50

van Bruggen, Coosje, 164
Vers Une Architecture (*Towards a New Architecture*) (Le Corbusier), 37, 107
Vienna's Academy of Fine Arts, 25
Villa Savoye, 36–45
    architectural promenade, 44
    circulation between levels, 41
    floor plans, 38, 39
    interior and exterior spaces, 42, 43
    Le Corbusier, 37–8, 41–2
    perspectives move, 38
    photograph, 36
    roof garden, 38
    site plan, 37
    viewing experience, 45
    visitor by vehicle, 40, 41
volume manipulation, Masters' Houses, 21
von Schnitzler, Georg, 31

Index

Warhol, Andy, 83
Winton, Mike, 161
Winton, Penny, 161
Winton Guest House, 160–7
    clustered objects, 164
    collection of shapes, 166–7
    floor plan, 162, 165
    Gehry, Frank, 161, 164–5, 167
    Johnson, Philip, 161, 165
    Morandi, Giorgio, as inspiration, 163, 164
    photograph, 160
    side view, 161
    site plan, 161, 163
World War I, 19
World War II, 107, 108
Wright, Frank Lloyd, 13
    Fallingwater, 55–63, 65
    Jacobs House, 47–53

Y House, 182–7
    branching masses, 182, 183
    Catskill Mountains, 183, 184, 186
    elevation, 183
    floor plans, 185
    Holl, Steven, 183, 184
    photograph, 182
    public and private areas, 186, 187
    roof plan, 185
    side view, 183
    site plan, 184

zone, Eames House, 76